Chaucer's Lyrics and *Anelida and Arcite*

Chaucer's lyrics pose more unique problems for Chaucer scholars than any other portion of his canon. Their relationship to his personal life, the court, and his circle of friends, and to the overall chronology is intricate, with many questions unresolved.

Peck's volume provides a concentrated survey of scholarly work on the lyrics between 1900 and 1980. In addition considerable attention is also given to the main currents of nineteenth-century scholarship. When it has been practical to do so, Peck quotes key phrases and passages which characterize the tone and thesis of the work as well as those passages which have been most influential on the writings of others. He has also annotated reviews which offer astute appraisal of the work under consideration or which advance their mutual topic in a substantive way.

RUSSELL A. PECK is a member of the Department of English, University of Rochester.

The Chaucer Bibliographies

GENERAL EDITORS

A.J. Colaianne *Virginia Polytechnic Institute and State University*
R.M. Piersol *Virginia Polytechnic Institute and State University*

ADVISING EDITORS

Emerson Brown, jr *Vanderbilt University*
E. Talbot Donaldson *University of Indiana*
John Hurt Fisher *University of Tennessee*
David C. Fowler *University of Washington*
Albert Friedman *Claremont Graduate School*
James J. Murphy *University of California, Davis*
Paul Ruggiers *University of Oaklahoma*

Chaucer's Lyrics and
Anelida and Arcite

AN ANNOTATED BIBLIOGRAPHY

1900 TO 1980

Russell A. Peck

UNIVERSITY OF TORONTO PRESS

Toronto Buffalo London

© University of Toronto Press 1983
Toronto Buffalo London
Printed in Canada
ISBN 0–8020–2481–5

Canadian Cataloguing in Publication Data

Peck, Russell A.
  Chaucer's lyrics and Anelida and Arcite: an
  annotated ibliography 1900 to 1980

  (The Chaucer bibliographies; 1)
  Includes index.
  ISBN 0–8020–2481–5

  1. Chaucer, Geoffrey, d 1400 – Poetic works –
Bibliography. I. Title. II. Series.

Z8164.P42   016.821'1   C82–095248–6

To Demaree Catherine Peck

Yet preye I yow that reden that I write,

Foryeve me that I do no diligence ...

And pray yow that ye wole my werke amende.

Contents

✒ General Editors' Preface

In 1870 James Russell Lowell asked, 'Will it do to say anything more about Chaucer? Can anyone say anything, not new, but even fresh, on a topic so well worn?' A century ago no one could have anticipated the course of modern Chaucer studies. Lowell believed that scholars had exhausted the possibilities of critical inquiry into Chaucer's works, and he saw no reason to expect that the twentieth century would produce more than ten times the amount of commentary published in all previous periods taken together.

In Lowell's time it was not unreasonable to expect an individual to read all the relevant Chaucer scholarship before recording and publishing his own findings. Today, however, it is virtually impossible to keep abreast of Chaucer studies published even during a single year. During the 1970s the *MLA International Bibliography* listed an average of 120 items each year dealing centrally with Chaucer. This level of activity is not likely to decrease; for several reasons – not all of them encouraging to scholarship – it is likely that the number of studies published each year will continue to grow as scholars develop their techniques of investigation, discovering new approaches and re-examining the assumptions of earlier criticism.

From Lowell's perspective the study of Chaucer might well have been thought 'exhausted.' To be sure, by 1900 the essential materials had been assembled for modern Chaucer scholarship. Texts of virtually all Chaucer's works had been published in relatively accurate editions; his major literary sources had been identified; the study of historical documents had yielded enough information for scholars to piece together a full if largely speculative biography. Yet these achievements marked not the culmination but rather the beginning, in the most crucial sense, of what we now see as the modern study of Chaucer. In working with the resources available at the beginning of the century, scholars would soon find themselves developing new methods of interpretation and looking to new areas of inquiry. And in time, through the re-examination of traditional views of medieval life and literature, the old answers would give way to new generations of questions.

Chaucerians during the present century have produced a body of literary commentary that is extraordinary in its vitality and variety. The techniques of traditional historical scholarship are continually being strengthened, with the result that we are able to place all of Chaucer's works more firmly within the culture that supported them. Our understanding of Chaucer's rhetoric, and of the relationships between style and meaning in his work, is much broader than it was fifty years ago. We have seen the influence of the New Criticism in the close reading of the Chaucerian text *qua* text, and a vigorous application of patristic doctrinal models in the reading of the same text as Christian allegory. The latter approach to Chaucer has led literary scholars into the study of medieval visual art, primarily in order to describe the iconography of motifs common to texts and pictures, but also as a means of understanding the aesthetics of medieval espression. Other scholars have begun to concentrate more specifically on the work of Chaucer in its relations with works in other media, with mixed and as yet very tentative results. None of the critical frameworks just mentioned excludes the others, of course, and though there has been much lively disagreement among Chaucerians on matters both general and particular, our knowledge has been enriched during the debate. Few would deny that the work of such critics, for example, as Charles Muscatine, E. Talbot Donaldson, and D.W. Robertson has permanently altered – and matured – our appreciation of Chaucer's art.

The study of Chaucer's texts has moved forward with equally significant results. Twentieth-century scholars, deeply indebted to the labors of Skeat, Furnivall, and other members of the original Chaucer Society, have been able to produce greatly improved texts of the verse and prose. The cooperation of modern textual scholars has led to the addition of the *Equatorie of the Planetis* to the canon, the sifting out of spurious Chauceriana, and, most recently, to the publication of the *Variorum* Chaucer.

The advances represented by the truly seminal twentieth-century work on Chaucer have stimulated in turn the publication of thousands of articles, books, monographs, essay collections, conference proceedings, notes, and doctoral dissertations. Many are original contributions to our understanding of Chaucer; more are primarily derivative; some are trivial; a few, if one wishes to 'lat the chaf be stille,' are best discarded altogether. But all have become part of the living record of Chaucer scholarship, and as such, they must be taken into account.

The proliferation of Chaucer studies is generally encouraging, but it is also a source of continuing frustration for both the experienced scholar and the beginning student. Chaucerians have for years relied on a number of valuable bibliographical tools, including those compiled by Hammond (1908), Griffith (1955), and Crawford (1967), and, more recently, the bibliographies by Lorrayne Baird (1977) and by John Fisher in his edition of Chaucer's works (1977). But bibliographies vary greatly in scope, organization, and depth of coverage, and scholars have found it necessary to supplement these compilations with the more selective bibliographies by Martin (1935) and Baugh (1968); with Wells's *Manual of the Writings in Middle English* (1916–1951); and with a number of serial bibliographies: the *MLA International Bibliography*, the Modern Hunamities Research Association *Annual Bibliography*, and the annotated bibliography apperaing annually in *Studies in the Age of Chaucer*. And in order completely to survey a topic, the Chaucer scholar must also consult enumerative bibliographies such as the *Cambridge Bibliography of English Literature* (and the *New Cambridge Bibliography*), as well as a variety of other checklists and bibliographical essays.

The difficulty of retrieving complete and accurate information from these disparate sources illustrates the need for a uniform and comprehensive Chaucer bibliography; and because of the immense number and variety of Chaucer studies published during the twentieth century, there is an equally pressing need for a bibliography that will offer some measure of guidance along the paths of modern Chaucer scholarship. The *Chaucer Bibliographies* are intended to satisfy these needs in several ways: by consolidating the contributions to modern Chaucer research published in all languages; by ensuring uniform bibliographical citation in order to improve the process of locating items; by including within each volume of the series a detailed index and an extensive system of cross-references among annotations; by introducing each bibliography with a substantial essay which traces the main lines of inquiry and suggests the most promising directions for future research on the works and topics treated in the volume; and by providing a full and detailed annotation for each item listed in the bibliography.

The corpus of commentary on Chaucer can be overwhelming simply because of its size, and the issues raised in annotating thousands of studies are additionally complicated by the uneven history – and conception – of annotated bibliography itself. The term 'annotated bibliography' embraces a wide range of possible formats, from checklists with brief parenthetical comments to bibliographical essays supported by extended commentary. From the inception of the *Chaucer Bibliographies* in 1979, members of the project have been particularly concerned to establish clear and consistent principles of annotation, and to incorporate them in bibliographies of the greatest possible value to scholars: scholars who typically will be turning to an annotation precisely because they are not familiar with the cited item, nor, in many cases, with related items to which the annotation may refer. With these and other issues in mind, we have determined that each volume of the *Chaucer Bibliographies* should be a comprehensive and self-contained reference guide to a single work or group of works, or to a major topic in Chaucer studies (e.g., 'Chaucer and Music,' 'Chaucer and the Sciences'). The bibliographies will provide annotations to books, monographs, articles, dissertations, notes and important reviews in all languages significant to modern Chaucer scholarship; where appropriate, editions will also be annotated. Annotations range in length from a single sentence to upwards of 300 words, or, as the occasion warrants, to several paragraphs – the length of an annotation is itself an indication of the value of an item. As the Guidelines for the series point out, annotations, to be useful, should be 'substantial and direct,' as objective and non-judgemental as possible: an accurate, comprehensive annotation will allow the piece of scholarship in question to speak for itself. It is our assumption, in short, that the usefulness of the *Chaucer Bibliographies* will depend at once on the quality of their annotations, their depth of coverage, and the accessibility of the information they contain. Although the first volume of the *Chaucer Bibliographies* embodies the the bibliographical principles and practices which will characterize the entire series, it differs somewhat from what we anticipate for future volumes: the relative size of the lyrics in the Chaucer canon and the corresponding proportion of relevant scholarship and criticism has made possible extensive annotation for each entry, a freedom which editors of other volumes may well not have.

The making of an annotated bibliography is sometimes thought to be dry and tedious work. Sometimes it is. But it can be invigorating work as well, especially when its subject is the study of Chaucer in the twentieth century. The scholars involved in the *Chaucer Bibliographies* have set out to produce reference guides that capture the spirit of modern Chaucer scholarship, an endeavor characterized by wit, learnedness, memorable brilliance, and only the very occasional absurdity.

The primary task of the bibliographer has always been to save other scholars time and labor in their researches. In an age when there is more and more to keep track of, and when scholarly books are so expensive that many academic libraries have difficulty in building collections, the work of the bibliographer becomes even more essential: it is the bibliographer to whom other scholars will turn increasingly for a perspective on what has been written over many years of discovery and debate. It is the bibliographer who helps give direction to future inquiry by ordering the individual contributions to scholarship – which, if it is to be of any genuine value, must be recognized as the ongoing collective enterprise that it is.

The inheritance of the modern Chaucerian is especially rich, and it descends directly from the great medievalists of the late Victorian period, who not only made possible our study of Chaucer, but who also helped

to establish a context for modern humanistic inquiry and textual
scholarship in general. We begin our coverage at the end of this era, the
energy and enthusiasm of which have left their mark on the best that
has been produced during the intervening years. Taken together, the
Chaucer Bibliographies should serve not merely as reference lists of published research, but more broadly, as detailed summaries of this first century of modern Chaucer scholarship. Clearly, the time has arrived for
such an undertaking. In his 1980 address to the New Chaucer Society,
Professor Muscatine voiced a concern shared by many Chaucerians:
'What Amounteth All This Wit?' We hope that the *Chaucer Bibliographies*
will open the way to some answers.

The present project has received generous support from a number of
individuals and organizations. We would like especially to thank
members of the English Department and the administration of Virginia
Polytechnic Institute and State University: Professors Arthur Eastman,
Hilbert Campbell, and Wilfrid Jewkes; Dean Henry Bauer and Assistant
Dean George Crofts; and the Provost of the University, Dr. John Wilson.
Dr. Raymond Smoot and the VPI & SU Educational Foundation have
been instrumental in funding editorial work on the project, and Ms. De-
anna Mersky of University Development has contributed much time and
energy in working with us. We would like also to thank Ms. Susan
Bright, of VPI & SU, who helped acquaint us with the use of computers
in the production of this volume; Mrs. Rebecca Cox, who entered and
programmed the final copy; and Leota Williams, who maintained her
sense of humor while helping us with correspondence.

Ms. Prudence Tracy, of the University of Toronto Press, has been a patient and helpful friend to the project. By hosting the first conference on
the *Chaucer Bibliographies*, the Department of English of the University of
Rochester provided contributors with the opportunity to discuss in detail
plans for the series: Professors Marjorie Woods, Rowland Collins, and
Russell Peck were especially helpful in arranging the meeting. Professor
Peck's commitment to the project has been manifested in many ways; the
result of his commitment, the present volume, marks an auspicious beginning for the publication of the *Chaucer Bibliographies*.

Until his death in December, 1981, Professor Richard L. Hoffman, of
VPI & SU, had served as an Advising Editor to the project; his dedication
to the study of Chaucer will continue to inspire those who knew him.

A.J. Colaianne
R.M. Piersol

❧ Preface

I began this bibliography in conjunction with another project on which I am presently engaged – a study of Chaucer's philosophical and scientific interests. At the outset I looked forward almost with glee to surveying scholarly efforts over the past century. I had some trepidation about the inevitable drudgery of the task, but my doubts were soon dispelled by sheer fascination with the ingenuity, variety, and depth of scholarly responses to Chaucer's lesser known works. Academics tend to be extraordinarily earnest when it comes to expounding their theories; it is exhilarating and sometimes astonishing to watch their zealous debates and curious insights unfold over several generations of intensive Chaucer studies. But in the end the experience of annotating so many studies was mainly humbling. When I began, I thought I would be able to provide a detailed coverage of all areas of scholarship assigned to me. But as I got further into the project the hope of being consistent, thorough, fair, and complete faded into a somber despair. The more intricate (and often the most interesting) arguments do not lend themselves well to condensation. Moreover, because of the eclectic subject matter of this particular volume of the *Chaucer Bibliographies,* I found myself usually excerpting portions from arguments which were devoted primarily to something else.

I apologize to any whose work I have misrepresented, distorted too egregiously, or inadvertently ignored. That I have made blunders and omissions seems inevitable. I have tried to be balanced and objective, though undoubtedly my own prejudices and enthusiasms have interfered. Because of the length of many of the annotations, the bibliography is likely to be more than a reference work. Students will probably use it as a summary of scholarship on the works I have treated. In my annotations I have attempted to indicate the scope of the work under consideration as it pertains to the purview of this volume and to provide a summary of the pertinent matter. When it has been practical to do so, I have quoted phrases or passages that characterize the tone or thesis of the work. I have also tried, within reasonable limits, to include exact quotation of material in influential studies that frequently gets quoted by subsequent studies. I have annotated some reviews – those that offer an astute appraisal of the work under consideration, or which advance their mutual topic in a substantive way. I have also included some unpublished doctoral dissertations.

Any bibliography of Chaucer studies owes a primary obligation to Dudley David Griffith, *Bibliography of Chaucer: 1908–1953* (Seattle: University of Washington Press, 1955); William R. Crawford, *Bibliography of Chaucer: 1954–1963* (Seattle and London: University of Washington Press, 1967); and Lorrayne Y. Baird, *A Bibliography of Chaucer, 1964–1973* (Boston: G.K. Hall, 1977). In my researches for Chaucer material in compiling this volume I always began with these three volumes. This volume does not, however, displace them. Baird especially remains valuable for her comprehensive listing of reviews and such unusual material as musical adaptations, phonograph recordings, films, and filmstrips. And Griffith and Crawford include dissertations and some items I was unable to obtain, as well as reviews that I ignored. I also have made use of the *New Cambridge Bibliography of English Literature*, which led me to a few items not found in Griffith, Crawford, or Baird. And, of course, I am indebted to the annual bibliography of the Modern Language Association, especially for recent items. Because of the peculiar range of topics included among the lyrics I have found some material in places not normally examined by Chaucer students in their general preparations – studies of prosody, histories of literature, studies in Catholicism, studies on *translatio*, and studies on writers other than Chaucer. Footnotes in various studies have yielded items that have not previously been noted in the published bibliographies. And sometimes I simply came across material by luck.

A word about the arrangement of this volume. I have divided the sections into those categories that reflect the most likely ways in which a user of the bibliography might be working. Editions are arranged chronologically, since that is the way scholars usually think of editions. Critical discussions of the works, however, are arranged alphabetically according to author, since we generally think of such material in terms of who wrote it. I find chronologically arranged bibliographies frustrating to use. One does not, in truth, get a good sense of historical sequence from such arrangements, simply because the influences of one author upon another do not get recorded in direct sequence. The two or three years' worth of other items that intervene between a statement and a response lose the item in the bibliographical mass, unless one is fortunate enough to have remembered the date. Even indexes do not help too much with chronological arrangements, since important issues are usually discussed by important scholars who have written on several other matters, which the researcher must then look up one by one until he lights on the right one. In short, an alphabetical arrangement is the easiest to use since it reflects the way we are accustomed to classifying material and thinking about it. If, however, an author is responsible for more than one entry in a section, then his works are listed chronologically, again, since that is the way we are accustomed to thinking about a single author's works. I list reviews chronologically immediately following the work being reviewed.

On the annotations: When quoting material directly I have restricted use of ellipsis to indicate material omitted *within* the quotation. In a few instances I have made silent emendations (eg, *Chaucer* for *he*) to fit the quotation more gracefully into the syntax in which I have place it. I have also adjusted capitalization and end punctuation to suit the new context. Numbers in boldface type indicate items located elsewhere in the bibliography.

I am indebted to Rossell Hope Robbins for his careful perusal of an early draft of the manuscript and to Alfred David for sharing with me the bibliography to the first volume of the *Variorum Chaucer: The Lyrics,* which will be published in 1982 by The New Chaucer Society. A.J. Colaianne, the general editor of the series, and R.M. Piersol, the associate editor, have overseen the progress of this volume with tolerance and good cheer. I am grateful to the John Simon Guggenheim Foundation for funding my researches on the philosophical Chaucer, some of which research went into the making of this bibliography. At the University of Rochester, Thomas Hahn has proven a patient counsellor and faithful friend to the project. I owe special thanks to the staff of the Rush Rhees Library at the University of Rochester, especially to Phyllis Andrews in the Reference Department and to Carol Cavanaugh and Sally Morsch of Interlibrary Loan, all of whom endured with good spirit numerous odd requests and helped me track down out-of-the-way references. Sheila Robertson, Jane Dever, and Helen Craven of the University of Rochester English Department have been helpful to me in the xeroxing of materials. I am especially grateful to Claire Sundeen, who typed the manuscript with great care, and to Carol Wilkinson, who assisted with the checking of references and proof reading. She works with the eyes of an eagle and duteous patience of Griselde.

R.A.P

Abbreviations

LBD   *La Belle Dame Sans Merci* (Roos)
LGW   *The Legend of Good Women*
MancT   *Manciple's Tale*
Mars   *The Complaint of Mars*
MB   *Merciles Beaute*
Mel   *Tale of Melibee*
MerchT   *Merchant's Tale*
MilT   *Miller's Tale*
MLT   *Man of Law's Tale*
MonkT   *Monk's Tale*
NPT   *Nun's Priest's Tale*
OM   *Ovide Moralisé*
PardT   *Pardoner's Tale*
ParsT   *Parson's Tale*
PF   *Parliament of Fowls*
PhysT   *Physician's Tale*
Pity   *The Complaint unto Pity*
PlowT   *The Plowman's Tale* (Apocryphal)
PriorT   *Prioress's Tale*
Prov   *Proverbs*
Purse   *The Complaint of Chaucer to his Purse*
Retr   *Chaucer's Retractation*
Romaunt   *The Romaunt of the Rose*
Ros   *To Rosemounde*
RR   *Le Roman de la Rose* (Guillaume de Lorris and Jean de Meun)
ReeveT   *Reeve's Tale*
Scogan   *L'Envoy de Chaucer a Scogan*
ShipT   *Shipman's Tale*
Siege   *The Siege of Thebes* (Lydgate)
SNT   *Second Nun's Tale*
SqT   *Squire's Tale*
Sted   *Lak of Stedfastnesse: Balade*
SumT   *Summoner's Tale*
T&C   *Troilus and Criseyde*
Thop   *Tale of Sir Thopas*
Truth   *Truth: Balade de Bon Conseyl*
Venus   *The Complaint of Venus*
WBT   *Wife of Bath's Tale*
WN   *Womanly Noblesse: Balade That Chaucier Made*

JOURNALS AND REFERENCE WORKS CITED

AB   *Anglia Beiblatt*
ABR   *American Benedictine Review*
Acad   *Academy*
AHR   *American Historical Review*
Ang   *Anglia*
AnM   *Annuale Mediaevale*
BL   *British Library*
BN   *Bibliothèque Nationale*
CBEL   *Cambridge Bibliography of English Literature*
CE   *College English*
ChauR   *Chaucer Review*
CHEL   *Cambridge History of English Literature*
CL   *Comparative Literature*
Crit   *Criticism*
DA   *Dissertation Abstracts*
DAI   *Dissertation Abstracts International*
DNB   *Dictionary of National Biography*
E&S   *Essays and Studies*
EETS   *Early English Text Society*
EIC   *Essays in Criticism*
EigoS   *Eigo Seinen* [The Rising Generation] Tokyo
ELH   *English Literary History*
ELN   *English Language Notes*
EM   *English Miscellany*
ES   *English Studies*
ESt   *Englische Studien*
Expl   *Explicator*
JEGP   *Journal of English and Germanic Philology*
JHA   *Journal for the History of Astronomy*
JHI   *Journal of the History of Ideas*
JMRS   *Journal of Medieval and Renaissance Studies*
MA   *Le Moyen Age*
MAE   *Medium Aevum*
M&H   *Medievalia et Humanistica*
MLN   *Modern Language Notes*
MLQ   *Modern Language Quarterly*
MLR   *Modern Language Review*
MP   *Modern Philology*
MRS   *Medieval and Renaissance Studies*
MS   *Mediaeval Studies*
Neophil   *Neophilologus*
NM   *Neuphilologische Mitteilungen*

NQ   *Notes and Queries*
NED/OED   *Oxford English Dictionary*
PLL   *Papers on Language and Literature*
PMLA   *Publications of the Modern Language Association*
PQ   *Philological Quarterly*
PRO   *Public Record Office*
RES   *Review of English Studies*
Rom   *Romania*
RomR   *Romanic Review*
SAC   *Studies in the Age of Chaucer*
SATF   *Societé des Anciens Textes Français*
SB   *Studies in Bibliography*
SELit   *Studies in English Literature* (English Literary Society of Japan)
SHR   *Scottish Historical Review*
SN   *Studia Neophilologica*
SP   *Studies in Philology*
Spec   *Speculum*
TLS   *Times Literary Supplement* [London]
TSL   *Tennessee Studies in Literature*
TSLL   *Texas Studies in Literature and Language*
UCTSE   *University of Cape Town Studies in English*
UMSE   *University of Mississippi Studies in English*
UTQ   *University of Toronto Quarterly*

Chaucer's Lyrics and *Anelida and Arcite*

✎ Introduction

Since the seventeenth century Chaucer's lyrics have posed more unique problems for Chaucer scholars than any other portion of the Chaucer canon. To begin with, several of his poems – *Origen upon the Maudeleyne, Book of the Lion, The Wrecched Engendrynge of Mankind,* and various balades, songs, roundels, and virelays – apparently have been lost. Those that survive appear in widely divergent contexts in nearly fifty manuscripts scattered throughout the fifteenth century. The manuscripts vary in quality, the later ones reflecting orthographic practices that differ markedly from early Chaucer manuscripts like the Ellesmere or Hengwrt. Of the twenty-two lyrics thought to be by Chaucer, six – *Womanly Noblesse, To Rosemounde, Lenvoy to Bukton, Adam Scriveyn, A Ballade of Complaint,* and *Merciles Beaute* – survive in only one manuscript. *Truth,* on the other hand, appears in more than twenty manuscripts and in one it even appears twice; yet, of the nearly two dozen manuscript authorities, only one (BL Addit. 10340) includes the famous envoy addressed to 'Vache.' *Gentilesse* appears in nine manuscripts, though in some it is embedded in the middle of 'A moral balade made by Henry Scogan squyer,' and is thus attributed to him. The fifteenth-century manuscript tradition raises intricate problems for all of Chaucer's poetry, but the problems of the lyrics are especially knotty in that the lyrics often appear anonymously in collections that include other anonymous poems by Chaucerian imitators, or in collections that attribute non-Chaucerian poems to Chaucer as well as those that are by Chaucer. Thus it is not possible to know in every instance which poems are definitively his. Modern editors usually include a section on short poems of doubtful authorship.

By the sixteenth century the practice of attributing poems to the legendary Chaucer had become almost pernicious. As England passed through the throes of the Reformation both sides invoked the great poet's name as a means of getting doggerel propaganda past the censors. Political complaints like the *Plowman's Tale,* some portions of which may indeed have originated as early as the fourteenth century, were adapted to suit the issues of the day and added to Chaucer's canon, which was exempt from censorship. Moreover, early editors, eager to sell copies, regularly sought out new 'Chaucer' poems their predecessors had missed to give their new editions greater completeness. John Stowe's blackletter edition of 1561 is 'newlie printed with diuers addicions, whiche were neuer in print before'; most of his additions are spurious, what the eighteenth-century editor Tyrwhitt called 'a heap of rubbish' (Hammond **37**, p 121), though Stowe does print for the first time *Adam Scriveyn, A Proverbe, Against Women Unconstant,* and *Complaint to His Lady.* He also includes *Gentilesse* as a poem separate from *Scogan's Balade,* though he presents the latter, nonetheless, with Chaucer's verses still embedded after the thirteenth stanza.

Thomas Speght's editions of 1598 and 1602 likewise add new 'Chaucer' poems. Speght is the first to print Chaucer's *ABC.* Among his spurious additions is the *Flower and the Leaf,* a poem that was thereafter esteemed one of Chaucer's best. Dryden modernized it, Pope and Hazlitt praised it, Keats wrote a sonnet about it, and the artist of the Chaucer window in Westminster Abbey chose subjects from it to shine down upon the poet's corner. No manuscript of the poem survives; so, although Speght perpetrated confusion upon centuries of Chaucer lovers, he preserved, nonetheless, a poem of great merit, regardless of its authorship.

It would seem that early printers – Caxton, Pynson, Julian Notary, Thynne, Stowe, and even a printer as late as Speght – had access to early manuscripts of excellent quality which no longer survive. Some may even have come directly from the household of Thomas Chaucer and his circle of friends. Once the type for a new edition was set, the copy text – in these instances often the best of the known manuscripts – was destroyed (or at least, it has disappeared). From the point of view of posterity the early editions are thus a mixed blessing. (Perhaps if Speght had not printed the *Flower and the Leaf,* the manuscript would have survived, and we could better understand its true relationship to Chaucer's work.) But because of these workshop practices the early printed editions are often of greatest importance in helping the modern editor to reproduce a more authentic Chaucerian text. This is especially true when the poem survives in a unique manuscript; in such instances the printed text, though made centuries after the poet's death, may be more reliable than the surviving manuscript, since it often was based upon a more authoritative text to begin with.

Modern editors, quite rightly, look for external evidence as proof of the authenticity of Chaucer's lyrics. Some evidence is to be found in references to his writings within his own works – lists like those in the *Man of Law's Introduction,* the *Retractation,* and the Prologue to the *Legend of Good Women.* Unfortunately, though such lists specify Chaucer's longer works, usually they lump the lyrics together as 'balades, roundels, virelayes' (Prol. *LGW* F 423), or as 'many a lay and many a thing' (Prol. *LGW*

F 430), or as 'many a song and many a leccherous lay' (*Retractation*), without specifying individual titles. John Lydgate devotes twelve stanzas of praise to Chaucer in the Prologue to the *Fall of Princes*. He speaks 'of Annelida and of false Arcite' and mentions 'a complaynt ... of the broche which that Vulcanus at Thebes wrought,' which surely alludes to the *Complaint of Mars*. But of the rest of the lyrics he simply states that Chaucer 'made and compiled many a freshe dittie, / Complaynts, balades, roundels, vyrelaies,' apparently following Chaucer's own statement in *LGW* rather than specifying more exactly.

A more precise testimony comes from John Shirley – one of the truly fascinating characters of the first half of the fifteenth century. According to Stowe, Shirley, who died October 21, 1456, lived past his ninetieth birthday. Born in 1366, he would have been in his mid-thirties when Chaucer died and might have known Chaucer directly. He certainly knew Chaucer's younger friends, for he played an active part for several decades in courtly literary circles that included Charles of Orléans, Thomas Hoccleve, John Lydgate, Henry Scogan, Duke Humphrey of Gloucester, and Thomas Chaucer, the poet's son. He loved books, copied them himself both at the request of his friends and to be lent and sold. The titles and colophons to the lyrics in some of his manuscripts include gossip and biographical tidbits as well as attributions. Sometimes the titles are in French, sometimes in English, which provides us with some indication of the audience for which his manuscripts were intended. Although editors, in their search for accurate texts, do not hold Shirley's renditions of Chaucer's poems in highest esteem (apparently he often wrote from memory and in some haste, without being too nice about accuracy), his attributions are held in highest regard. His testimony upholds the genuineness of Chaucer's *ABC, The Complaint unto Pity, The Complaint of Mars, The Complaint of Venus, Chaucer's Words unto Adam Scriveyn, Fortune, Truth, Gentilesse, Lak of Stedfastnesse, The Complaint of Chaucer to his Purse,* and *Anelida and Arcite*. Shirley is not the only scribe to attribute poems to Chaucer. Among the most reliable of the non-Shirley manuscripts is Fairfax 16. And there are others. See Skeat **1**, I, 25–91; Hammond **37**, pp 325–463; and Brusendorff **28**, pp 178–295, 453–71.

But a uniquely complex textual tradition and an uncertain canon are not the only problems that set the lyrics apart from the rest of Chaucer's writings. As a group, these poems have undergone an odd reversal in reputation. For nearly the first two hundred years of their literary life Clere Laude trumpeted their fame and influence even more boldly than the sustained glory of the *Canterbury Tales*. C.S. Lewis **118**, Rossell Hope Robbins **136**, and others have emphatically demonstrated that it is the Chaucer of the lyrics and dream visions who found imitators in the fifteenth century and who established the prosody and verse forms out

of which the great age of English lyricism in the sixteenth century
would grow. But so great were the progeny of his latter day benefactors
that the source was eventually quite overshadowed. Moreover, changes
in the language itself made Chaucer's pronunciation and measures uncertain, and for the next three centuries his lyrics fell into relative ob-
livion. More recently, a few have dared sing their praises again, though
in this judicious age there have been echoes of Sklaundre as well. In our
own day, as in Chaucer's, nothing, it would seem, is certain.

The renewed interest in the lyrics has not always been due to their
literary merit. At the beginning of the twentieth century scholars found
in them valuable scraps for filling in Chaucer's biography, which had
been sadly depleted when the more scientific nineteenth-century biogra-
phers rejected the foolish legends of the Renaissance that had grown up
around Chaucer. All the lyrics seem to be occasional pieces, whether the
chastising of a scribe, a begging poem to the king, an exhortation to
Vache, or an allegory on some court intrigue. The Envoys to Scogan and
Bukton link Chaucer to real people, though which Scogan and which
Bukton is not easily determined. Some of the new researchers saw autobiography in Chaucer's woeful complaints against unconstant women,
Venus, Pity, and female pride – signs, perhaps, of an unhappy marriage
to Phillipa and rotten luck in getting away from her. More recently,
such views are thought to be leaden compared to the radiant sophistication of new critical approaches that study the rhetoric, style, and fictive
techniques of the witty and ironic Chaucer.

Over the past decade the dominant voice in studies of Chaucer's lyrics
has been that of Rossell Hope Robbins. His assessment – 'they're just
minor poems' – has riled many a graduate student, who gladly comes to
their defence. But more important than such prickly dogmatisms have
been Robbins' suggestions that the manuscripts and the culture that produced them be looked at afresh. The poems can only be understood just-
ly when the court for which they were written is understood. Robbins
has been so bold as to suggest that Chaucer's earliest lyrics may have
been written in French and that it is to the great number of unpublished
manuscripts containing late fourteenth- and early fifteenth-century court
verse to be found in France, Spain, Portugal, and perhaps even Italy, that
scholars should be turning if they hope to discover a more firm basis on
which to build stable criticism of this oddly elusive portion of Chaucer's
canon. But even if more delving into French courtly poetry does reveal
further the conventional qualities of Chaucer's poems, identify
Rosemounde, or even add to the canon more poems by Chaucer, it will
become increasingly clear how Chaucer triumphs within the conventions
as no other English or French poet does. And even though his lyrics
were originally written for a coterie of people attuned to courtly rhetoric,

those poems will doubtless continue to enjoy a modern-day coterie, if only of academics, who will find their quiet manner as pleasing in wit and gentilesse as the more strikingly original work on the grand scale, like *Troilus* and the *Canterbury Tales*, for which Clere Laude sounds perpetually.

❧ Editions

1 *The Complete Works of Geoffrey Chaucer.* Ed. W.W. Skeat. London: Oxford
University Press, 1894. *The Oxford Chaucer*, in six volumes with a supplementary volume VII, *Chaucerian and Other Pieces*, 1897; rpt 1899.
Volume I: *The Romaunt of the Rose and Minor Poems.* The introduction to
the Minor Poems (pp 20–91) discusses the canon on the basis of external
evidence (ie, Lydgate's list of Chaucer's writings in *The Fall of Princes*;
lists in Chaucer's own writings; the testimony of John Shirley and other
scribes; Caxton, and other early editions). Skeat lists forty-six mss containing Chaucer lyrics, discusses the more important ones found in Oxford, Cambridge, and London libraries, and comments on each poem and
the mss in which it occurs. To the Chaucer Society's list of genuine
poems Skeat adds three more as certain: 'Compleint to his Lady,' which
Stowe says is 'by Chauciers,' perhaps from the authority of a manuscript
now lost; 'Merciles Beaute,' the only poem which Skeat admits to the set
of minor poems with incomplete external evidence; 'To Rosemounde,'
which he discovered in the Bodleian in 1891. He also includes an additional three which he relegates to an Appendix 'because they are not ex-
pressly attributed to Chaucer in the mss' (p 91), but which he thinks are
probably genuine: 'Against Women Unconstant'; 'An Amorous Complaint'; and 'Balade of Compleynt.' Three others, 'Womanly Noblesse,'
'Complaint to my Mortal Foe,' and 'Complaint to my Lodesterre,' which
Skeat had included in *The Minor Poems*, revised and enlarged, 1896, appear at the beginning of volume IV, pp xxv–xxxii, prior to *CT*. Skeat's
notes are detailed, especially in verbal glosses, notices of sources, and
suggestions of literary parallels; but they are also a treasure trove of general information. The Oxford Chaucer has remained influential
throughout the twentieth century and has been reprinted many times
and as recently as 1963. The list of genuine poems includes (in order):
ABC (with French original); *Pity*; *BD*; *Mars*; *PF*; *Lady*; *AA*; *Adam*; *FA*; *Fortune*; *MB*; *Truth*; *Gent*; *Sted*; *Scogan*; *Bukton*; *Ros*; *Venus* (with French original); *Purse*; *and Prov. WN*, *CMF*, and *CML* appear in Volume IV, as noted.
– See Eleanor Hammond **37**, pp 144–6, on Skeat's edition: 'The limitation

of the editor to a portion of the possible evidence is a ... radical weakness' (p 145). Skeat does not explain his editorial decisions, nor is he always consistent but rather 'is guided by the erroneous supposition that the true Chaucerian readings may be picked out intuitively, instead of by the laborious and impartial comparison of all authorities' (p 146). Nonetheless, as Kittredge has said, 'The edition will remain a monument of learning and sagacity which few similar works in English can rival' (p 146). The notes and annotations are the best accessible to students. It is in the notes 'that his prolonged labors in medieval literature and in etymological pursuits enable him to speak as one having authority' (p 146).

2 *The Student's Chaucer*. Ed. W.W. Skeat. New York and London: Macmillan, 1894. Rpt 1929. Pp 79–129.
More recently printed as the Oxford Standard Authors edition. Includes the same list of Minor Poems as 1, adding *WN* from vol 4 with the note: 'This genuine poem was first printed in June 1894' (p 129).

3 *The Works of Geoffrey Chaucer* [The Globe Chaucer]. Ed. Alfred W. Pollard, H. Frank Heath, Mark H. Liddell, W.S. McCormick. London: Macmillan, 1898/rev 1928. Pp 627–37.
This edition was chosen as the basis of the Tatlock-Kennedy *Concordance* (**53**) on the grounds that it was less heavily emended than Skeat's edition and is thus closer to the best mss. Tatlock and Kennedy made some corrections where there were 'undeniable mistakes'; in 1928 Pollard then revised the Globe Chaucer to retain 'wherever possible' the readings recorded in the *Concordance*. The sections on the minor poems are edited by H. Frank Heath, whose Introduction (pp xxxii–liii) discusses problems of editing the lyrics: 'A text of Chaucer's Minor Poems which shall be even fairly satisfactory is no easy achievement. There is scarcely one of his shorter works which does not offer serious difficulties to the editor' (p xxxii). The introduction provides notes on date of composition, sources, versification, and any known surrounding historical circumstances, and gives a ms stemma for each entry. Heath divides the poems into early, late, and doubtful categories, and includes: *Pity, ABC, Mars, Lady, AA; Adam, Ros, FA, Fortune, Truth, Gent, Sted, Scogan, Bukton, Venus, Purse, Prov*; and, as doubtful, *MB*, 'Madame, for youre newfangelnesse,' *CD, BC*, and *WN*.

4 *The Works of Geoffrey Chaucer and Others, Being a Reproduction in Facsimile of the First Collected Edition 1532* [Thynne]. Introduction by Walter W. Skeat. Oxford: Oxford University Press, 1905.
Skeat's introduction discusses both William and Francis Thynne and all early editions and their contents. Skeat prints in full Sir Brian Tuke's preface to the 1532 edition (pp xxii–xxiv). Of the twenty-two new works never before printed which Thynne includes, only six are Chaucer's. But he is the first to print the *Romaunt, LGW, BD, Pity, Sted*, and the *Astrolabe*.

Moreover, his edition of the *Romaunt* is sole authority for a good portion of this text. He also includes *Boece*, first published by Caxton. Other lyrics included by Thynne are *Bukton* (only one known ms; thus Thynne, along with a printed copy by Julian Notary, ca 1499, is of great textual importance); *Pity* ('The ms followed by Thynne seems to have been neither very good nor very bad,' p xxxv); *AA* (Caxton's text was corrected from a ms still preserved at Longleat; 'it is so instructive to see him at work that I give some account of what he has done,' p xxxvi); *Mars* (uses Notary and Longleat ms); *Venus* (does not follow Notary but some ms similar to Fairfax 16, but not Fairfax 16); *Truth; Fortune; Scogan; Purse*. Besides the genuine Chaucerian works, Thynne includes: *Testament of Creseyde; Flour of Courtesy; La Belle Dame Sans Merci; Assembly of Ladies; Complaint of the Black Knight; A Praise of Women; Testament of Love* (sole authority); *Lamentation of Mary Magalene; Remedy of Love; Letter of Cupid; A Balade in Commendation of Our Lady: To My Soverain Lady; Gower to Henry IV; Cuckoo and Nightingale; Envoy to Alison; Scogan to the Lords; Go Forth, King; A Balade of Good Counsel; Epitaphum Galfridi Chaucer.*

5 Chambers, E.K., and F. Sidgwick, eds. *Early English Lyrics: Amorous, Divine, Moral, and Trivial*. London: Sidgwick and Jackson, 1907. Pp 20–6, 172–6, 203–6.

An anthology of English lyric poetry antecedent to Wyatt, Surrey, and the sonnet, which includes Chaucer's roundel from *PF* 'Now welcom somer'; 'Hyde, Absolon, thy gilte tresses clere' (*LGW* F 249–69); *Ros; MB; AWU; Truth; Gent; Sted; Purse; Bukton*. The essay 'Some Aspects of Mediaeval Lyric' (pp 259–96) surveys the history of the lyric in medieval Europe, with a focus on England, beginning with folk traditions and including trouvère-songs, carols, *chansons populaires, chansons d'aventure, chansons de mal mariée, pastourelles*, and *chansons courtois*. 'Literary poetry during the fifteenth century is ... wholly under the domination of Chaucer ... His *balades* and *rondels* ... represent a fresh wave of continental influence' (p 280). But Chaucer also diverted the lyric toward narrative techniques; 'so far as Lydgate and Occleve and their fellows write lyric at all, they follow his models, and show but little spontaneity' (p 280).

6 *The Complete Poetical Works of Geoffrey Chaucer*. Trans. John S.P. Tatlock and Percy MacKaye. The Modern Reader's Chaucer, with 32 Illustrations by Warwick Goble. New York: Macmillan, 1912/rev 1938. Reissued without illustrations in paperback; Toronto: Collier-Macmillan, 1966, from the original plates. Pp 310–77.

The minor poems follow Skeat's text (twenty-three items including *BD, PF*, and *AA*), except that the translators exclude *BC* and *WN*. 'To Merciless Beauty' and 'To Rosemounde' are given colour illustrations: the first, a swain peering through brambles at a bare-breasted and garlanded blonde reflecting upon herself in a mirror (quite erotic), and the second, an elegant damsel with grand hairpiece at her ease on a stone seat beneath Cupid in a rose garden while a timid pilgrim figure approaches hesitantly from behind. The text in this edition is bowdlerized (nb, what the translators do to the *Miller's Tale*), though the translation of the minor poems is straightforward.

- Review by Clark S. Northup, 'Chaucer in Prose,' *Dial*, 53 (1912), 436–9. With excellent modern editions like the Globe why do we need modernized texts? Quotes Landor's preference of Chaucer in Middle English: 'I would rather see Chaucer quite alone in the dew of his sunny morning than with twenty clever gentlefolks around him, arranging his shoestrings and buttoning his doublet. I like even his language. I will have no hand in breaking his dun but richly-painted glass to put in (if clearer) much thinner panes' (p 436). The attempts by Dryden, Wordsworth, and Leigh Hunt to modernize Chaucer in verse miss the mark; if we *must* have modernization, 'let it be in prose' (p 437).

7 Cook, Albert Stanburrough, ed. *A Literary Middle English Reader*. Boston: Ginn, 1915/rev 1943. Pp 389–98, 416, 417, 420–1, 428, 431.
Under *Translations* Cook includes the 'joys of spring,' 'the river and garden,' and 'pictures of old age' sections of *The Romaunt*, and the 'former age' section of *Boece*. Under *Lyrics* he includes 'Now welcom, somer' (roundel from *PF* which he entitles 'Chaucer's Bird-Song'); *MB*; 'Hyd Absolon' (from *LGW* F Prol., listed as 'Chaucer, Ballade'); *Purse*; *Truth*; the Invocation to Venus (*T&C* III.1–14); and Invocation to the Trinity (last stanza of *T&C*).

8 Kaluza, Max. *Chaucer-Handbuch für Studierende*. Leipzig: Bernhard Tauchnitz, 1915/rev 1927. Pp 13–23.
Under 'Die Kleineren Gedichte' (pp 13–23) Kaluza includes the first three stanzas of *ABC* with their French source; *Mars*, lines 191–217; Anelida's lament, *AA*, lines 220–80; *Adam*; *Ros*; *Sted*; *Bukton*; the *Envoy to Venus*; and *Purse*.

9 Koch, John. 'Chaucerproben.' *ES*, 53 (1919), 161–7.
Translations into German of *Ros* and *MB*, with announcement of a new edition of the minor poems. See **10**.

10 *Geoffrey Chaucer's Kleinere Dichtungen*. Ed. John Koch. Heidelberg: Carl Winter, 1928.
Koch's edition includes a life of the poet based on autobiographical and political interpretations of the life records and poems, a chronology of works, headnotes for individual items discussing sources, a fresh classification of mss, and textual notes at the foot of the page for all poems including *ABC*, *BD*, *Pity*, *Lady*, *CD*, *Mars*, *PF*, *AWU*, *Ros*, *MB*, *Adam*, *HF*, *AA*, *LGW*, *FA*, *Fortune*, *Truth*, *Gent*, *Sted*, *Venus*, *Scogan*, *Bukton*, *Purse*. The *Romaunt*, *Prov*, *BC*, and *WN* are excluded as inauthentic. *T&C* and *CT* are excluded because they are not *kleinere*. Koch published supplementary

notes, bibliography, and an explanation of his method of determining his readings in *Anglia*, 53 (1929), 1–101.

11 *The Poetical Works of Chaucer*. Ed. F.N. Robinson. Cambridge, Mass.: Houghton Mifflin, 1933. Text, pp 612–39; explanatory notes, pp 969–83; textual notes, pp 1034–40.

'Short Poems' (pp 612–39) includes *ABC, Pity, Lady, Mars, Ros, WN, Adam, FA, Fortune, Truth, Gent, Sted, Venus, Scogan, Bukton, Purse;* and under 'Poems of Doubtful Authorship' *AWU, CD, MB, BC,* and *Prov.* The explanatory notes include some discussion of historical criticism, source studies, and biography; the textual notes are extensive and valuable. (See second edition, **12.**)

12 *The Works of Geoffrey Chaucer*. Ed. F.N. Robinson. New Cambridge Edition. Cambridge, Mass.: Houghton Mifflin, 1957. Text, pp 524–43; notes, pp 854–67, 915–20.

'Short Poems' (pp 524–43). Includes the same items as **11.** Under 'Textual Notes' Robinson acknowledges the important studies of G.B. Pace, which have been taken into consideration in this revised edition. 'Since the authorities used for the text of the Short Poems often depart from the orthographical practice of the best Chaucer mss, it has seemed best to the editor to normalize the spelling of these pieces' (p 915). This section of the second edition is one of the least revised. Occasionally *(ABC, Mars, Ros, Sted)* a sentence or two has been added at the end of the earlier statement in **11** acknowledging studies after 1933.

13 *The Canterbury Tales (Selections), together with Sections from the Shorter Poems*. Ed. Robert Archibald Jelliffe. The Modern Student's Library. New York: Scribner's Sons, 1952. Pp 307–12.

Includes *Truth, Gent, Scogan, Bukton,* and *Purse.* The frontispiece, a British Library ms scene of the lover's entrance to the Garden of Delight in the *Romance of the Rose,* is in colour. Glossary, pp 315–77.

14 *Chaucer's Poetry: An Anthology for the Modern Reader*. Ed. E. Talbot Donaldson. New York: Ronald Press, 1958/rev 1975. Text, pp 532–48/693–709; notes, pp 959–64/1123–8.

The selection and the commentary on the short poems is the same in both editions, though the pagination of the texts is different. Donaldson includes *ABC, MB, Ros, Purse, Adam, Bukton, Scogan, Sted, Gent, Truth.* His comments are often cited by other scholars; I have thus included annotations of them as separate entries under the separate poems. One Donaldson comment in particular frequently recurs as a prod in getting new essays under way: 'We have enough of [Chaucer's] short verse ... to make us glad that he did not dissipate too large a portion of his energy on such compositions' (p 959). See **168, 210, 448, 467, 499, 529,** and **546.**

15 *Chaucer's Major Poetry*. Ed. A.C. Baugh. New York: Appleton-Century-Crofts, 1963. Pp 535–40.

Includes *Ros, Adam, Gent, Truth, Sted, Scogan, Bukton, Purse*. Textual and explanatory notes at the foot of the page. The language is well glossed in this edition. The critical commentary is minimal. The glossary is analytic.

16 Davies, R.T., ed. *Medieval English Lyrics: A Critical Anthology*, with Introduction and Notes. London: Faber and Faber, 1963; Evanston, Ill.: Northwestern University Press, 1964. Texts, pp 132–9; notes, pp 328–30. Of the 181 entries six are by Chaucer: 'Welcome, Summer' (roundel from *PF*, 'almost certainly for public delivery on St Valentine's Day' [p 328]); *Ros*; 'Hide, Absolon' (from *LGW*, 'a ballade ... in which the poet is superbly sure of himself' [p 329]); *Truth; Purse; MB*.

17 *Geoffrey Chaucer: A Selection of his Works*. Ed. Kenneth O. Kee. College Classics in English. General Editor, Northrop Frye. Toronto: Macmillan; New York: Odyssey, 1966. Pp 2–13.

Includes *MB, Ros, Sted, Bukton, Adam, Purse*. 'The text of the short poems is based on the manuscript materials published by the Chaucer Society, with the exception of "To Rosemounde", which is derived from W.W. Skeat, *Twelve Facsimiles of Old English Manuscripts* (Oxford, 1892), 36–7' (p xlv). Introduction to the Short Poems includes general comments about the roundel and ballade forms.

18 Griffin, Russell Morgan. *Chaucer's Lyrics: Selected and Edited with Commentary, Canon, and Text*. Case Western Reserve PhD Dissertation. 1970. Dir. Paul M. Clogan. See also *DAI*, 32 (1971), 1452A.

Griffin divides the twenty lyrics into three groups: Early (1360–80), mainly courtly complaints which lead to questioning of moral implications of courtly conventions; Middle (1380–90), the balades which deal with moral philosophy and are distinguished by technical virtuosity; and Late (1390–1400), the envoys and complaints which parody earlier forms to convey a serious sentence through humour. Griffin does not include 'embedded' lyrics such as 'Hyd Absolon' from *LGW* in the study. Appendix I discusses the canon of the lyrics, and Appendix II the problems of editing them. Griffin's texts are based mainly on Robinson, **12**, though he has restored ms readings where Robinson emended on 'metrical grounds' without ms support. Griffin notes that some of the poems were not quite finished and that to regularize them metrically is to do what Chaucer himself did not yet do. For Griffin's comments on the poetry, see **173, 300, 343, 408, 424, 435, 451, 516, 569**.

18a Stemmler, Theo, ed. *Medieval English Love-Lyrics*. Tübingen: Max Niemeyer, 1970.

The anthology of 112 lyrics includes *Lady, Ros, WN, Venus, AWU, CD, MB, BC,* and the following embedded Chaucerian lyrics: *BD* 475–86, *BD* 1175–80, *PF* 680–92, *T&C* I.400–40, *T&C* II.827–75, *T&C* III.1–44, *T&C* III.1422–42, *T&C* III.1450–63, *T&C* III.1744–71, *T&C* V.638–44, *T&C* V.1317–1421, *T&C* V.1590–1631, and *LGW* Prol. F 249–69. Stemmler includes with the appropriate Chaucerian texts the three Ballades by Oton de Granson which Chaucer translates in *Venus,* Petrarch's Sonnet 132 and Boccaccio's *Filostrato* III.74–9 which are sources for *T&C* I.400–20 & III.1–44, and Chaucer's translation of *Boece* II.m.8, which Stemmler parallels with *T&C* III.1744–71.

19 *Chaucer: Lyric and Allegory.* Ed. James Reeves. London: Heinemann, 1970; New York: Barnes and Noble, 1971.
Selections include excerpts from the A Frag. of the *Romaunt; AA,* and seventeen Chaucer lyrics; also excerpts from *BD, PF, HF, T&C,* and *LGW.* Introduction (pp 1–23), glossary, and brief notes. 'Even without the *Tales* Chaucer must still be regarded as, in any significant sense of the word, a major poet' (p 11). Reeves reviews and refutes Matthew Arnold's assessment of Chaucer (pp 18–23); *Truth* exemplifies 'high seriousness' and *T&C* reveals pathos 'touched with irony in a manner unexcelled outside Chaucer, even in Shakespeare' (p 23).

20 Luria, Maxwell S., and Richard L. Hoffman, eds. *Middle English Lyrics.* Norton Critical Editions. New York: W.W. Norton, 1974. Pp 11, 44, 166–9.
An anthology of 245 poems, including *Pity, Truth, Sted, Gent,* and *Purse,* taken from Robinson 12. The volume includes essays on critical and historical background of Middle English lyrics by Peter Dronke, 'Performer and Performance: Middle English Lyrics in the European Context'; Stephen Manning, 'Game and Earnest in the Middle English and Provençal Love Lyric'; Raymond Oliver, 'The Three Levels of Style'; and Rosemary Woolf, 'Lyrics on Death.' Also, eleven brief discussions on specific lyrics, none of which are by Chaucer, and a Select Bibliography.

21 Donahue, James J., tr *Chaucer's Lesser Poems Complete in Present-Day English.* Dubuque, Iowa: Loras Coll., 1974.
The translation, based on Skeat's *Oxford Chaucer* 1 2, includes all certain works apart from *CT* and *T&C* except *RR, Astrolabe,* and *Boece.* Each translation has a brief introduction, which includes a synopsis and such information as sources, date, versification, and a few critical observations. See **169, 209, 236, 283, 288, 298, 310, 338, 380, 392, 404, 422, 447, 466.**

22 *Geoffrey Chaucer. The Works, 1532, with supplementary material from the editions of 1542, 1561, 1598, and 1602.* A facsimile edition, ed. with introduction by Derek S. Brewer. London: Scolar Press, 1974.
Brewer's introduction comments on all early printings from Thynne's 1532 edition to the 1687 reissue of Speght. As well as providing a facsimile of the 1532 edition, he prints in facsimile all new material added

after 1532. He discusses the contents of each volume item by item: first the forty-four entries in Thynne's 1532 edition, then the additions of 1542, especially the *Plowman's Tale*; then the twenty-six new items in Stowe's 1561 edition; then the seven new items of Speght's 1598 edition, including *FL*, for which Speght is sole authority; then eight new items from Speght's 1602 edition, including the first printing of *ABC*, *Jack of Upland*, and Speght's expanded glossary of 'Old and Obscure Words,' which incorporates annotations from the 1598 edition; and finally Brewer comments on the 1687 edition, the last of the black letter editions, which, along with an edition ca 1550, is not represented in facsimile text, since neither includes new material. Brewer notes that a copy of the 1532 edition was sold at Sotheby's of London in October 1971 for £850; another was sold in November 1973 for £23,000.

22a Sato, Tsutome, ed. and trans. *Chaucer no Renai Shi: Shujaku to Kaishaku*. Tokyo: Kobundo Souppansha, 1976.
Chaucer's love poems translated into Japanese with annotations and résumés. Includes Didactic Poems: *FA, Truth, Sted, Gent, Fortune*; Love Poems: *Ros, WN, AWU, MB*; Complaints: *BC, CD, Pity, Lady, Mars, Venus, AA, Purse*; Scraps: *Scogan, Bukton, Adam, Proverbs*.

23 *The Complete Poetry and Prose of Geoffrey Chaucer*. Ed. John H. Fisher. New York: Holt, Rinehart, and Winston, 1977. Pp 667–708.
Fisher's edition includes the various titles for each poem given in mss and in the explanatory and textual notes at the foot of the page is mindful of Shirley's involvement in the history of the lyrics. Fisher presents the poems attributed to Chaucer in the mss in this order: *ABC, AA, Mars, Venus, Pity, Lady, WN, Ros, Prov, Fortune, Truth, Gent, FA, Sted, Adam, Bukton, Scogan, Purse*; poems not attributed to Chaucer in mss but which he includes are *MB, AWU, BC, CD*. This edition provides an extensive bibliography for Chaucer's works, pp 975–1018.

24 Burrow, John, ed. *English Verse: 1300–1500*. Longman Annotated Anthologies of English Verse. London and New York: Longman, 1977. Pp 146–233.
Includes *Ros; Hide, Absolon; MB; Scogan*; and *Truth*; as well as excerpts from *T&C* and *CT*. Extensive notes and annotations.

24a Norton-Smith, John, ed. *Bodleian Library MS. Fairfax 16*. London: Scolar Press, 1979.
A facsimile edition of an important lyrics ms which contains *Pity, ABC, Fortune, Scogan, Purse, Bukton, Sted, AWU*, and *AA*, as well as other minor poems. Norton-Smith's introduction speculates on the circumstances and rationale of the book's compilation. He suggests that Chaucer may have circulated the minor poems in six small booklets – *LGW, HF, Mars* and *Venus, PF, AA*, and the lyrics – which proved too fragile to survive. Thus no mss of the minor poems antedate Fairfax 16, which was the first

collection of such poems. Norton-Smith emphasizes Chaucer's casual attitude toward 'publication.' The edition includes a full-scale, full-colour reproduction of the *Complaint of Mars* illustration, the iconography of which Norton-Smith discusses.

– Review by Donald C. Baker, *SAC*, 3 (1981), 165–9: 'Norton-Smith's notes on the texts of the individual poems are quite useful, citing in each case the place of the Fairfax 16 text in the editorial tradition of the poem. His comments are careful, and his remarks upon the classification of the manuscript copies of *Lack of Steadfastness* make a contribution, suggesting a new way of grouping the manuscripts on the basis of a convincing authorial variant' (p 166). Baker challenges Norton-Smith's assumptions about Chaucer's lack of concern over the text of his poems, noting *Adam* to the contrary and pointing out the scruples of Gower, Lydgate, Dante, Petrarch, and Boccaccio on textual accuracy. Surely we are not to assume Chaucer 'to have been the lone standard-bearer of the now current "medievalism"' (p 167).

24b Parkes, M.B., and Richard Beadle, eds. *Poetical Works: Geoffrey Chaucer. A Facsimile of Cambridge University MS Gg.4.27* [With Introductions]. 3 vols. Norman, Oklahoma: Pilgrim Books, 1979.

Harley 1239 contains *T&C* and five *CT*; Harley 7333 includes *CT*, *PF*, *Mars* and various shorter poems. But Cambridge University ms Gg.4.27 is the only surviving fifteenth-century attempt to collect all of Chaucer's major poetical works into one volume. Its contents include: *ABC, Scogan, Truth,* 'In May when every herte is ly3t' (fifteen 8-line stanzas, *The Bird's Praise of Love*), *De Amico ad Amicam, T&C, CT, LGW, PF, Temple of Glass* and Lydgate's *La Compleyn,* plus an independent quire of the seventeenth century which includes *Gent, Purse,* and *Adam.* The ms was 'copied sometime in the first quarter of the fifteenth century, and most probably in the second half of that quarter' (III,7). The editors print a few plates in colour, including one of the first stanzas of *ABC*. The legibility of the colour plates is much better than that of the black and white facsimiles. The ms was mutilated in the late sixteenth century by someone collecting pictures and borders.

❧ Bibliographies, Indexes, Manuscript and Textual Studies

See also **24A, 24B, 57, 307, 321.**

Specific Chaucer manuscripts containing lyrics may be conveniently identified by consulting the textual notes in Robinson **12.** Robinson gives the location of each manuscript, which is necessary information if one wishes to investigate the manuscript further, since manuscripts are catalogued by location. Most of the lyric manuscripts are to be found in the British Library or in the college libraries of Oxford and Cambridge. The student of Chaucer's lyrics may obtain detailed information on the contents of individual manuscripts in these libraries by consulting the following catalogues.

British Library

- *A Catalogue of Additions to Manuscripts in the British Museum.* 22 vols. London: British Museum, 1848–/ Rpt 1964–. [All volumes in this sequence are well-indexed. Most contain Chaucer entries for life records as well as for his poetry and prose. For Addit. 10340 see vol for 1836–40; for Addit. 16165 see vol for 1846–7; for Addit. 22139 see vol for 1854–60; for Addit. 34360 see vol for 1888–93; for Addit. 36983 see vol for 1900–5.]
- Smith, Thomas. *Catalogus Librorum Manuscriptorum Bibliothecae Cottonianae.* Oxford: Sheldon, 1696. [This catalogue is valuable in that it was compiled before the fire of 1731.]
- *A Catalogue of the Manuscripts in the Cottonian Library deposited in the British Museum.* London: L. Hansard, 1802.
- *A Catalogue of the Harleian Manuscripts in the British Museum.* 4 vols. London: G. Eyre and A. Strahan, 1808–12.
- *A Catalogue of the Lansdowne Manuscripts in the British Museum.* London: R. and A. Taylor, 1819. Scott, Edward J.L. *Index to the Sloane Manuscripts in the British Museum.* London: Printed by Order of the Trustees, 1904. (See **534**).

Oxford Libraries

- Black, William Henry. *A Descriptive, Analytical, and Critical Catalogue of the Manuscripts Bequeathed unto the University of Oxford by Elias Ashmole.* 2 parts. Oxford: University Press, 1845.
- Coxe, Henry O. *Catalogus codicum manuscriptorum qui in collegiis aulisque Oxoniensibus hodie adservantur.* 2 vols. Oxford: University Press, 1852.
- Madan, Falconer. *A Summary Catalogue of Western Manuscripts in the Bodleian Library.* 7 vols. Oxford: Clarendon Press, 1895–1953.

Cambridge Libraries

- Cowie, Morgan. *A Descriptive Catalogue of the Manuscripts and Scarce Books in the Library of St John's College, Cambridge.* Cambridge: University Press, 1843.
- Hardwick, C. *A Catalogue of the Manuscripts in the Library of the University of Cambridge.* 5 vols. Cambridge: University Press, 1856–67.
- James, Montague Rhodes. *Catalogue of Western Manuscripts in the Library of Trinity College.* 4 vols. Cambridge: University Press, 1901.
- — *Descriptive Catalogue of the Manuscripts in the Library of Gonville and Caius College.* 2 vols. Cambridge: University Press, 1907–8.
- — *A Descriptive Catalogue of the Manuscripts in the Library of St John's College, Cambridge.* Cambridge: University Press, 1913.
- — *Bibliotheca Pepysiana.* 3 vols. London: Sidgwick and Jackson, 1923.
- — *A Descriptive Catalogue of the Manuscripts in the Library of Lambeth Palace.* Cambridge: University Press, 1932.

For the Bannatyne ms in the Advocates Library, Edinburgh, see **460a** below. For the Longleat 258 ms, in the possession of the Marquis of Bath, see **35a.** For a description of Leiden University ms Vossius 9, see **32b**; for the Lambeth Palace ms, see **41.** For the Mellish ms (University of Nottingham) see **29**; for Cosin V.1.9 (Durham) see **30a.** For Coventry ms see **31**; for the Melbourne ms see **32.** For information on early printed editions, in addition to specific items annotated below (see especially entries on Caxton, Thynne, Stow, and Speght), see the following:

- McKerrow, Ronald B. *A Dictionary of Printers and Booksellers in England, Scotland and Ireland, and of Foreign Printes of English Books, 1557–1640.* London, Printed for the Bibliographical Society by Blades, East & Blades, 1910.

– Nixon, Howard M. 'Caxton, his Contemporaries and Successors in the Book Trade from Westminster Documents.' *The Library*, 31 (1976), 305–26.
– Plomer, Henry Robert. *Abstracts from the Wills of English Printers and Stationers from 1492 to 1630*. London: for the Bibliographical Society, by Blades, East & Blades, 1903. [Pertinent selections from 40 documents.]
– — *Richard Pynson, Glover and Printer*. In *The Library*, 4th Series, 3, London, 1923.
– — *William Caxton*. London: L. Parsons; Boston: Small, Maynard and Company, 1925.
– — *Wynkyn de Worde and His Contemporaries from the Death of Caxton to 1535*. London: Grafton & Co., 1925. [Chapters on Pynson and Notary.]

25 Blodgett, James Edward. 'William Thynne and His 1532 Edition of Chaucer.' *DAI*, 36 (1976), 5311A. Indiana University Dissertation, 1975. Dir. Alfred David.
After discussing Thynne's life and work as a bureaucrat in Henry VIII's household, Blodgett attempts to establish Thynne's editorial practices. Thynne used Caxton and two surviving mss which bear Caxton's printer's marks in the making of his edition. Strong cumulative evidence indicates that he emended his base-texts by collating them against other texts of the same works, choosing a reading found in two mss against a single third one. Thynne liked to archaize Chaucer's language and to classicize spelling of proper names; he also made efforts to adjust Chaucer's lines for regular syllable counts. 'In the case of the *Romaunt of the Rose*, Thynne seems to have derived many of his emendations from a copy of the French original.' Blodgett's concluding chapter sketches cultural influences on Thynne – humanism, scholarly interest in the past, new uses of medieval love poetry at court. 'Because of Thynne's practices in emending his texts, any variants unique to his edition should be treated cautiously; on the other hand, because of Thynne's access to and use of manuscripts no longer extant, his variants should be given careful consideration' (p 5311A).

25a Bühler, Curt F. *The Fifteenth Century Book: the Scribes, the Printers, the Decorators*. Philadelphia: University of Pennsylvania Press, 1960.
Bühler discusses the scarcity and value of books and the relationship of poet and scribe (pp 15–39). He notes the vehement wrath of Cicero, Strabo, Roger Bacon, Petrarch, Leonardo Bruni, Chaucer, and Reginald Pecock against the ignorance and carelessness of scribes (pp 17, 97).

26 Brown, Carleton. *A Register of Middle English Religious and Didactic Verse*. Oxford: Oxford University Press, vol 1, 1916; vol 2, 1920.
See index, vol 2 for mss of *ABC* and the moral balades.

27 Brown, Carleton, and Rossell Hope Robbins. *The Index of Middle English Verse*. New York: Columbia University Press, 1943.
See p 746 for Chaucerian and pseudo-Chaucerian lyrics. A supplement appears below (**51**).

28 Brusendorff, Aage. *The Chaucer Tradition*. London: Oxford University Press, 1925; Copenhagen: V. Pio and Povl Branner, 1925. Pp 178–294.
Ch 4: 'The Minor Poems': 1) *The MS Collections* (pp 178–207) describes and discusses the principal mss containing lyrics. Some mss include attributions, but if they are late mss (two generations after Chaucer) the attributions are often of little value. 'It appears to have been a common publishers' custom during the latter half of the fifteenth century to make one or more scribes copy a number of short poems in separate quires and to unite these very much at random, merely with a view to get up such collections as would command a good price and a quick sale' (p 179). Brusendorff notes how regularly Lydgate's poetry is mixed with Chaucer's, along with that of Clanvowe and Hoccleve, and with anonymous lyrics. Some mss contain French titles, indicative perhaps of the buyer and audience. Brusendorff categorizes the manuscripts into a 'Shirley Group,' a 'Bradshaw Group,' and a 'Hammond Group.' 'It seems practically certain ... that no complete ms edition of Chaucer's Minor Poems – not to speak of his Collected Works – ever existed' (pp 206–7). 2) *The Shirley Group* (pp 207–36) considers the six more or less complete Shirley autograph mss and an additional five others copied from lost Shirley mss. The best two are BL ms Addit. 16165, containing numerous minor poems, *Boece*, and a poem by the Earl of Warwick on his wife Isabella (ca 1422); and Cambridge ms Trin. R.3.20, containing shorter pieces, including several Lydgate poems. John Shirley (ca 1366–1456), a great lover and copier of books, possessed 'a sort of circulating library,' which was fashionable in London in the days of Henry VI. He began his work at an advanced age, seems to have known personally most of the literary men of his day, and produced signed mss with elaborately decorated flyleaves. Sometimes his titles contain instructions or admonitions to the reader; sometimes they contain gossip. The texts have little critical value, though three Chaucer poems (*Adam, WN, BC*) are found uniquely in his mss. His texts are very idiosyncratic with 'extraordinary perversions,' apparently due to his writing from memory, in some instances 'from a very enfeebled memory' (p 233). 3) *The Separate Poems* (pp 236–94) discusses textual matters pertaining to *ABC, Fortune, Truth, Purse, Gent, AA, Mars* and *Venus, Pity, Sted, Adam, WN, Balade of a Reeve, Prov, PF, Scogan, Bukton, FA, BD*. Brusendorff includes an appendix on Lydgate and Shirley, pp 453–71.

28a Caldwell, Robert A. 'Joseph Holand, Collector and Antiquary.' *MP*, 40 (1943), 295–301.

Holand (ca 1552–after 1605) once owned ms Arundell XXII, containing Geoffrey of Monmouth's *Historia* and the *Seege of Troye*, and the mutilated Cambridge University Library ms Gg.4.27, to which Holand added a fascicle 'obviously to supply the lost passages in the text' (p 299). Holand was acquainted with Thynne, Camden, and Cotton and contributed to the Society of Antiquaries. He is descended from John Holland, fourth son of Robert, Lord Holland (d 1328–9), that is, the family Shirley alludes to in his glosses on *Mars* and *Venus*. Caldwell traces what is known of Holand's life and involvement in antiquarian activities of his day.

28b — 'The Scribe of the Chaucer MS. Cambridge University Library Gg.4.27.' *MLQ*, 5 (1944), 33–44.

Gg is carefully executed by a competent scribe. Nevertheless, 'many errors ... indicate that the scribe was uncertain of what he was doing, that he often failed to understand what he was writing, and that he was perhaps not thoroughly familiar with the English language' (p 34). The simplest hypothesis, in view of the kinds of errors, is that he was a Fleming or a Dutchman (p 36). Caldwell presents numerous instances of Dutch morphology and phonology in the ms, which explain why the ms 'in many ways very good came to be in other ways very bad' (p 44). See **57**.

29 Davis, Norman. 'Chaucer's *Gentilesse:* A Forgotten Manuscript, with some Proverbs' *RES*, 20 (1969), 43–50.

The Nottingham University Library MeLMI (Mellish), written in the fifteenth century for John Harpur of Rushall in Staffordshire, includes *Truth, Gent,* and several proverbs with Chaucerian affinities copied in vacant spaces by hands other than the original. *Truth* has been cited by editors and the *Index of Middle English Verse* **1** 27; but *Gent* has been ignored. The Mellish ms offers an eleventh text of *Gent* according to Doyle and Pace's count (**31**), though one of the eleven (Camb. University Lib. Gg.4.27) should be deleted from the *Index*, since it is a copy of Speght's 1598 edition and has no independent value. Mellish, on the other hand, is a 'genuine witness' (p 46); it has no unique readings, but its textual affinities are complex. Davis cites various cross-connections with other mss and transcribes the text. But see **49** and **57**.

30 Doyle, A.I. 'More Light on John Shirley.' *MAE*, 30 (1961), 93–101.

A concise summary of known biographical details from public records, mss, guildhall rolls, calendar of close rolls, etc, to shed light on Shirley beyond that found in Hammond **37** and Brusendorff **28**. The essay ends with 'To be continued' (p 101).

30a — 'Unrecorded Chaucerian Manuscript.' *The Durham Philobiblon,* 8 (1953), 54.

Refers to Cosin ms V.1.9, a late fourteenth- or early fifteenth-century copy of Book I of Giles de Rome, *Le Livre du gouvernement,* with the first two stanzas of *ABC* added on fol 203r below the colophon. Doyle prints the two stanzas.

31 Doyle, A.I., and George B. Pace. 'A New Chaucer Manuscript.' *PMLA,* 83 (1968), 22–34.

A ms from the King Henry VIII School at Coventry, long thought lost, has reappeared and is now held in The Coventry City Record Office. Containing *ABC, Bukton, Purse, Gent, Sted,* and *Truth,* 'the new ms is the fourth largest collection of Chaucer's Short Poems extant. Yet virtually nothing has been known about the ms beyond the entry in Bernard, which dates from 1697' (p 22). The ms illuminations are in a style of ca 1430–60; its texts belong to the Bradshaw Group (see **28**) and exhibit 'a relatively large number of unique readings. Unique readings do not necessarily lessen greatly the usefulness of a ms; the scribe cannot know which readings will be significant. Even so, a valid characterization of the Coventry ms is to say that it is an uneven rendering, varying from fairly poor in parts of the *ABC* to good in *Truth.* But deficiencies in quality, such as they may be, are offset by the generous quantity of texts' (p 34).

32 — 'Further Texts of Chaucer's Minor Poems.' *SB,* 28 (1975), 41–61.

In response to Nichols **42,** can it be said that 'all the manuscript evidence is available for the student?' (p 42). Evidently not, for Doyle and Pace publish transcriptions of *ABC* from Melbourne MS State Library of Victoria, Felton Bequest; *Truth* in Nottingham University Lib. ms MeLM1 (Mellish); and *AWU* in Bodleian ms Fairfax 16. None of these has been published before, though 'the Fairfax copy is the best version of that poem' (p 42). Doyle and Pace also bring together mss (all of lyrics) which have been referred to as unpublished and also certain early printed editions which have never been reprinted.

32a Doyle, A.I. and M.B. Parkes. 'The Production of Copies of the *Canterbury Tales* and the *Confessio Amantis* in the Early Fifteenth Century.' In *Medieval Scribes, Manuscripts & Libraries: Essays presented to N.R. Ker.* Ed. M.B. Parkes and Andrew G. Watson. London: Scolar Press, 1978. Pp 163–210.

The essay studies the five hands in Trinity College Cambridge ms R.3.2 as a key to the relationship between scribes copying English works in London during the first quarter of the fifteenth century. Although few of the mss discussed contain Chaucer lyrics, the essay is informative in describing workshop procedures as well as the efforts of individual scribes. Appendix C (pp 208–10) considers evidence for original owners, early owners, and speculative production of mss.

32b Dorsten, J.A. van. 'The Leyden "Lydgate Manuscript".' *Scriptorium*, 14 (1960), 315–25.

Leiden University Library ms Vossius Germ. Gall.Q.9 contains Lydgate pieces, a few anonymous pieces including *Guy of Warwick* and unique copies of 'Preservaryum,' 'On Fortune,' 'A Nightingale Poem,' and 'An ABC Hymn to Christ and the Blessed Virgin,' and two of Chaucer's lyrics, *Fortune* and *Truth*. The anthology is in three hands from the last quarter of the fifteenth century. It bears similarities to Lansdowne 699 and Harley 2255 and others, though the relationship is not direct.

 33 *The Findern Manuscript: Cambridge University Library ms Ff.1.6*. Introduction by Richard Beadle and A.E.B. Owen. London: Scolar Press, 1977.

A facsimile edition of a manuscript that includes excerpts of Gower's *CA*; Chaucer's *Pity, PF, Purse, Anelida's Complaint*, 'Tale of Thisbe' from *LGW, Venus*; several Lydgate lyrics; Clanvowe, *Boke of Cupide (CN)*; *Sir Degrevant*; Roos' *LBD*; and a large number of anonymous lyrics. Sixty-two items in all. For discussion of this ms see Robbins **50** and Hanson-Smith **38**.

33a Fletcher, Bradford Y. 'Printer's Copy for Stow's Chaucer.' *SB*, 31 (1978), 184–201.

'In the course of editing ms R.3.19 in Trinity College, Cambridge, I have had an opportunity to examine Stow's work at length and can now identify most of his printer's copy and testify to the remarkable accuracy with which he reproduced it' (p 184). Stow printed directly from this ms without an intermediary transcription. His additions to the Chaucer canon in the Renaissance included *Gent, Lady*, and *Adam*, as well as *AWU, Proverbs*, and nineteen spurious poems associated with Chaucer until Tyrwhitt's ringing denunciation of Stow. Fletcher discusses each of the twenty-four entries in R.3.19, comparing them with other mss as well as Stow's edition. Stow modernizes spelling and to some slight extent regularizes. But in the 2170 lines that he prints from R.3.19, 'he varies substantively less than 200 times' (p 200). Occasionally he corrects obvious errors; occasionally he introduces errors of his own. Fourteen of his additions to the Chaucer canon come from R.3.19; four come from R.3.20; and one each (with less certainty) may come from Cotton Cleo.D.v, Fairfax 16, and Harley 78. 'Finally, in two cases (7, 8) Stow's print is certainly itself an authority and one (24) awaits further investigation' (p 201).

 34 Hammond, Eleanor Prescott. 'Omissions from the Editions of Chaucer.' *MLN*, 19 (1904), 35–8.

In emphasizing our indebtedness to John Shirley, Hammond points out that 'the amount of knowledge which we have of his work and of his personality gives to his testimony a something which no unsigned and undated copy, however excellent in itself, can possess' (p 35). Often we have only the testimony of Shirley in determining the authenticity of

Chaucer's lyrics. Moreover, his ' "gossippy" headings ... often give us knowledge as to contemporary conditions which no other copyist has preserved' (p 36). Hammond considers lost Shirley mss, his friendship with Lydgate and personal addresses to Thomas Chaucer and the Duke Humphrey of Gloucester, his errors, and his account that Chaucer wrote *Truth* on his deathbed. After relating Shirley mss to other mss and emphasizing the need for more research in this area, Hammond prints the texts of two balades in Shirley that 'should be again brought to the notice of Chaucer-students' (p 36), namely, 'Of alle the crafftes oute blessed be the ploughe' and 'Hit is no right alle other lustes to leese.'

34a — 'MS Pepys 2006 – A Chaucerian Codex.' *MLN*, 19 (1904), 196–8.
The ms is in six hands, according to the following distribution: 1) *Complaint of the Black Knight* and part of *Temple of Glas*; 2) the rest of *Temple of Glas, LGW, ABC, HF, Mars, Venus, Fortune, PF*: 3) Three *Kings of Cologne, Cesar and Pompey*, and *Cato*; 4) *Melibeus* and most of the *ParsT*; 5) the rest of *ParsT* and the *Retractation*; 6) *Mars, Venus, Anelida, Scogan, ABC, Purse, Truth*, and *MB*. The second set of Chaucer texts (hand 6) was once a separate fascicule. The title for the first copy of *Mars* (hand 2) seems to have been *The broche of Thebes*. This title occurs elsewhere only in Harley 7333. Hammond would date the ms in the latter part of the fifteenth century.

35 — 'Two British Museum Manuscripts (Harley 2251 and Adds. 34360.). A Contribution to the Bibliography of John Lydgate.' *Anglia*, 28 (1905), 1–28. Both mss contain several Chaucer items *(Purse, WN, Pity, Lady)*; Harley 2251 also has *Fortune*. Hammond considers the relationship of the two mss to each other and to the Shirley mss, listing contents and comparing sequences with each other. Entries 13–23 of the Addit. ms and 1–11 of the Harley 'are copies from the same original, executed by the same scribe' (p 25). Hammond assumes a lost Shirley volume, four leaves of which remain bound into the scrapbook now called Harley 78 (p 26). 'It is possible that a detailed comparison of these and other codices would result in showing that a large body of Lydgate's work is derived en masse from one or two archetypes' (p 24). But there is a great need for more comparative study of groups of mss.

35a — 'MS Longleat 258 – A Chaucerian Codex.' *MLN*, 20 (1905), 77–9.
The ms, in a late fifteenth-century hand on a mixture of vellum and paper, is related to the Bodleian group (Fairfax 16, Bodley 638, Tanner 346, and Digby 181). Its contents include *Temple of Glas*, three stanzas by Rycharde Hattfield, *Mars, Pity, AL, AA, PF, LBD*, and *Churl and Bird*. Sixteen leaves have been lost, which contained *FL* and the first six stanzas of *Mars*.

35b — 'Ashmole 59 and Other Shirley Manuscripts.' *Anglia*, 30 (1907), 320–48.
Ashmole 59 was owned by William Browne in 1614, who also owned
Ashmole 45, Addit. 34360, Lansdowne 699, Durham V.ii.15 and 16 (main-
ly Lydgate mss, and Durham V.iii.9. Hammond describes the contents of
Ashmole 59, which though dominantly comprised of Lydgate materials
includes *Scogan's Moral Balade* in which *Gent* is embedded, *Fortune*, 'The
Chronicle Made by Chaucer' which Furnivall (*Trial Forewards*, p 97) said
'could not possibly be by Chaucer,' 'Ballad in Commendation of Our
Lady' which Thynne (1532) printed as Chaucer's but which Tyrwhitt rejected, and *Venus* beside which Shirley has written 'Lenvoye by Thomas
Chaucier to alle princis and princesses of this translacon of this compleynte and laye' (p 326). The mss includes sixty-five works in all. Hammond compares its contents with those of Addit. 16165, Trinity R.3.20,
and Harley 2251, which are also in Shirley's hand, in an attempt to establish a Shirley chronology. She also considers Harley 7333 which is
not in Shirley's hand but is copied from a Shirley ms or mss which were
executed earlier than were Trinity and Ashmole (p 338). Hammond suggests that much of Ashmole was written by Shirley from memory. 'No
editor should adopt Ashmole's lections in preference to those of other
manuscripts' (p 345). Several of Shirley's mss must have been written in
the same scriptorium where Harley 2251 and Addit. 34360 were executed.
More than a few of these mss were in the possession of Stow.

36 — 'On the Editing of Chaucer's Minor Poems.' *MLN*, 23 (1908), 20–1.
Constructs a stemma for Fairfax 16, Bodley 638, and Tanner 346. 'The
great value of the Oxford group lies ... in the clearness with which each
step of its descent can be traced, and the certainty with which we can
work back to a ms two degrees nearer Chaucer than the existing
volumes' (p 21). The competing authority is Cambridge ms Gg.4.27; its
value is 'still unproven' (p 21).

37 — *Chaucer: A Bibliographical Manual*. Boston: Macmillan, 1908; rpt, New
York: P. Smith, 1933.
Ch 1, 'The Life of Chaucer,' pp 1–50, with subdivisions on the Chaucer
Legend, the Appeal to Fact, the Portraits of Chaucer, and Chaucer as a
Character in Fiction; Ch 2, 'The Works of Chaucer,' pp 51–149, with a
survey of the Chaucer canon, Chaucerian imitators, earlier editors, lost
works, chronology of accepted works, sources, and recent editions; Ch 3,
'The *Canterbury Tales*,' pp 150–324, with discussion of mss, chronology,
and separate tales; Ch 4, 'Works other than the *Canterbury Tales*,'
pp 325–405, see below; Ch 5, 'Verse and Prose Printed with the Work of
Chaucer,' pp 406–63, including seventy-two entries; Ch 6, 'Linguistics
and Versification,' pp 464–509 (see **62**); and Ch 7, 'Bibliographical
Matters,' including descriptions of the main library collections of
medieval mss. In Ch 4, Hammond offers detailed analyses of the

manuscripts containing the shorter poems, and includes a table comparing the contents of Fairfax 16, Bodley 638, and Tanner 346, the three principal Oxford sources for Chaucer's lyrics (pp 333–9). In this chapter, Hammond lists all works other than the tales in alphabetical order, and for each work discusses known mss, title and authenticity, printed editions, sources, date, and other notes. Ch 5 includes several works probably by Chaucer, including *WN, AWU, BC, Lady, CD, MB, Prov, Romaunt,* and *Ros.* Hammond's study remains an indispensable reference work.

38 Hanson-Smith, Elizabeth. 'A Woman's View of Courtly Love: The Findern Anthology Cambridge University Library, ms Ff.1.6.' *Journal of Women's Studies in Literature,* 1 (1979), 179–94.

Several of the twenty-four poems in the ms are probably by women and 'supply a needed corrective balance to the generally accepted critical version of medieval courtly love' (p 180). Robbins **50** noted the prominence of female signatures in the ms but thought the women were scribes, not authors. Evidence of female authorship in the poems is 1) direct reference to men as the object of love; 2) the unique occurrences of these poems in this ms, which suggests that they were not 'the stock in trade of an itinerant copier' (p 181); 3) originality within the pieces and the fact that in no other ms is there a group of poems employing a female *persona.* The poems are marked by an 'awareness of the female condition' (p 182). They also reveal 'dialect occurences [sic] and authorial errors in the text' (p 182). Hanson-Smith stresses the limitations placed on women in the male-dominated fifteenth century. The woman is constrained by social circumstances not felt by men. 'Nor do we ever find poems where a woman rides out seeking adventure' (p 183). A woman's defence against unwanted lovers was to fall back on arguments of virtue and chastity. 'We may well speculate whether the whole vast Neo-Platonic superstructure of medieval courtly love service were not built upon women's refusal to give in to men they did not fancy' (p 190). The Findern poems reflect female psychology with a satisfying artistry and are surely authored by women.

39 Holt, Lucius Hudson. 'Chaucer's "Lac of Stedfastnesse." A Critical Test.' *JEGP,* 6 (1907), 419–31.

'The object of editing Chaucer should be to present us with the poems as nearly in the form in which Chaucer wrote them as possible ... Again and again we find that the editors ... scorn the spelling of the mss. only to insert their own, which is utterly out of keeping with the surroundings' (p 429). Holt sets up a stemma with four groups to conclude that the text of *Sted* must be formed from collaboration of mss Harl 7333, Trin. Coll. Cambr. R.3.20, and Fairfax 16, with Hatton 73, Trin. Coll. Cambr. R.14.51, and Bannatyne, the latter three to be used to check up results and aid in doubtful cases. Thynne also should be consulted. Holt then prints the text devised according to these principles, noting the preference of 'Lenvoy' or 'Envoy' to 'Lenvoy to King Richard,' which appears only in a Shirley ms. Also he thinks 'dryve thy peple agayne to stedfastness' found in Harl, Cambr. R.3.20, and Hatton is preferable to 'wed thy folk,' as in Skeat. (But see **46**.)

40 Kökeritz, Helge. 'Chaucer's *Rosemounde*.' *MLN*, 63 (1948), 310–8.

Kökeritz objects to Skeat's 'unnecessarily normalized spelling' (p 311) and prints the text as it appears in the ms (Bodl. Rawl. Poet 163, f 114r), where Skeat discovered it on the flyleaf to *T&C*. Kökeritz agrees with MacCracken **534** that Tregentil was meant to be a scribal compliment. The ms has fewer errors than Skeat assumed; Kökeritz then discusses Skeat's emendations, accepting some but rejecting most.

41 MacCracken, Henry Noble. 'Notes Suggested by a Chaucer Codex.' *MLN*, 23 (1908), 212–4.

A note on ms Lambeth Palace 344, which contains *Truth* and *Sted* here printed for the first time, and a supplement to Holt's 'ingenious reconstruction' (p 212) of *Sted* (**39**) which gives ms Hatton 73 secondary status. MacCracken defends the importance of Hatton, noting that it and Lambeth 344 probably had identical contents. Both are mid-fifteenth century; Hatton is in three hands, Lambeth in one and derived from Hatton 'in every case. Its readings where different are always inferior and are the result of careless transcribing' (p 213). The contents of Hatton tell something of its later audience – Queen Margaret and Dame Elizabeth Windsor in the reign of Henry VIII. 'Surely a volume enjoyed by all these noble ladies deserves a prime place in the noble role of Chaucer mss' (p 214).

42 Nichols, Robert E., Jr. 'Chaucer's *Fortune, Truth,* and *Gentilesse:* The "Last" Unpublished Manuscript Transcriptions.' *Spec*, 44 (1969), 46–50.

The 'Last' in the title refers to the last of the four mss discussed by Pace **43** which remain unpublished. Following the Chaucer Society system of line and stanza numbering in preparing his transcriptions, Nichols presents *Fortune* and *Truth* from the Leiden University Codex Vossianus variarum linguarum, quarto 9, and *Gent* from ms Cambridge University Lib. Gg.4.27(b). See Pace's response, with Doyle, to the idea of a 'last' ms (**32**).

43 Pace, George B. 'Four Unpublished Chaucer Manuscripts.' *MLN*, 63 (1948), 457–62.

Pace prints the texts for *Truth* from BL ms Add.36983, f 262, and Cambridge Magdalen College ms Pepys 2006, pp 389–90; *Sted*, from Dublin Trinity College ms 432, f 59a; and the last stanza and envoy to *Purse*, Cambridge Caius College ms 176, p 12. 'With the printing of these texts, there remain unpublished only four manuscripts of Chaucer's Short

Poems. One of these is now the subject of study [Cambr. University Lib. Gg.4.27(b) ms of *Gent*]; the most significant readings of the second and third can be found in Robinson's notes [Leyden University Lib. Vossius 9 ms of *Truth* and *Fortune*]; but the fourth, a casualty of the war, seems lost for some time if not for ever [Phillipps 11409, Cheltenham ms of *Truth*]. Of the nature of its text nothing is known' (p 462).

44 — 'The Text of Chaucer's *Purse*.' *SB*, 1 (1948), 105–21.

Pace argues against a bifid arrangement of *Purse* mss. 'The confusion arises from the slightness of the variations' (p 106); he suggests instead a trifid arrangement: F, Ff; A, CC_1, P, Cx, Black letter texts; and H_2, CC_2, H, AZ, M. Four mss seem one remove from the original (F, Ff, A, H_2); 'of these Ff (Cambr. University Lib. Ff 1.6, Fol 59a) has the fewest unique readings and is in general a good text' (p 117). Pace uses it as the basis for the text he then prints.

45 — 'Otho A. XVIII.' *Spec*, 26 (1951), 306–16.

Otho A. XVIII, containing saints' lives, chronicles, four Chaucer poems, and a picture of Chaucer, burned in the Cotton Library fire of 1731. Pace has discovered a transcription of the Chaucer portion pasted into a copy of Urry's *Chaucer* which William Thomas presented to the British Museum. The titles of the poems are given as *A balade by Geffrey Chaucier uppon his dethe bedde lyinge in his grete Anguysse* [*Truth*, without the envoy]; *Balade Ryalle made by Poetecall Chaucyer a Gaufrede [Sted]; Balade by Chaucier etc [Purse]; Cantus Troili* [from Bk I]. Signed Otho A.18 28 June 1721. 'Thus we have in effect a new Chaucer Manuscript' (p 308). Pace demonstrates that none of the texts is derived from a Shirley original. He compares the text with others of *Purse* and *Truth*, to establish two possible manuscript trees. Since the Otho *Truth* seems to precede Shirley, Shirley's statement of *Truth*'s having been made on Chaucer's deathbed, which some have rejected, must be reconsidered. But the real value of the ms lies in helping to establish firmly the text of *Sted* for the first time. Pace compares eight mss of *Sted* to show that Otho is in the same line of descent as the Shirley texts, but is their ancestor.

46 — 'Chaucer's Lak of Stedfastness.' *SB*, 4 (1951), 105–22.

The mss of *Sted* fall into two groups, with disagreement on lines 5, 19, and especially 28, where one group reads 'dryve thi peple' and the other 'wed thi folk.' With the discovery of the transcription of Cotton ms Otho A. XVIII (see **45**) 'it is now possible to show that one set of readings is the work of scribes' (p 105). Pace reconstructs a stemma of fifteen mss to conclude that 'Is no thing lyke,' 'For amonge us now,' and 'wed thi folke' are to be preferred, since competing readings are of scribal origin. He then uses Cotton Cleopatra D. VIII, fol 188b ('decidedly the best,' p 119), as basis of the text he prints. Pace also finds interpretative reasons for preferring 'wed thi folk.' Chaucer 'can hardly ask the king to cherish his folk in line 23 and five lines later to drive them with the sword' (p 122).

47 — 'The True Text of the *Former Age.*' *MS*, 23 (1961), 363–7.
Brusendorff **28** suggests that *FA* is 'clearly a fragment copied from one of
the poet's drafts,' but does not offer good reasons. Pace shows why that
theory is likely, namely, because of the poem's lack of a definite conclusion, its uncompleted stanza, and its unmetrical line. 'The lines ... are
not of the sort usually associated with scribes (misreadings of the sense,
eyeskips, and the like) but rather with an author who is still seeking his
phrasing' (p 367). Emendations on grounds of meter are thus unfounded.
The Cambr. Univ. Lib. ms Ii.3.21 scribe is very reliable. 'There is at least
a chance that he had Chaucer's ms, or something very close to it, before
him for this one ... The evidence allows us little choice other than to regard his copy – his unemended copy – as being as near to the true text
of Chaucer's poem as we are likely to get' (p 367).

48 — 'The Chaucerian *Proverbs.*' *SB*, 18 (1965), 41–8.
Adding Stowe (1561) as a genuine authority to Fairfax 16, Harley 7578,
and Addit.16165 (Shirley), Pace offers a detailed textual analysis of *Proverbs* in an effort to set the record straight on their authenticity. He concludes that 1) all the authorities are from the same archetype; 2) none of
the unique readings is in the archetype; and 3) H is derived from F. 'The
major reason for believing that Chaucer wrote the *Proverbs* is the ascription of them to him in the titles of two of the mss' (p 46). Stowe's edition is also 'tantamount to an ascription' (p 46). Pace uses F as basis for
correcting *shul* (line 1) to *shal* and *my* (line 6) to *myn*, and can see no reason to doubt the authenticity. What we are dealing with is 'a fragment, a
work begun but abandoned, or, alternatively, quotations, appealing because of their sententious cast, from a work now lost' (p 48).

49 — 'Speght's Chaucer and [Cambridge Univ. Lib.] ms Gg.4.27.' *SB*, 21
(1968), 225–35.
ABC was first printed by Speght in 1602. Though it is found in sixteen
mss it appears on the opening folios of Gg, a ms in the possession
ca 1600 of 'Joseph Holland, antiquarian and lover of Chaucer' (p 225).
There are a sufficient number of marked eccentricities of the version in
Gg to leave no doubt that Holland's volume is Speght's source. We have,
then, 'a rarity – the actual copy underlying an Elizabethan printed book'
(p 226). Pace explores Speght's editorial treatment of the text. He also reflects upon the tradition which says Chaucer composed the poem for
Blanche, Duchess of Lancaster, noting that there is a special reason for
believing that this ms might have preserved such a tradition; its earlier
owner was probably Humphrey, Duke of Gloucester, Chaucer's 'great
nephew (half blood) ... [whose] grandmother was Blanche, Duchess of
Lancaster' (p 235). See **29** and **57**.

50 Robbins, Rossell Hope. 'The Findern Anthology.' *PMLA*, 69 (1954), 610–42.

Noting the rarity of ms anthologies of vernacular lyrics, Robbins catalogs the contents of Cambr. Univ. Lib. ms Ff.1.6 to show the typical non-religious entertainment verse known to a wealthy and educated provincial group in the later fifteenth century. After discussing curious marginalia in other mss pertaining to the Finderns, Findern hall, and family history, Robbins suggests a possible method of compilation for the polite Findern anthology 'through the cooperative efforts of itinerant professional scribes and educated women living in the neighborhood' (p 611). Perhaps Nicholas Findern obtained a blank ms 'for making a permanent record of his favorite poetry' (p 626). The ms contains many women's names – Elizabet Koton, Elisabet Frauncys, Anne Schyrley, Margery Hungerford, and ffraunces Crucken. Robbins traces their family ties, then speculates: 'Can it be that young women of these neighboring families, when visiting Findern, copied into the big book texts of poems which they enjoyed, from mss of their own or mss borrowed for the occasion?' (p 628). Robbins notes that the bulk of the poems are not in their same hands, though some are. Other scribes are named in the explicits – W. Caluerley, a leweston, Nicholaus, and Godwin. On the basis of other practices in the ms it is possible that the 'explicit Clanvowe' after the *Cuckoo and Nightingale* indicates that 'Clanvowe is simply a scribe' (p 630). The essay concludes with the printing of nine unpublished lyrics from the ms. (See **33** and **38**).

51 — and John L. Cutler. *Supplement to the Index of Middle English Verse.* Lexington: University of Kentucky Press, 1965.

See p 529 for ms with extracts from *Sted*, and several spurious ascriptions to Chaucer.

52 Root, Robert K. 'Publication before Printing.' *PMLA*, 28 (1913), 417–31.

'It is the purpose of this paper to set forth on the basis of contemporary evidence the conditions of publication which prevailed in Western Europe during the fourteenth and early fifteenth centuries' (p 417). Root begins with letters of Boccaccio and Petrarch that discuss publication, that is, the releasing of a ms to go forth to the public *(in publicum)*. Once a dedicatory copy was given it could be freely lent; indeed, 'it would seem that the patron was even under some obligation to further its circulation *(emittere in publicum)*' (p 419). Once the ms was in circulation the literary fame of its author was at the mercy of the critics. Petrarch seemed full of terror of the irrevocableness of publication (p 420). Unauthorized publication was common through the promise-breaking of a friend. (Cf the premature publication of Boccaccio's *De Genealogia Deorum*.) Petrarch personally revised mss of his works prepared by the scribes he employed. 'Continually and bitterly Petrarch complains of the difficulty of getting scribes, and of the carelessness of those whom he can get' (p 425). It seems that in Italy the author was in the first instance his own publisher. In England and France authors were more dependent on patrons. Like Petrarch, Chaucer was concerned with textual accuracy (cf *Adam*); such proofreading might lead to revision as well as correction. 'The author's concern for the purity of his text which led him to revise each several copy prepared under his orders would also lead to a continual and progressive alteration in phrasing and metre. Each copy might in this way take on the character of a new recension' (p 431).

53 Tatlock, J.S.P., and A.G. Kennedy. *Concordance to the Works of Geoffrey Chaucer, together with the Middle English Versions of Le Roman de la Rose.* Washington: Carnegie Institution of Washington, 1927.

The *Concordance* is based on the Globe edition of Chaucer's *Works* 3 rather than Skeat because 'its text is rather more conservative, and in some parts is based on a larger number of mss' (p iii). All works contained in the Globe edition have been concorded and no others. The *Astrolabe* is included, but not Skeat's 'Supplementary Propositions.' Concerning the decision to include all of the *Romaunt* the editors observe: 'It may seem odd to print words from its certainly non-Chaucerian portions among Chaucer's words, but the inclusion suggestively exhibits the likenesses and unlikenesses of the two vocabularies. Students of Chaucer are aware of the spuriousness of at least the middle part of the work and the doubt as to any of it, and other readers are sufficiently warned by the title page and this introduction' (p iv). The editors feel that on the whole Chaucer's text is in as good condition as that of 'any other important medieval author except Dante, and much better than Shakespeare's' (p v). The Introduction includes an historical account of the plans for making a Chaucer Concordance, going back to the inception of the Chaucer Society as an offshoot of the Early English Text Society in 1868.

54 Utley, Francis Lee. *The Crooked Rib.* Columbus: Ohio State University Press, 1944.

A survey of medieval treatments of women, beginning with introductory chapters on 1) 'The Motive Forces behind Medieval Satire and Defense of Women'; 2) 'The Genres of Satire and Defence'; 3) 'The History of English Satire and Defence to 1568'; and concluding with an analytic index (pp 93–350) of works satirizing or defending women. Utley makes frequent reference to Chaucer and *RR* in his introduction. His Index includes *AWU, Ros, Romaunt, Bukton, Truth, Purse, Scogan, MB*; several excerpts from the *CT, T&C,* and other narrative works; and a large number of poems ascribed to Chaucer in Thynne, Stowe, and Speght.

55 Wells, John Edwin. *A Manual of the Writings in Middle English: 1050–1400.*
New Haven: Connecticut Academy of Arts and Sciences, 1916.
Pp 599–747; bibliography, 866–81; index, pp 885–941. [With nine supplements, two in 1923 (bound into the third edition) and others published
by the Connecticut Academy in 1925, 1929, 1932, 1935, 1938, 1941, with
continuous pagination. The eighth supplement (1941) includes an index
to all the supplements. Wells died in 1943. A ninth supplement was issued in 1951, by Beatrice D. Brown and others.]
Originally his Yale dissertation (1915), Wells's *Manual* was for many
years the standard bibliographical reference for Middle English studies.
His bibliographical entries on Chaucer are somewhat erratic, though occasionally, especially in the supplements, he picks up on bits which other bibliographers have ignored. Complete revision of the *Manual* was
undertaken in 1967 under the general editorship of J. Burke Severs and
then Albert E. Hartung. The Chaucer section has been made obsolete by
Hammond **37** and the bibliographies of Griffith, Crawford, and Baird (see
Preface to this volume; the Editorial Board of The MLA Bibliographical
Committee decided not to revise the Chaucer section so as to avoid du-
plication of effort).

Wells's introductory comments reveal a generally low opinion of
Chaucer as a poet, placing him 'in the third or fourth class of great
poets' (p 606) – a poet without vision, 'scarcely at all interested in the
human heart or the ways of the soul,' showing 'limited emotional range'
and 'little enthusiasm' (p 602). Wells comments briefly on Chaucer's
achievements in versification, noting the many new stanza forms he experiments with in the lyrics (p 600), but concluding: 'Though Chaucer
wrote graceful and pleasing stanzas, he had success with but the form of
lyrics – his best lyrical efforts are incidental bits of a line or two in his
narratives' (p 602). Wells divides his discussion into the Life, Canon,
Chronology, and Works, commenting briefly on mss, dates and circumstances. His section on Minor Poems (pp 628–48) includes *ABC,
AWU, CD, AA, BC, BD, Adam, Mars* ('Whatever be its actual significance,
the piece is a glorification of illicit love,' p 635), *Venus, Lady, Purse, Pity,
FA* ('Its late printing in 1866 was no slight addition to the Chaucer
canon,' p 639), *Fortune, Gent, Sted, Bukton, Scogan, MB* ('the manner is his,'
p 642), *PF, Prov, Ros, Truth, WN.* Also sections on *Romaunt* (pp 648–50;
'That any of the extant translation is Chaucer's is doubtful,' p 649), and
Boece and *Astrolabe* (pp 650–3), where Wells speculates on the possibility
that little Lewis might be Chaucer's son by Cecilia de Chaumpaigne.

56 Windeatt, B.A. 'The Scribes as Chaucer's Early Critics.' *SAC*, 1 (1979), 119–41.

'With varying levels of attainment, the scribes – as the near-contemporaries of Chaucer – can offer us the earliest line-by-line literary criticism of Chaucer's poetry, a reaction to what in the poet's text makes it distinctive and remarkable in its own time' (p 120). Using *T&C* mss as his principal sources, Windeatt explores scribal alterations which reveal personal responses to the poetry but also recurrent difficulties scribes had with Chaucer's text. Seldom do scribes invent whole lines; usually the change 'focusses on a limited number of words within the body of a line' (p 125). Scribes gloss what strikes them as strange or awkward in Chaucer's diction, which suggests concern for meaning; they also often reduce poetic or fresh wording to cliché. Chaucer's difficult or elliptical syntax tends to get clarified or simplified by scribes who find it hard 'to cope with this flexibly various approach to syntax by the poet' (p 138). They often alter verb forms and modal auxiliaries to accommodate the text to their sense. 'To read all the extant mss for a Chaucer poem is like taking up – to look at the same object – a number of sets of binoculars each adjusted to somebody else's eyesight' (p 139).

The footnotes to the essay contain references to several recent studies on scribal relationships with Chaucer's text.

Metrics, Versification, and Vocabulary

See also **56, 93, 100, 193, 256.**

57 Bateson, F.W. 'Could Chaucer Spell?' *EIC*, 25 (1975), 2–24.

Emphasizing the oral delivery of Chaucer's poetry Bateson differentiates two textual levels, one seen on the page and the other heard. Chaucer was conscious of the distinction in *T&C*, when he lists three interconnected risks – that the scribe *myswrite*, that he *mysmetre*, or that whoever reads or sings what is written might not be understood (p 7). Unlike spelling, *metre* operates at both textual levels. Its syllables can be counted on the page but primarily their function is to be heard. It may be that Chaucer intoned his poems in a rhythmic monotone, but more likely he preferred 'a more dramatic presentation' (p 9). *Myswrite* and *mysmetre* are words of his own coinage. The latter probably meant 'to offend against or misrepresent the syllabic regularity of his lines' (p 10). (Cf *HF* where Geoffrey would be forgiven should he 'fayle in a sillable.') The French had already begun to read their poetry *privately* with eyes on the page. (Cf Richard II's 'excited retirement into a private room on the arrival of a brand-new poem from France,' pp 10–1). But oral delivery mitigates octosyllabic or decasyllabic rigidity 'by a complementary prosody of stress, which was to some extent antagonistic to syllabism. As they were read by Chaucer himself the lines will have been heard as more or less syllabically consistent within a loose iambic pattern of unstressed/stressed syllables – sounding equally regular in the number of its feet as in the number of its syllables. In the cold light of analysis of Chaucer's words on the page ... the two prosodies are in continuous conflict – nine-syllable and eleven-syllable lines offending against the *syllabic* norm and the stresses distributed so casually that an *iambic* norm is often almost lost' (p 11). Bateson borrows Robert Bridges' term 'hybrid' (*Milton's Prosody*, 1901) to describe Chaucer's metrics (p 11). By analyzing *Emelye/Emelia* and *Arcite/Arcita* distinctions in *KnT*, Bateson concludes that the *–a* spelling represents an additional syllable. Chaucer's elisions and apocopation were possible because of the instability of Middle English (p 14). For Chaucer, elision is essentially a spelling convention (p 15). 'A skilful reader, as Chaucer must surely have been, mitigates the superficial syllabism of the mature work by allowing an unstressed syllable to hover between full articulation and the merest whisper' (p 15). Bateson suggests that the ms closest to Chaucer's own spelling is Cambridge ms Gg.4.27, although its scribe was apparently Dutch or Flemish (see Robert A. Caldwell, *MLQ*, 5 [1944], 33–44). The fact that the scribe was foreign gives him a 'negative evidential value' – at least he does not knowingly improve or miscopy' (ie, edit) as the Ellesmere-Hengwrt scribe did (p 21). Bateson examines *LGW Prol.* in Gg, noting the prominence of different vowels in the inflectional endings (–i– or –y– is prominent as well as –u– and –e–). Chaucer may well have intended all three alternatives (p 20). Bateson concludes that Chaucer could spell – 'at least as well as Shakespeare, perhaps even a little better' (p 21). By intention he was a phonetic speller. His phonemes are 'primarily those of his "advanced" London speech as his audiences will have heard it when he read his poems aloud' (p 21). [ms Gg.4.27 includes *ABC, Truth, Scogan*; also *Gent.*]

58 Baum, Paull Franklin. *Chaucer's Verse.* Durham, N.C.: Duke University Press; Cambridge University Press, 1961.

With the good Chaucer texts now available ('except for the Minor Poems,' p 4), it should be possible to explore Chaucer's principles of versification and 'by deductive methods come reasonably close to an appreciation of his verse and its rhythms' (p vii). Baum devotes separate chapters to 'Meter,' in which he considers the five-stress line, short couplets, rimes, and stanzaic forms; 'Prosody;' and 'Art Poetical.' He uses lyrics throughout as specimens (see his Index). In discussing metrical feet, inversions, and kinds of stress in Chaucer's five-stress line he compares *Pity* (as an early work) with the *GP*. For the short couplet he relies mainly on *BD* and *HF* for examples. For rimes he starts with *Venus*, where the poet complains of the 'skarsete' of 'rym in English,' then discusses a wide range of specimens, especially from *T&C*. In the discussion of stanzaic forms Baum draws extensively on the lyrics, especially the *Compleynt of Anelida*, which is 'Chaucer's most gorgeous metrical display' (p 51). In Ch 2, pp 52–79, Baum finds that Chaucer obtains metrical variety by 1) deliberate use of irregular lines, which do not easily conform to theoretical scansion; 2) use of enjambement to subordinate the line to the syntactic unit (in early works like *ABC* and *Pity* most lines end with a pause, though there are notable exceptions; but later Chaucer uses run-on lines frequently, with great variety in *T&C*); 3) the placing of grammatical or rhythmic pauses at regular or varied positions; 4) different weighting of consecutive lines (four-beat lines are common, and even three-beat). Though 'Chaucer was first of all a narrative poet' (p 80), in his lyrics, especially in *AA*, he practices 'art poetical' (see Ch 3, pp 80–107; and p 222). Nonetheless, for Chaucer, 'naturalness is the key.

Chaucer's verse is eminently natural' (p 110). There were no rhetoricians to tell him about the art of writing verse as verse; rather he relied on his 'good ear' (cf Dorothy Everett, *RES*, 23 [1947], 201–8, on 'Chaucer's Good Ear'). 'Chaucer had no need for the complex rhythms of Milton or the elaborate orchestration of line and stanza of Shelley and Swinburne, or of the artistic subtleties of Tennyson. Nor should we expect them. His business was to tell a story that would please a none too exigent audience, and for this he created a style and a method of versifying which were perfectly suited to his aim' (p 116). He knew that 'the beauty of a line is its modulation away from the fixity of meter' (p 126). Baum concludes with three appendices, one on the four-beat heresy (a refutation of Southworth 76 on grounds that he fails to differentiate between rhythm and meter); a second on metrics in *CYT*; and a third on metrical revision in *T&C*.

- Review by E. Talbot Donaldson, *Spec*, 39 (1964), 112–4: *Chaucer's Verse* is 'disappointing as a study of the "whole subject" of Chaucer's verse' (p 113). The economy of presentation often produces puzzlement; there is 'a good deal of inconsistency in Baum's method, which tends to treat every line as a unique problem unconnected with any other line' (p 113). Baum should have made better use of the Chaucer *Concordance* (53), which is 'the basic text for any consistent metrical study' (p 114). Though Baum bases his study on the premise that good texts now make metrical analysis possible, in his argument he shows little respect for any of the editors: 'A reader faced with the fact that the best editors are damned if they do, damned if they don't, and sometimes damned for doing what they didn't, is apt to wonder whether their texts could supply any firm base for a metrical study' (p 114). Baum's skepticism of systems 'seems to forget that versification by definition implies a system and that dogmas sometimes rest on observable fact' (p 114).
- Review by Gardiner Stillwell, *JEGP*, 63 (1964), 141–7: Baum's case for the four- and five-beat iambic lines is 'strongly presented' (p 141); in the appendix he lays to rest the four-beat heresy 'as definitively as any one could' (pp 141–2). Stillwell challenges several of Baum's rhythmical analyses; nonetheless, '*Chaucer's Verse* is unquestionably a contribution to the discussion [of versification]' (p 147).
- Review by P.J. Frankis, *MAE*, 35 (1966), 78–82: *Chaucer's Verse* is 'the most thorough and sensible survey of Chaucer's verse-technique so far published' (p 78). But Baum's attempt to avoid the recondite terminology of specialists leads to a 'lack of exactness'; the controversy on metre should not be 'side-tracked into an appendix' (p 80). Baum relies in his analysis too heavily on the foot as a unit of metrical composition.

See also Gaylord 61 for further response to Baum.

59 Cowling, G.H. 'A Note on Chaucer's Stanza.' *RES*, 2 (1926), 311–7.
Cowling challenges ten Brink's theory (**78**) of a tripartite structure for
the Chaucerian stanza; rather, the stanza is usually bipartite. After examining all the seven-line stanzas which occur in Chaucer's canonical
poems Cowling concludes: 1) 'The Chaucerian stanza is normally, but
not invariably, terminated by a full pause after the seventh line. 2) The
Chaucerian stanza ordinarily has a half-pause or *volta*, determinable not
by punctuation, but by the sense. This half-pause is followed by an am-
plification, a re-statement, or by the consequences of, or a contrast to the
preceding lines; and is recognisable by the fact that it is a break in the
unity of the stanza, if not a break in narrative. 3) There is no fixed place
for this half-pause. Chaucer observed it wherever it best suited his purpose; but it will be found in about 90 per cent of his stanzas. Usually it
occurs at the end of a line. More rarely it is found in the middle of a
line. The varied position of this half-pause indicates that the stanzas
were not written to be sung' (p 312). 4) The most common type consists
of two *pedes* (ab,ab) and a *cauda* (bcc). 5) Other common types are a tercet
(aba) followed by a quatrain of couplets (bb,cc) – about 20 per cent are of
this type. 6) Irregular types, especially a couplet (ab) followed by a quin-
tet (abbcc) and stanzas with interlinear pauses, make up the rest. Cowling finds that Chaucer's early verse is more regular (4–3 type) than the
later verse. *Pity* and *AA* are early types; *Mars* is a late type. See **64.**

60 Eliason, Norman E. *The Language of Chaucer's Poetry. An Appraisal of the
Verse, Style, and Structure.* Anglistica, vol 17. Copenhagen: Rosenkilde and
Bagger, 1972.
Eliason works inductively to identify the particular way in which
Chaucer uses language. 'Style in English poetry begins, in a sense, with
Chaucer. Before him there had been style, which at its best was excellent. But it lacked the variety that he was to give it, and this stylistic
variety gives his poetry a range of tone which is remarkable even today
and in his day was unique' (p 10). Ch 1, 'The Sound of the Verse,'
pp 16–59: 'The delight which Chaucer's poetry affords the ear is remarkable. Clearly he wrote for the ear, intending his verse to be heard rather
than silently read and taking pains therefore to give it auditory appeal'
(p 16). Eliason thinks the skepticism sometimes expressed about Middle
English stress or Chaucer's handling of it is unwarranted. 'Any latitude
he took ... for the sake of meter or rime ... would have escaped censure
from even the most captious critic of his meter at the time, for Chaucer's
usage was in accord with that which prevailed in the spoken language
then' (p 33). Perhaps the most important achievement of nineteenth-
century Chaucer scholarship was 'the rehabilitation of Chaucer's versification by establishing its regularity of meter and rime' (p 39). In his early poetry Chaucer had trouble with versification; his rime, instead of

seeming easy and natural, 'is often laboriously contrived, and its true-
ness is sometimes gained by questionable means, such as using dialect
forms not yet established in London speech' (p 55). Ch 2, 'The Style,'
pp 60–136: Style is not transportable across linguistic boundaries;
every language has its own way of putting things (p 61). Chaucer borrows from the French 'only a special literary *genre* or mode' (p 62). Eliason discusses the problems of relating rhetoric and its principles to style.
Chaucer's style is rarely dazzling (p 74); its most conspicuous feature is
its naturalness. Of the major poets he is one of the least quotable. When
he resorts to elaborate rhetorical figures the style becomes 'conspicuously
artificial' (p 75). Eliason stresses the vividness, freshness, and precision
of Chaucer's vocabulary (pp 86–113), and his skill at arranging details ef-
fectively, a skill he learned not from other poets, French or English, 'who
in this respect provided him only with anti-models' (p 95). Ch 3, 'Chaucerian Structure,' pp 137–244: this portion of Eliason's argument concentrates on Chaucer's narrative work and does not deal with the lyrics,
though some mention is made of *AA*, but only as example of traditional
narrative types. See **237**.

- Review by Charles A. Owen, Jr., *Spec*, 49 (1974), 727–30: Owen finds
  Eliason's book disappointing in its failure to come to grips with the issues it raises and in its cavalier attitude toward *BD, HF,* and *KnT*. The
  book is at its best in the first chapter, which provides 'a sensible discussion of the language Chaucer spoke and the use he made of it in
  his meter and rhyme.' But 'there is not much that is new here and
  what there is needs considerably more supporting evidence than it
  gets' (p 728). Owen finds Eliason's generalizations to be too sweeping
  and 'asserted rather than demonstrated' (p 728). The chapter on style
  lacks a systematic approach to the subject. The 'distinctive traits'
  which Eliason identifies – naturalness, oral appeal, freshness and vividness, and stylistic variety – are too vague to be informative, and the
  three levels of style – artificial, simple, and colloquial – though 'more
  germane to the subject of the chapter' (p 729), are not explored with
  subtlety of depth. In the chapter on structure 'Eliason gives overriding
  emphasis to considerations of genre' (p 730).

  See also Gaylord **61**.

61 Gaylord, Alan T. 'Scanning the Prosodists: An Essay in Metacriticism.'
ChauR, 11 (1976), 22–82.

Advocating that more attention be paid to Chaucer's prosody, Gaylord
raises a number of basic issues by going back to mss which do not look
like the Chaucer we are accustomed to seeing. 'The prosodist is handi-
capped by having to deal with reports about, rather than words directly
from, the poet. He deals with overlapping, even opposing versions.
There is no such thing as Chaucer's own line. There are only scribal versions

of it' (p 27). Gaylord compares discussion on *AA* by Baum **58**, Eliason **60**, Knight **63**, and Ian Robinson **71** to point up the limitations of their methods. To show how much 'prosodic matters must depend upon textual scholarship,' Gaylord begins his argument with a transcription of a stanza of *AA* from Fairfax 16, which Robinson **12** used as his basic text, to show 'many differences between a medieval original and the modern critical texts most critics take for granted' (p 59). In viewing what the critics say about the passage 'we discover more about their author's proclivities than Chaucer's poetry' (p 59). Baum **58** sees *AA* as a bizarre piece of engineering – 'art poetical' – with its 141 end rhymes, 36 internal rhymes, and 177 rhyming words: 'There was nothing like it before; one would be hard pressed to find anything like it since' (**58**, p 101). This method of analysis Gaylord compares to the 'more pungent formulation by the film critic, James Agee: "The goddamndest thing I ever did see"' (p 59). Ian Robinson **71**, on the other hand, avoids the poem because it is a ridiculous deviation from the less mannered English tradition; he brushes it aside, along with Gower, by observing: 'Gower is always trying to be a Great Poet (an affliction from which Chaucer made an almost complete recovery after *Anelida and Arcite*)' (**71**, p 181). Eliason **60** points to the poem as a kind of sport, a strange, perhaps even grotesque, begonia in a petunia shed. He quotes the heavily edited version of Robinson, then slips away with, 'The poem remains a mystery to critics, who can make nothing of it except as a dazzling display of technical virtuosity. Very likely its unfinished state indicates Chaucer's feeling that such displays were not worth his time or effort' (**60**, p 38). Knight **63** provides the first sustained discussion of *AA*. He tries to evaluate the movement of the verse but falls victim of 'the perils of "affective" prosodic analysis' as he 'makes Chaucer begin to sound like a bite of celery' with his 'crisp' prosody (p 61). Gaylord notes that Knight does not in fact scan the verse or solve any of the difficulties in figuring out precisely what is there. Gaylord then goes back to Fairfax 16, noting that its scribe did not care for the final –e and that there is no punctuation. Robinson **12** makes many silent emendations and other emendations which are not noted by Knight. Gaylord then concludes: 'Surely the moral of this sortie into the manuscripts is that one had better be careful to locate just where the text is that he thinks he is discussing, especially in matters metrical, where so much depends upon the interpretation of scribal vagaries and the multiplicity of mss' (p 62). The latter part of the essay deals with prosodic studies and linguistics and the directions Gaylord thinks future studies should proceed.

62 Hammond, E.P. *Bibliographical Manual*. 1908. See **37**.

Ch 6, 'Linguistics and Versification,' pp 464–509, lists early discussion of Chaucer's prosody from 1575–1847, quoting in full the crucial passages. Hammond also lists later nineteenth-century studies of Chaucer's language and verse, presents an essay of her own 'On the Language and Verse of Chaucer,' pp 481–91, and comments on Chaucer's line and strophe forms, his modes of varying line flow, bibliography on the rime test for determining authenticity, and on Chaucer's use of alliteration and rime and on his style. 'Chaucer's use of padding phrases has not received adequate treatment' (p 504). The chapter concludes with discussion of glossaries and dictionaries.

63 Knight, Stephen. *Rymyng Craftily: Meaning in Chaucer's Poetry*. Sydney: Angus and Robertson, 1973.

The book proposes a close reading of Chaucer's texts to explore ways in which his prosody generates and supports meaning. Ch 1, *Anelida and Arcite* and the *Parlement of Foules* pp 1–48: Knight finds the stylistic pattern of *AA* to be 'on the whole unsatisfactory' and that of *PF* in 'the subtle and various style typical of the poems that are commonly thought to be his greatest' (p 1). Knight begins with a review of criticism on *AA*, then, with 'open mind,' enters into a stanza by stanza reading of the poem. Eg, on lines 8–14: 'The opening lines have that easy demotic movement that we associate so much with Chaucer; it is a relaxed, firm progress in which no element seems to jump out at us, and in which nothing seems redundant. Just as before, though, there seems some trouble in filling out the stanza, for in the last three lines the organisation is complicated without seeming subtle, and the unsophisticated repetition of "frete" emphasizes this' (p 5). 'It is tempting to suggest that this is a first attempt at the rhyme royal stanza by Chaucer, for here the stanza seems too hard for him, and I can think of no other reason to explain this phenomenon' (p 6). (See **248** for further annotations of Knight's discussion of *AA*.) The other chapters in Knight's book fall outside the purview of this bibliography. See **61** for comments on Knight's methodology.

64 Lineberger, Julia E. 'An Examination of Professor Cowling's New Metrical Test.' *MLN*, 42 (1927), 229–31.

Cowling's tests (**59**) for determining the chronology of Chaucer's works on the basis of stanza structure are unconvincing. 'A theory which bade fair to be the objective test that we are looking for came to be as subjective, perhaps even more subjective, than any test it aspired to supersede' (p 231).

65 MacCracken, Henry Noble. 'King James' Claim to Rhyme Royal.' *MLN*, 24 (1909), 31–2.

The editors of the *NED* perpetuated an error which has gone uncorrected: 'This is the statement, apparently a mere guess of some scholar of the nineteenth century, that *rhyme royal*, or *ballade royal*, owes its name to the fact that King James I of Scotland, a 'royal' poet, wrote *The Kingis Quair* in that metre' (p 31). This derivation is altogether inaccurate. Gower uses the term 'ballades ryal' in his French Balades. The stanza was, of course, that of Chaucer. John Shirley labels three items with the term ca 1430: 'Balade Ryal de saine counsylle'; 'Balade moult Bon et Ryal'; 'Balade Ryal made by oure laureat poete of Albyon,' that is, Chaucer. 'Rime royal' first appears as a term in George Gascoigne, where rime substitutes for balade, since *ballade* had now become reserved for a new six-line stanza. James VI of Scotland refers to an eight-line stanza as Ballat Royal. He also calls the seven-line stanza 'Troilus stanza.' 'It has remained for modern critics to fasten the term *rhyme royal* definitely upon the seven-line stanza, and then to justify it by a plausible legend of its kingly origin' (p 32).

66 Masui, Michio. *The Structure of Chaucer's Rime Words: An Exploration into the Poetic Language of Chaucer*. Tokyo: Kenkyusha, 1964; rpt Folcroft, Pa.: Folcroft Library Editions, 1975.

The analysis deals mainly with *KnT, BD*, and *T&C*, though many of the lyrics are included as specimens at various points in the study. There are chapters on the structure of nouns in rime; position and structure of pronouns; position and structure of adjectives, adverbs, and adverbial phrases; position and structure of verbs; separation; transposition, place, and structure of prepositions and prepositional phrases; rime phrases; rime clauses; expansion; enjambement; rime-breaking; internal rime; structure of rime in seven-line stanzas; feminine and masculine rimes; subjective utterances; for the nones words and expressions; emotive utterances; and the semantic and stylistic structure of Chaucer's rime words. Appendix 1 lists rime words in *CT*; Appendix 2 lists rime words in *T&C*. Bibliography, pp 307–19.

67 Maynard, Theodore. *The Connection Between the Ballade, Chaucer's Modification of It, Rime Royal, and the Spenserian Stanza*. Washington, D.C.: Published Catholic University of America dissertation, 1934.

Ch 1, 'The Literary Background,' pp 1–36, a preliminary summary of medieval Latin, Old French, and Anglo-Saxon verse. Ch 2, 'The Ballade,' pp 37–48, on variations and intricacies of the form in French. Ch 3, 'Chaucer and the Ballade,' pp 49–63: 'Though most of the ballades of Machaut, Froissart, and Deschamps were somewhat mechanical, demanding ingenuity rather than poetic genius, at least this practicing of ballades was useful as literary discipline, at a time when discipline was necessary as a preliminary to further poetic development' (p 49). Chaucer observed all the accepted ballade rules in his various lyrics. We can only speculate upon the fate of the 'mery songs and lecherous lays' he claims to have written. 'Chaucer may have destroyed them in later life, because he disapproved of them on moral grounds ... [Or he] may not have thought them worth keeping. And this merely because he was ashamed of their artistic immaturity' (p 50). He does refer to them with pride, however, in *LGW*. Maynard cites *Hyd Absolon* and *Truth* as the two main types of Chaucer ballades and discusses the multiplicity of French stanza forms which he reduced to rime royal. 'With such models before him [as the various forms of Froissart, Deschamps, and Machaut] it is no wonder that Chaucer had no uniform mould for his ballades; the wonder, rather, is that he conformed as closely as he did to the standard ballade' (p 54). Still, he avoids the complexity of the French. The ballades which we possess are from a late period of his life. Maynard disagrees with Hammond 37, p 71, that Chaucer's poetic powers decayed in old age, causing him to return to earlier French models. The lyrics represent the mature Chaucer. Yet, 'the more of the extant ballades that are assigned to Chaucer's later years, the more we have to assume a number of lost ballades written by Chaucer in his youth' (p 62). Ch 4, 'Italian Influence upon Chaucer,' pp 64–82: Chaucer remained loyal to the seven-line stanza even after he became acquainted with the Italian *ottava rima*. Although he experimented with eight-line stanzas in *ABC* and terza rima in *Lady*, rime royal remained his principle stanzaic form. Maynard puzzles over Chaucer's failure to experiment with the sonnet. 'It would seem that for such work [as short amatory or reflective poems] the fourteen lines of the sonnet would have been more convenient than the much more complicated and artificial pattern of the ballade' (p 73). He knew the sonnet from Petrarch, and 'it is unthinkable that he could have failed to perceive the nature of a sonnet. But, as in the cases of *terza* and *ottava rima*, he decided that the form was not for him' (p 73). Perhaps this is evidence against his meeting Petrarch in Italy. But there may be other reasons for his turning to rime royal. The decasyllabic line was already being experimented with in English before Chaucer, and the seven-line stanza probably would have become the dominant form even without him (p 78). But it became for him his main vehicle, and in that sense it is his great innovation. Tatlock is wrong in thinking that it was not until after the Italian journeys that Chaucer learned poetic form (**146**, p 18). He learned that from the French ballades. Ch 5, 'Chaucerian Stanza or Rime Royal': 'Chaucer must be given full credit for seeing what could be done with the seven-line ballade stanza after it had been set free from the ballade restrictions' (pp 83–4). He never regarded rime royal as appropriate for anything except a noble subject. Still, Maynard stresses the variety of effects Chaucer achieves with it – 'tenderness, simplicity, complexity, roguishness, brilliance, color, and power' (p 87). Maynard reiterates the importance of MacCracken's correction (65) of the error in the *NED* in attributing the term 'rime royal' to King James I of Scotland and adds further details to confirm MacCracken. The term was practically synonymous with ballade royal. 'But it is no more than just to Chaucer that it should bear his name' (p 92). Ch 6, 'Chaucer's Influence on his Successors,' pp 93–107: Maynard emphasizes Chaucer's gift of rime royal to the Chaucerians; they do not pick up on the decasyllabic couplet, however, which is just as well. Ch 7, 'Formation of the Spenserian Stanza,' pp 107–27: The Spenserian stanza grows 'naturally, and inevitably, from native stock, which, though ultimately derived from the French ballade, was employed only in England: rime royal' (p 131).

68 Mersand, Joseph. *Chaucer's Romance Vocabulary*. Brooklyn: Comet Press, 1937.

See Ch 8, 'Romance Words in the Minor Poems,' pp 62–74: Mersand discusses the Romance words which appear for the first time in English in each of the poems and concludes: 1) Chaucer introduced more new Romance words than Gower and Mandeville together; 2) the new words he introduced are now more familiar than those introduced by Mandeville and Gower; 3) Chaucer imported fewer new Romance words in earlier works than in later works. *Boece* and *T&C* contain the largest number of new words, respectively (p 73); 4) Almost 60 per cent of the new words are used only once by Chaucer; 5) about one-fourth of the new words are used for rhyme; 6) Chaucer used more new Romance words in his translations than in original work; 7) Romance originals can be found for about 10 per cent of his new words. 'He either made up the rest, – which seems improbable – or gave literary currency to words in use in literary and social circles' (p 74); 8) most of his new Romance words have been preserved to this day and some are our most useful words; 9) 'Chaucer was extremely careful in his desire to select *le mot juste*. This accounts for many of his compound words' (p 74); 10) 'It is possible to adjust the works of Chaucer into the accepted chronology of his works by the conclusions stated above' (p 74). See also pp 75–89; 100–4; 119–22, for comments on *AA, Pity, Ros, FA, Fortune, BC, Venus,* and *AWU*.

69 Owen, Charles A. 'Thy Drasty Rymyng ...' *SP*, 63 (1966), 533–64.

'Though Chaucer recognized the difficulty of such intricacy [as that required by the French balade] in English with its "skarsete" of rhyme, and though he put his main emphasis on "sentence," yet the purity of his rhymes sets him off from his English contemporaries and enables scholars to separate the grain from the chaff in poems attributed to him. Furthermore, the balades and complaints show him on occasion meeting the exigencies of the strict French forms. In some of his mature works he goes beyond the artificially difficult to draw from rhyme and stanza pattern unobtrusive support for his "sentence"' (p 534). Most of the lyrics of interest are 'the finger-exercises of the poet' (p 534). Owen discusses *Truth, Mars,* and *AA* (see **258, 362, 557**), then considers the poet's preference for the seven-line stanza with its flexibility, especially for rhythms of dialogue. 'When Chaucer turned from rime royal to the decasyllabic couplet as a medium for narrative poetry, he apparently did so with a view to reducing the importance of rhyme' (p 555). 'What we experience in Chaucer's use of the couplet is what we experience in his poetry as a whole, a freedom from system or repetitive form. The unobtrusive rhymes and the disregard of the couplet as a determinant of syntax and "sentence" make possible the varied special effects. Chaucer was willing to experiment with rhyme, and on occasion, usually in short poems or short sections of longer poems, he tried out what could be effected by elaborate and difficult stanza forms' (p 563).

70 Preston, Raymond. *Chaucer*. London and New York: Sheed and Ward, 1952.
Ch 1, ' "Many a lecherous lay",' pp 17–31: Beginning with the scene in the *Romaunt* where the lover enters the garden amidst caroling and dancing, Preston discusses relationships between music and lyric verse in Machaut and Chaucer. Chaucer uses musical forms, though probably not with musical setting. Chaucer's lyrics lack the purity and intense emotion of Machaut. Instead we get irony and dramatic narrative devices. 'Taking hints, perhaps, from Deschamps' practice, he extended the range of tone of the *ballade* to a degree which would perplex a musician trying to set his words' (pp 19–20). Preston stresses the Englishness of the rhythm in Chaucer's lyrics and the *Romaunt*, as opposed to the French (pp 21–4). He then discusses Chaucer's development of the Chaucerian stanza to its perfection.

71 Robinson, Ian. *Chaucer's Prosody: A Study of the Middle English Verse Tradition*. Cambridge and New York: Cambridge University Press, 1971.
Through an inductive procedure Robinson develops a new theoretical basis for Chaucer's pentameter line. His chapters concentrate on *CT*, though some mention is made of lyrics (see **509**). Robinson challenges the circular reasoning of traditional views of Chaucer's iambic decasyllabic line: a predetermined iambic pentameter causes editors and readers to emend what they see to fit what they are predisposed to hear, sounding –e when it is necessary, shifting accent to fit the iambic foot, etc. Robinson insists that Chaucer's line should be read without preconception: 'we might hope, if we can be good enough and delicate enough readers, that the language of the fourteenth century is not too far from us to communicate its own rhythms' (p 66). The final arbiter should be the line

itself. What Robinson hears is a balanced pentameter line in which the rhythm works in half-lines as well as feet. 'If there is a perceptible metrical development in Chaucer it is almost certainly away from pentameter as usually understood towards an increased dependence on half-line movement' (p 174). The latter part of the argument is devoted to the Chaucerians – Hoccleve, Lydgate, and lesser colleagues like Ashby, Bokenham, Burgh, and Capgrave, who seem to understand the balanced half-lines; but not the Scottish Chaucerians who write in a tradition of 'foot metre.' Hawes, Skelton, Barclay, and Wyatt, however, continue working with half-line prosody (pp 189–212).

- Review by Charles A. Owen, Jr., *Spec*, 49 (1974), 148–51: 'When not obsessed by theory – his own or the ones he opposes – Robinson shows himself a sensitive reader of poetry' (p 149). His advocacy of manuscript punctuation as a guide to reading the line is instructive up to a point. 'No one but a zealot, however, can fail to find instances in any extended passage of the Hengwrt or the Ellesmere where the punctuation reflects a nervous scribal habit rather than a reading of the poetry' (p 150). Moreover, the breaking of all of Chaucer's lines into two reasonably equal halves 'can only be seen ... as intruding on the subtleties of rhythm within the line and from one line to another' (p 150). But parts of the book are stimulating. 'By bringing into question once again the basic assumptions about Chaucer's metrics, it forces us to face uncertainties and choose the most acceptable of the alternatives. Its emphasis on the manuscript readings and punctuation shows us, perhaps unintentionally, how little our texts have been falsified by editing, and suggests certain advantages in at least returning occasionally to the sources on which they rest' (p 150). Unfortunately, his method excludes recognition of the influence of French and Italian metrics.

72 Saintsbury, George. *A History of English Prosody.* 2 vols. London and New York: Macmillan, 1906. Volume I: *From the Origins to Spenser.*
Ch 4, 'Chaucer,' pp 143–78: See comments below on *ABC, Pity, AA.* The lessons of Chaucer's early poems are clear: the poet finds an English prosody thoroughly broken to the use of foot-divisions arranged in metrical groups. Chaucer does not attempt 'startling innovations or reformations' as far as feet go (p 154). 'In metres ... he is decidedly eclectic and experimental, and calls both French and Italian to his aid,' but the diction and versification of the early poems 'shows no very brilliant accomplishment' (p 155). That comes with *T&C* and *CT*. Saintsbury emphasizes that whatever formal training Chaucer might have had would have been in the classics: 'There was up to Chaucer's time absolutely no school-instruction even with English as a vehicle, let alone any school-instruction in English itself' (p 167). Any influence in theory of prosody would thus be from Latin.

73 Skeat, W.W. *The Chaucer Canon.* Oxford: Clarendon Press, 1900.
Skeat's object is 'to explain clearly the chief peculiarities of Chaucer's grammar and versification' in order 'to distinguish his genuine poems from those that have been attributed to him ... by the carelessness or wantonness of editors and critics' (p 1). Beginning with the postulate that Chaucer was author of *CT* he establishes criteria which characterize Chaucer's language. The poet's 'grammar remains unaltered' throughout the tales; the style develops, however, becoming easier but with richer vocabulary (p 4). Skeat uses the *Ormulum* as evidence on pronunciation, grammar, and syllabic awareness especially of –e and –en in the generation before Chaucer. He then analyses *SqT* to establish grammatical criteria for endings (–es, –en, –e), substantives, adjectives, verbs, adverbs and prepositions; and various rime–tests, especially –y/–yë and –iht/–yt. Skeat separates by external evidence works identified as Chaucer's from those sometimes attributed to Chaucer. Those claimed by Chaucer in his own works and by Shirley's testimony all satisfy the rules of grammar and rime that Skeat has established (p 60). He then examines *MB, AWU,* and *WN,* to conclude that internal evidence is satisfactory and that we should accept all three as genuine (pp 61–4). *CD, CMF,* and *CML* present difficulties, however, and should be retained among the doubtful poems. *BC* 'should certainly be excluded' (p 64); it is probably by Lydgate. Skeat devotes three chapters to the *Romaunt* and provides separate discussions for each of the early editions.

74 Smith, Egerton. *The Principles of English Metre.* Oxford: Oxford University Press, 1923. Pp 243–5.
Smith rejects ten Brink's theory (**78**) of a tripartite structure in the Chaucerian stanza. 'Clearly ... Chaucer, if he divided the stanza at all, did so at whatever point suited him best, and sometimes within a line instead of at the end; and there is no sufficient evidence that he regarded as essential any subdivision of the stanza' (p 244).

75 Stevens, Martin. 'The Royal Stanza in Early English Literature.' *PMLA,* 94 (1979), 62–76.
Rhyme royal was not a stanza spontaneously generated by Chaucer: nor did it take its regal title from James I of Scotland. Perhaps the dedicating of balades to royalty reflects practices of the London *puy* in the fourteenth century. How far back the rhyme royal stanza was employed as a ceremonial device is an open question (p 65). Chaucer may have 'taken part in the literary performances of the *puy,* where we know that royal songs were performed' (p 66); perhaps *PF* was such a poem. But whether Chaucer took part or not, 'there seems to be little doubt that rhyme royal existed as a conscious form of higher poetic address in Chaucer's time and even that antecedents of its name were already in use during that period' (p 66). Stevens offers reasons why Chaucer wrote his various

works in the seven-line stanza. He goes on to argue that the phrase 'tale in prose,' used to describe the verse of *MLT*, refers to rhymed prose, that is, 'organized stanzaic units with long lines, usually endecasyllabic' (p 69); the phrase has nothing to do with 'prose' as we now define it. At the beginning of the second day of the *CT* Chaucer and the host conspire to introduce 'high style'; thus the 'tale in prose.' See also **65** and **67** on the origins of rhyme royal.

76 Southworth, James. *Verses of Cadence: An Introduction to the Prosody of Chaucer and his Followers.* Oxford: Blackwell, 1954.

By returning to the fundamentals of prosody Southworth attempts to free Chaucer and his followers from the fallacies of nineteenth-century scholars who would place Chaucer in a tradition which came into existence in England only in the sixteenth century. 'Music exerts a stronger influence [on Chaucer] than classical prosody' (p 1); his texts have been edited 'on a preconceived prosodic principle ... By a return to original sources the student will have brought more forcefully to his attention the truth of the matter' (p 3). Southworth argues that –e had died out in the speech of Chaucer's day and that the poetry does not give it syllabic value. Various 'myths' perpetrated by scholars of Chaucer's prosody include: final –e; French mute –e; analogy between Chaucer's and Goethe's practice; Chaucer's not rhyming words in –er/–ere; foreign sources for Chaucer's prosody; the endecasyllabic line; and the French endecasyllabic line. Unfortunately no published text can give us what we need; we must have recourse to the mss themselves. Southworth uses musical notation to study the prosody of the Hengwrt ms in order to show that the iambic theory fails miserably in dealing with Chaucer's verse and that of his fifteenth-century followers. Throughout his argument Southworth frequently cites T.S. Eliot, Pound, Ransom, and Stevens as examples of twentieth-century poets who get away from nineteenth-century prosody to rediscover flexibility like that of Chaucer and 'pre-classical' prosody.

77 — *The Prosody of Chaucer and his Followers: Supplementary Chapters to 'Verses of Cadence.'* Oxford: Blackwell, 1962.

Southworth's first attempt (**76**) presented a partial theory which did not cover from the point of rhythm all the types of verse Chaucer used. He now elaborates, still insisting 'it is useless to attempt to develop or substantiate a theory of prosody on anything but the manuscripts themselves' (p xi). Ch 1: 'Ecclesiastical and Secular Influences: Rhythm, Intonation, Punctuation,' investigates marks of punctuation (rhythmic, intonational) in mss, following the suggestions of Peter Clemoes on the ecclesiastical origin of such marks in works meant to be read aloud (Clemoes, *Liturgical Influence on Punctuation in Late Old English and Early Middle English Manuscripts*, Cambridge, 1952). Ch 2, 'Chaucer and his Contemporaries,' advances the theory by examining several poems, including some of Chaucer's lyrics. 'I am anxious to show that the superficial classification of his work into iambic octosyllabic couplets, iambic decasyllabic couplets, iambic quatrains with alternating rhyme, and rime royal stanzas obscures both the nature of his achievement and his development. It is not the external appearance of his verse that matters but rather the internal structure of his verse – his rhythms' (p 29). *ABC* is written in series of cadences which, if the reader forgets old rules for final –e, are decasyllabic following 'the hemistich tradition of being divided by the virga into arsis and thesis' (p 30). The half lines should be of equal time. 'Let the reader read to an imaginary metronome with one beat for each part of the line, and I think he will hear the music' (p 30). In *Sted*, 'every line concludes with a *cadence*' (p 33). *MB* is also an example of Chaucerian cadence; Southworth argues that Chaucer did not pronounce final –e in *herte, deere,* or *herte made,* using Fairfax 16 examples from *Mars, Venus,* and *AA* to support his theory. 'I am glad to see ... that a rapidly increasing body of scholars takes the view that the scribes knew what they were doing' (p 34). Southworth argues for an increasing flexibility of line as Chaucer matured as a poet. Noting the virga in early *T&C* mss, he suggests that they are intonational marks, a guide to the person reading aloud: 'My experience has been that in every case, if these marks are heeded, the reading is good. The marks in some mss indicate a very subtle reading' (p 49). Some of the marks may be from the poet himself. Ch 3 is on *CT*; Ch 4, on Chaucer's Disciples. 'Chaucer's mature style is the perfect distillation of the speech of his England – that of the urbane, sophisticated court of Richard II; that speech reflecting the strong influences of ecclesiastic writing and sermoning; that of persons who have steeped themselves in popular romances; that of the court, the counting house, the village, and the field. His great achievement lies in the artistry with which in his poetry he has eradicated the prolixity of daily speech without sacrificing its rhythms' (p 78).

Nb, Both of Southworth's books include detailed disputes with previous writers on medieval prosody and thus constitute a good source of bibliography on the subject in general. Southworth's thesis on Chaucer's final –e first appeared in 'Chaucer's Final –e in Rhyme,' *PMLA*, 62 (1947), 910–35. E. Talbot Donaldson attacked the argument in 'Chaucer's Final –e,' *PMLA*, 63 (1948), 1101–24. Southworth replied in *PMLA*, 64 (1949), 601–9; then Donaldson replied, *PMLA*, 64 (1949), 609, with a final rejoinder by Southworth on the same page. In both the subsequent books Southworth continues to maintain his original position.

– Review by P.J. Frankis, *MAE*, 35 (1966), 78–82: Southworth's new book is as contentious as its predecessor and 'displays the same kind of anti-rhetoric that seems calculated to convince the reader that the writer is wrong' (pp 80–1). One of Southworth's basic contentions is 'clearly important and right: namely, that Chaucer editors over the past hundred years have generally constructed an eclectic text from a number of manuscripts in accordance with a preconceived idea of Chaucer's metre, even on occasion introducing emendations on metrical grounds' (p 81). Other main arguments are erroneous, namely the refusal to allow for the pronunciation of final –e, and the insistence that pronunciation of verse must be the same as that used in ordinary speech. This latter point ignores what little is known about early verse declamation and reflects an odd unawareness of the recorded readings of modern poets (p 81).

78 Ten Brink, Bernhard. *The Language and Metre of Chaucer.* 2nd ed. Rev by Friedrich Kluge, trans. M. Bentinck Smith. London and New York: Macmillan, 1901.

See 'The Stanza,' pp 252–65, where ten Brink stresses the tripartite structure of the Chaucerian stanza, which originates in the traditional musical division described by Dante in *De Vulgari Eloquentia* II.10–3 (*pes* 1: ab; *pes* 2: ab; *cauda*: bcc). 'Chaucer often observes this tripartition, even in the logical structure of his argument, without pedantically binding himself to it' (p 255). The stanza originates in Old French and Provençal art poetry. 'Although not its creator, Chaucer may claim the stanza as his own. The skill with which he constructs it and the extent to which he uses it have given it a far greater significance than it originally possessed. The English poet has set his own peculiar seal upon the system, especially by the consistency with which he employs a new rime for the last couplet; whereby the structure becomes more clearly outlined and the conclusion more defined' (pp 255–6). Chaucer remained loyal to it 'even after he had become acquainted with the Italian ottave-rime in Boccaccio's epics' (p 256). Ten Brink discusses the complex stanza of *AA* (pp 257–8), *ABC* (p 261). See **74.**

❧ General Studies

79 Baldwin, Charles Sears. *Three Medieval Centuries of Literature in England: 1100–1400*. Boston: Little Brown, 1932; rpt New York: Phaeton Press, 1968. Ch 7, 'Medieval Lyric,' pp 142–56: Baldwin cites 'Hyd, Absolon,' from *LGW*, as the courtly balade 'heard at its prettiest in Chaucer' (p 152); he traces the 'enumeration of famous persons' trope to Machaut. The roundel from *PF* is Chaucer's best example of that form (p 154). Baldwin quotes *Truth* in its entirety, since 'among the hundreds of *balades*, French and English, in Chaucer's time' few have its 'lyric depth' (pp 154–6). 'Before the *balade* had faded, Petrarch had made the sonnet the occasional form of the future' (p 156).

80 Baskervill, Charles R. 'English Songs on the Night Visit.' *PMLA*, 36 (1921), 565–614.
Baskervill traces the *aube* back to 'a very ancient pagan custom ... which allowed a youth to visit a girl secretly and spend the night with her before marriage' (p 565). Features of the night visit lie behind *Romaunt* ll. 2640–80 where the God of Love tells the lover how it will be at night 'without rest, in payne and wo' (pp 569–70). Chaucer also draws on the aube tradition in *T&C* and *Mars*. 'Open the door' and 'Go from my window, go' poems are related to the tradition. Chaucer draws on these variations in *T&C* and his fabliaux.

81 Baugh, Albert C. 'The Middle English Romance: Some Questions of Creation, Presentation, and Preservation.' *Spec*, 42 (1967), 1–31.
Minstrels, like actors, were primarily performers, not authors (pp 4–5). Baugh cites numerous references to minstrels in Middle English romances.

82 Bethurum, Dorothy. 'Chaucer's Point of View as Narrator in the Love Poems.' *PMLA*, 74 (1959), 511–20.
Bethurum warns against the assuming of autobiographical interpretation of the French love poets and Chaucer. Chaucer's notions of love were strongly influenced by the Neoplatonic ideas of Alain de Lille, Macrobius, Boethius, and *RR*. 'Love of man leads to love of God, and this belief also gave stimulus and approbation to the great interest in sexual love displayed in the Middle Ages' (p 512). 'Whether it was that he was widely read in all of this or whether the appeal of the Neoplatonic Eros was

naturally congenial to him it created the atmosphere in which the love visions and *Troilus* were conceived. His trust in a beneficent Nature, autonomous and intelligible because she is the 'Vicaire of the almighty Lord,' forms the basis of his all-embracing sympathy. This sympathy expresses itself in different forms in the *Book of the Duchess* and in the *Miller's Tale*, but it is always there' (p 512). The discussion then concentrates on the dream visions and *T&C*.

83 Birney, Earle. 'The Beginnings of Chaucer's Irony.' *PMLA*, 54 (1939), 637–55.

In exploring the beginnings of Chaucerian irony Birney discusses in detail six lyrics (*Pity, Lady, CD, AWU, Ros, MB*) in addition to the early dream visions. See **281, 294, 389, 397.**

84 Braddy, Haldeen. *Chaucer and the French Poet Graunson*. Baton Rouge: Louisiana State University Press, 1947; rpt Port Washington, N.Y.: Kennikat Press, 1968.

Ch 1 assesses the great fame of the Savoyard poet in the fourteenth century. Chaucer's praise of Graunson in *Venus* as 'flour of hem that make in Fraunce' reflects the views of other courtiers as well, whether in England, France, Spain, Portugal, Prussia, or Italy. 'His was a narrow field for operation; but within the limited area of his talents he was capable of turning out more than one happy version of hackneyed themes' (p 21). His poems share the blemishes of his age; he 'could not free himself from the traditions [of *RR*] which almost suffocated even Machaut' (p 18). Ch 2, 'The Savoyard Knight of Chaucer's Circle,' traces the history of friendly relations between Savoy and England. Oton's chronology closely parallels Chaucer's. Born ca 1340; married 1356; knighted at 18 years of age; had two sons; served in the diplomatic service in England, Spain, Italy; died in 1397. He was friends with Philip la Vache and Thomas Bukton. Chaucer may have met him first at the wedding of Prince Lionel. He was in London in 1372 where he entered the service of Pembroke for the expedition against Spain. Ch 3, 'Graunson in England and the Canterbury Tales': Part of Graunson's family had migrated to England at the time of Edward II, so the name was well established throughout England in the fourteenth century. Oton I and Oton II, the ancestors of Chaucer's friend, both served in the court of the English king. After 1374 Oton III served John of Gaunt; Chaucer at this time was staying with Gaunt at the Savoy. Braddy includes a chart outlining Graunson's many activities with English courtiers in the last two decades of the century. Ch 4, 'Some French Influences on Chaucer's Minor Poems,' explores kinships between Chaucer's poems and Graunson's. 'Many of Chaucer's poems, some of which are unfortunately now apparently lost, belong to a type of poetry that was much cultivated in mediaeval England and France' (p 55). Braddy draws parallels between Graunson's poems and

CD, BD, *Venus, Mars, PF,* and *Sted* (see separate entries below). Ch 5, 'Personal Allegory in the Valentine Poems,' relates *Le Songe Sainct Valentin* to *PF* and *Mars*. Braddy discusses Graunson's acrostics on Isabel (of York) whom Shirley associates with *Mars* and *Venus*. 'The data here given should serve somewhat to rehabilitate the reputation of John Shirley' (p 83). Ch 6, 'The Courtly Tradition and Chaucerian Chronology': Courtly tradition flourishes in *Troilus,* but also in the minor poems where 'the poet is unquestionably writing in observance of the doctrine *amour courtois*' (p 87). Braddy is inclined to agree with Galway **101** that these poems are filled with autobiographical hints.
  – Review by J.A.W. Bennett, *MAE,* 18 (1949), 35–7: In his 'lavish use of the we-may-suppose formula' and his 'leap-frog method of argument' Braddy attributes more importance to Graunson's influence on Chaucer than the facts warrant (p 36). His transcriptions sometimes lack accuracy and his interpretation of documents is occasionally faulty (p 37).
85 Brewer, D.S. 'The Ideal of Feminine Beauty in Medieval Literature, Especially "Harley Lyrics," Chaucer, and Some Elizabethans.' *MLR,* 50 (1955), 257–69.
Although Brewer's essay does not devote much attention to Chaucer's lyrics, as background to their use of stock conventions it is essential. Part 1 traces the conventions of description from classical literature through Matthew of Vendôme and Geoffrey of Vinsauf (whose descriptions are 'much fuller than Matthew's, though without his trifling indecencies' [p 258]), and discusses applications of such formulas by Gerald of Barry, Benoît de Ste-Maure, Chrestien de Troyes, and Guillaume de Lorris. Part 3 is devoted to Chaucer (mainly Good Faire White in *BD,* Criseyde, Emily, and Alisoun). Chaucer's Emily differs from Boccaccio's; his 'achievement is to describe girl and garden so that it is our own imaginations which pour in all the pure and fresh associations of flowers and dewy scents and spring and dawn and girlhood' (p 266). Using Emily as his primary example of a stock convention with its stock response, Brewer goes on to generalize about the power of such a technique: 'We respond to Emily because of the scores of other golden-haired girls, bright, pure, gay, which literature has created – even later than the Middle Ages, but first then – which have been vehicles for so many daydreams, secret desires, aspirations, hopes, and fears. Such girls, in medieval literature at least, represent not realistic individuals, unique, never to be met with again ... They represent universals in concrete form. A convention in feeble hands loses particularity and vividness; but in capable hands, like Chaucer's, it achieves the kind of power which no mere reportage of individuals can attain. The convention both formulates and releases that 'stock response' ... The idealized beautiful girl

corresponds to a basic element in man's experience ... A great poet needed only to touch on an essential detail or two to suggest the whole and, indeed, to bring it more powerfully alive than could be done by a full description. Even Dante's Beatrice perhaps draws life from this tradition' (p 267). In a character like Alisoun in *MilT* Chaucer 'has created an amusing incongruous literary and social pattern which because of the steadiness of accepted conventions is quite without the irritability that would almost inevitably accompany it today. There is an element of parody, burlesque, which a firm literary tradition always makes possible and which by no means implies that the tradition itself is scorned' (p 268). (See **523** below for further comment.) The concluding part of Brewer's essay examines the survival of the tradition in Shakespeare and Donne.

86 Brown, Emerson, Jr. 'Chaucer and the European Literary Tradition.' In *Geoffrey Chaucer.* Ed. George Economou. New York: McGraw-Hill, 1975, pp 37–54.

Designed for beginning students, this essay stresses the importance of literary tradition to Chaucer. Noting the familiar tag that Chaucer is the first great poet in English, Brown suggests: 'it is far closer to the truth to view Chaucer as standing at the end of a long literary tradition,' like a figure in 'a tapestry crowded with the poets and thinkers of 1,500 years of the European literary tradition' (p 51). 'Rarely has a poet had so much confidence as Chaucer in the capacity of his audience to participate imaginatively in the creative relationship between text and reader that produces, in its fullest sense, the work of literature' (p 41). 'From the evidence of a list of books owned by King Richard in 1384 to 1385, his tastes were clearly for French literature' (p 42). Brown jokingly suggests that Chaucer is 'the greatest French poet of the Middle Ages' (p 43). 'While we can imagine him becoming a very good poet without ever setting foot in Italy or reading a word of Italian, we can hardly imagine him becoming a poet at all without the incalculable influence of France' (p 43). 'If we are to concentrate on "the poem itself," we must broaden our definition of the poem to include passages and whole literary contexts which the poem alludes to' (p 48).

87 Burnley, J.D. '*fine amor:* Its Meaning and Context.' *RES,* 31 (1980), 129–48.

Burnley analyses the 'linguistic architecture' of *fine amor,* to explore its senses in relation to each other. *Fin,* from *finitum,* connotes the perfect, complete, consummate, pure, and is so used by Jean de Condé, Machaut, and Gower. Meanings of *amor* range from *caritas* to sexual passion. *Fine amor* is thus a kind of excellence in love evaluated in terms of medieval psychological theory (p 137), a motion of will, which, guided by reason, may be virtuous and distinct from foolish secular love. It is an affect. 'It is plain ... that English usage is merely the reflection of French with the exception that, in English, the phrase is relatively rarely applied to secular and extramarital love. There is no great mystery why this should be. It is simply because the idealizing and elaborate treatment of sexual love does not appear until relatively late in English, by which time a new philosophical vocabulary had emerged. Chaucer does not speak of the *herte fyne*, but of the *gentil herte*; Gower speaks, not of *love fin*, but of *honeste love*' (p 147). *Fine amor* is a product of *fins cuers*, drawn from a theory of *amicitia*, and ultimately defined by the heart. Whether it is sexual or divine, marital or extramarital, pure or true is not directly relevant. It refers rather to a quality and intensity of the act itself.

88 Burrow, J.A. *Ricardian Poetry: Chaucer, Gower, Langland, and the Gawain Poet.* London: Routledge and Kegan Paul, 1971. Pp 43–5, 47.
The style of Ricardian poetry is essentially 'a long-poem style. One can see this in the short poems of Chaucer, the *Envoy to Scogan* or *Truth*, where much careful and intelligent workmanship somehow fails to produce a fully memorable result. There is something a little mysterious about the failure of Chaucer's not inconsiderable body of short poems to make the expected impression; but one reason is surely that the verbal texture remains, despite efforts on Chaucer's part to exclude "verse tags" and "fillers", too open and loose for poems of this magnitude. What is lacking is just that fundamental harmony between the scale of the poem and the scale of the language which we feel to be achieved without effort in the longer poems both of Chaucer and of his contemporaries. Just as John Donne's habitual style, which seems right in the short poems, seems overwrought in long poems such as the *Anniversaries,* so Chaucer's style seems right in long poems but underwrought in short ones' (pp 43–4). 'Gower says that Chaucer "filled the land" with love-songs; but even Chaucer's lyrics, charming as they are, fail to amount to very much. No doubt many have been lost, however' (p 47).

89 Carter, Thomas. 'The Shorter Poems of Geoffrey Chaucer.' *Shenandoah*, 11 (1960), 48–60.
Carter stresses the universality of Chaucer's later lyrics and their strong appeal even to a modern American audience. In contrast to *ABC* (a poem with 'neither animation nor feeling'), *Pity* (a poem without emotion, 'certainly not any passion') and *Mars* (an exercise which 'reeks with cleverness'), a poem like *Ros* is rich in wit and playful humour, 'not, after all, so very far from what we consider light verse today' (pp 51–6). It is in such poems that we begin to get what Ezra Pound has called 'the particular Chaucerian enrichment, or humanity,' a Chaucer who can speak to us 'without benefit of conventions' (p 56). Carter contrasts *FA* ('merely perfunctory') with *Sted* and *Truth*, whose 'very "common-ness" ... gives these poems their genuine folk quality; one feels at once that the poet is, in a way reflecting his entire culture. It is important that we need to

know nothing of that culture – for the world is always turned around, and we hope that truth will deliver us – to feel the quiet strength of the lines' (p 57). Carter praises *Purse, Scogan,* and *Bukton* for their wit; he concludes with *MB,* which 'could only have been written by Chaucer' (p 60).

90 Chiarenza, Frank John. 'Chaucer and the Medieval Amorous Complaint: A Study in the Evolution of a Poetic Genre.' *DAI,* 31 (1970), 2337A. Yale Dissertation, 1956.
Chiarenza traces forms of amorous complaint from classical antiquity to the mid-fourteenth century, then concentrates on Chaucer's use of the genre both as independent lyrics and as interpolated poems within the framework of larger narratives. 'The complaint in the hands of Chaucer sometimes follows the most familiar patterns of the convention, but it more frequently attains a degree of complexity and perfection not easily recognized and rarely appreciated when considered apart from the tradition from which it stems. Chaucer's use of the complaint to heighten the dramatic moment of a larger narrative, and as a form of direct discourse, represents the fullest realization of its potential' (p 2337A).

91 Clemen, Wolfgang. *Chaucers frühe Dictung.* Gottingen und Zurich: Vandenhoeck und Ruprecht, 1963.
An enlarged version of *Der junge Chaucer* (Bonn, 1938). See **92.** For a full listing of reviews see Lorrayne Y. Baird, *A Bibliography of Chaucer, 1964–73* (Boston: G.K. Hall, 1977), pp 28–9.
 – Review by Siegfried Wenzel, *JEGP,* 64 (1965), 165–6: An improvement as well as a revision of *Der junge Chaucer.* Clemen has benefitted from the critical studies of others to provide 'a more complete and a more mature study' (p 165). 'A most stimulating and influential analysis of the young poet' (p 166).

92 — *Chaucer's Early Poetry.* Trans. C.A.M. Sym. London: Methuen, 1963.
Early poems are those written before 1380. Chs 1–3 are on *BD, HF, PF.* Ch 4, 'Minor Poems,' pp 170–209: 'Machaut's lyric poems are possibly the most artificial and conventional products of the whole fourteenth century. With Machaut all personal and original expression is paralysed by the exaggeration and over-elaboration of rules and forms. What mattered in these poems was not what was said but that the same rhyme should be used fifty or more times on end, with numerous other artistic devices introduced as well. The technical, formal element was employed more and more for its own sake; and this brought with it a considerable weakening in the content and range of themes' (p 170). Critics of Chaucer have overemphasized the French and Italian influence on Chaucer. Though Chaucer uses Machaut as his 'model,' what strikes Clemen is the Englishness of the result. Chaucer's choice of pattern 'ran clean counter to his own nature as a poet' (p 171). Chaucer seeks diversity, change,

variety of images, individual characterization in his lyrics, as in his narrative poems. His poems tend toward dramatic dialogue. 'A dislike of pedantic rigidity and stiff formalism lies ... so deep in Chaucer's nature and is so obvious throughout his work that it requires no exemplification' (p 171). Probably Chaucer wrote many conventional poems, which have not come down to us, after the pattern of Machaut in the first decade of his productive period. His early complaints (*Pity* and *Lady*) are 'as impersonal and conventional as their models' (p 172). The early lyrics are inferior achievements to the three early dream visions, but still they are important as stages in Chaucer's linguistic and poetic development. 'He is rightly regarded as the first great versifier in English literature' (p 172). Probably many of the lost poems were free translations like the *ABC* and *Venus*, the value of which in Chaucer's development 'can hardly be exaggerated; for here we often have a creative type of translation that leads on to something new' (p 173). Chaucer 'succeeds in making the most diverse styles and texts so completely and so unequivocally his own that they melt into one with his own modes of expression. He felt the other writer's idiom as a welcome enrichment, not a restriction' (p 174). Clemen gives specific treatment to *ABC*, *Pity*, *Lady*, *Mars*, and *AA*. See **163, 229, 334, 390, 401.**

– Review by Charles Muscatine, *MLQ*, 25 (1964), 473–8: '*Der junge Chaucer* was incomparable in its time for its sensitivity to the actual aesthetic and poetic character of the early poems' (p 474). The good qualities of the earlier work are preserved in the revision, along with a 'sensitive continuous account of Chaucer's alteration of sources' (p 474). The revision is 'more overtly and confidently concerned with rhetorical tradition' (p 475).

93 Cohen, Helen Louise. *The Ballade.* New York: Columbia University Press, 1915.

Cohen discusses the history of the balade form in Middle English (pp 222–99), with special attention to Chaucer as its first practitioner. 'In all probability, it will never be explained to our entire satisfaction why the *ballade*, which had met with so much favour in France and which won its way with the greatest Middle English poet, did not achieve greater popularity with Chaucer's contemporaries and successors. In England, the fifteenth century man of letters seems to have been susceptible to a variety of French conventions, but only occasionally did he feel impelled to use the form that in France had become a favourite means of literary expression' (p 222). Because of the scarcity of rhyme in English, the rigour of the French form is relaxed. Cohen abandons the French definition of ballade to consider any Middle English poem of three stanzas with a refrain to be one (p 224). Cohen discusses ballade nomenclature as understood by Lydgate, Shirley, and other fifteenth- and

sixteenth-century writers up to the point at which the term becomes
synonymous with *ballet*. She considers Chaucer's ballades (pp 233–52),
giving special attention to formal experimentation, which ranges from
strict accord with French rules in some to expansion through double ballades and freer rhyme schemes in others. She devotes brief attention to
Chaucer's moral ballades, contrasts *Purse* with French begging poems,
then moves on to discuss Lydgate, Quixley's translation of Gower's
Traitée, and anonymous ballades of the fifteenth century.

94 Crosby, Ruth. 'Oral Delivery in the Middle Ages.' *Spec*, 11 (1936), 88–110.
'In the Middle Ages the masses of the people read by means of the ear
rather than the eye, by hearing others read or recite rather than by reading to themselves' (p 88). Crosby traces the oral tradition from Greece,
noting objections by Roman poets to too many recitations or too large audiences. In England the scop was the cultural purveyor in Anglo-Saxon
times, the source of Alfred's education until he learned to read. The popularity of the professional storyteller 'cannot be overestimated' (p 93).
Crosby comments on allusions to recitation in the romance. The chief
characteristic of such literature is the 'use of direct address not to the
reader, but to those listeners who are present at the recitation' (p 100).
Such poems are marked by set phrases, fillers, inclusive phrases, alliterative pairs ('blod and bon'), redundancy ('on the morn when it was day'),
formulaic phrases, repetitive transitions, asseverations, and oaths.

95 — 'Chaucer and the Custom of Oral Delivery.' *Spec*, 13 (1938), 413–32.
Crosby begins by discussing reading-scenes in Chaucer's poetry, some
peaceful like Criseyde's reading to her friends, some not so peaceful like
Jankyn's reading to Alisoun. Chaucer uses all the devices of the oral tradition, especially direct address, introductory phrases, formulaic pairs,
transitional passages, oathes, and colloquialisms. His narrator clearly
imagines himself to be before an audience (eg, in *AA*). These devices are
found in Chaucer's lyrics as well as in his narrative poetry. *Truth* and
Bukton end in prayers; *AA* begins with an 'invocation in the classical
manner' (p 428). Chaucer, his genius notwithstanding, 'was conventional
... Though unquestionably many characteristics of Chaucer's style are to
be traced to his Latin, Italian, and French reading of a literary character,
many others can be accounted for only by understanding his relations to
the popular traditions engendered by the custom of oral delivery. These
traditions are above all French and English ... We may say that Chaucer
... wrote primarily for a listening public and that in doing so he naturally adopted many of the tricks of style familiar to him through his
knowledge of literature intended to be heard' (pp 431–2). Bateson **57,** p 5,
singles out Crosby's essay as 'incomparably the most useful contribution
to Chaucer studies.'

96 Dodd, William George. *Courtly Love in Chaucer and Gower.* Harvard Studies in English. Vol 1. Boston: Ginn, 1913.
Dodd divides the lyrics into two categories: those which contain little or nothing but ideas common in conventional French love poems; and those, though French in form, 'infused with the personality of the poet and ... in the racy style characteristic of Chaucer at his best' (p 91). The first group includes *Pity, Lady, Venus, AWU, CD,* and *WN*; the second *MB, Ros, Purse, Scogan, Mars,* and *AA.* See **235, 282, 297, 379, 498, 567.**

97 Ehrhart, Margaret Jean. *Chaucer's Contemporary, Guillaume de Machaut: A Critical Study of Four Dits Amoureux.* Illinois Dissertation, 1974. Director, Jackson Campbell. See also, *DAI,* 35 (1975), 7299A.
Introduction; Ch 1, 'Le Dit dou Lyon'; Ch 2, 'Le Dit de L'Alerion'; Ch 3, 'Le Jugement dou Roy de Navarre'; Ch 4, 'Le Dit de la Fonteinne Amoureuse'. Conclusion. Appendix A: 'On the Placement of the "Lai de plour"'; Appendix B: 'On the Duc de Berry as a character in the *Fonteinne Amoreuse.*' Machaut is the most important of Chaucer's fourteenth-century French influences. Chaucer scholars too frequently disparage his poetry. After exposing various misconceptions of the French poet (especially the failure to understand his use of classical mythology), Ehrhart shows that Machaut, very much like Chaucer, 'purposely employed a fictional, first-person narrator in order to achieve various humorous and ironic effects, and so Machaut's narrators ought not to be viewed as always expressing Machaut's own point of view' (p 7). 'Machaut appears to have been an important force in the reawakening of interest in mythology which characterized the mid-fourteenth century' (p 10). He ranks with Bersuire, 'a remarkably learned man,' and Philippe de Vitri in his popularizing of the classics (p 11). He wrote nine dream visions, but did not progress beyond the genre as Chaucer did. Ehrhart's chapters on the individual poems include a good plot summary and running commentary for each. She concludes: 'Those critics who characterized Machaut's *dits* as attractively decorated but hollow confections were simply being unobservant' (p 205).

98 Flügel, Ewald. 'Chaucers Kleinere Gedichte.' *Anglia,* 23 (1901), 195–224.
A collection of textual notes to *Pity, Adam,* and *Truth.* See **211, 405,** and **548.**

99 French, Robert Dudley. *A Chaucer Handbook.* New York: Appleton-Century-Crofts, 1927/rev 1947.
Ch 3, 'The Lesser Works,' pp 75–134, contains brief essays on each of the works other than *T&C* and *CT,* which summarize ms information, date, source, metrical form, and major critical disputes.

100 Friedman, Albert B. 'Late Mediaeval Ballade and the Origin of Broadside Balladry.' *MAE*, 27 (1958), 95–110.

Long before Machaut the ballade had lost all actual connection with the dance and had become a very nearly fixed form: three stanzas with the same rime scheme, common rime sounds, and a last line of each stanza recurring as refrain. The envoy, 'the addressing of the *balade*, so to speak, attached itself to the type during the *puys*,' fourteenth-century contests among ballade-makers, and became a regular feature through Deschamps, 'who wrote over a thousand such pieces and framed archly legalistic formulas for contriving them' (p 98). Gower wrote ballades in French which are 'dilute in thought and strained in execution'; 'it remained for Chaucer to introduce the *genre* into English with his "sovereyn ballades" modelled on those of his admirer Deschamps' (p 98). The form had only a 'moderate success' in England. Many of Chaucer's minor poems may be lost, but only ten survive which are ballades 'of reasonably certain attribution ... complying with the French rules' (pp 98–9). Lydgate provides only two examples of independent ballades complying with the rules. Hoccleve captions many poems ballades, but none meets the French requirements. Of strict Middle English ballades, the bulk are translations from the French and survive in two collections: Quixley's Englishing of Gower's *Traitie* and the 120 pieces in Harley 682 (mostly Charles of Orléans). The rime royal stanza was not the reason for the ballade's failure but rather the requirement that the three rimes run throughout the poem (p 100). The villanelle, another popular French form, proved almost impossible in English. 'In view of these difficulties, it is no wonder that almost from the beginning of ballade writing in England, a simplified form was evolved in which the stanzas did not have rimes in common, with the exception of the c-rime, which was preserved by the refrain' (p 100). English writers also showed less variety in stanza structure than the French. Chaucer works with seven-, and eight-line staves; the nine-, ten-, eleven-, and even fourteen-line ballade stanzas common in French are rarely found. 'To lengthen the stanza ... is to complicate the rime scheme, and rime, of course, is the English writers' principal difficulty' (p 101). Most English ballades lack the envoy. The French create length by writing double and triple ballades. Chaucer complicates the form by adding narrative elements. And Chaucer's principal ballade stanza (rime royal) becomes the dominant narrative stanza throughout the fifteenth century. Single-stanza ballades and political broadsides developed from the pseudo-ballade in the fifteenth and sixteenth centuries. 'Apparently the doggerel style which became standard on broadsides for the next several centuries had already rooted itself before 1550 ... The wares these much reviled "toss-pot poets" scribbled and sold were a far cry from Chaucer's gracefully turned

ballades, but ... there are historical reasons for both kinds of poetry
bearing the same label' (p 110).

101 Galway, Margaret. 'Chaucer's Sovereign Lady: A Study of the Prologue to
the *Legend* and Related Poems.' *MLR*, 33 (1938), 145–99.
Galway argues that Chaucer's noble queen Alceste in *LGW* is Joan of
Kent in real life; the G revision of the F Prol. was necessary after her
death. The God of Love is the Black Prince, and the poet's offence has to
do with events surrounding Thomas Holland, her first husband. Galway
also argues that Chaucer's eightyear love sickness in *BD* refers to his
passion for Joan, who married the Black Prince in 1361, eight years before Blanche's death. This unrequited love lies behind such poems as
Pity, Lady, and the envoy to *Venus:* all are autobiographical and refer to
the rejected suitor who would render life-long service to her (cf also *BC*
and *WN*). The crux of Anelida's complaint may be Holland's rejection of
Joan in her early youth (see **239**). The same heartbreak is perhaps
represented in the *SqT*, while the *KnT* alludes to the rivalry of Holland
and Salisbury for the fair maid of Kent. *Mars* presents 'in allegorical
form' the story of the liaison between Thomas Holland (Mars) and Joan
of Kent (Venus) before their official marriage, the departure of Holland
with Edward III (Phoebus) and Joan's flight to Salisbury (Cilenius). John
Shirley's note on the poem comes close to being right; he only had the
parties wrong (ie, the wrong Holland, the wrong woman, and the wrong
generation). 'The symbol of Chaucer's Canterbury period, it might be
said, is the Wife of Bath; the symbol of his pre-Canterbury period the
Fair Maid of Kent' (p 199). See also **341**.

101a — 'Chaucer, Graunson, and Isabel of France.' *RES*, 24 (1948), 273–80.
The 'princesse' addressed in *Venus* and Graunson's poems is the same
'Isabel,' 'but we cannot assume that Graunson was actually in love with
her, or even that she was an adult. The love-poems of court poets for
grandes dames ... normally were conventional compliments, often border-
ing on the obligatory, and sometimes the *grande dame* was very young'
(p 273). Galway suggests that Graunson's Isabel and Chaucer's 'princesse'
is the daughter of Charles VI, whom Richard II married on 4 November
1396, on the eve of her seventh birthday, the child for whom, as Manly
has suggested [*Canterbury Tales* (London, 1940), p 40], 'Chaucer wrote his
love-poem *To Rosemounde*' (p 274). Chaucer addresses the child bride not
only in *Venus* and *Ros*, but also in *AWU, MB,* and the revised Prologue
to *LGW* (p 275). In *Venus* Chaucer alters Graunson's ballades, changing
pronouns so that Isabel might present the poem 'to Graunson as an expression of *her* devotion to *him*' (p 277). Chaucer's 'ten-line envoy
outshines Graunson by having only two rhymes' (p 277). 'The child
bride of Richard II made her journey from Calais to England in

November 1396 in the charge of Chaucer's sister-in-law the Duchess of Lancaster. At Eltham palace in Kent, which became Isabel's headquarters, she had for her chamberlain Chaucer's friend Sir Philip Vache, the son-in-law of Sir Lewis Clifford. Chaucer himself ... was a near neighbour of the new queen. When he had met her in person he composed for her the ballade To Rosemounde' (p 278). The signature 'Tregentil Chaucer' possibly originated in the child's 'imperfect attempt to say "Tres gentil,"' which she pronounced in her 'smal' voice upon first hearing the poem (p 278). Chaucer had written PF to celebrate Richard's betrothal to Marie of France in 1377; perhaps Isabel objected to his having produced nothing comparable for her, 'hence Chaucer's second ballade to "Madame," Against Women Unconstant, where he complains of her overfondness for "newe thing"' (p 279). MB forms 'a natural sequel to the lively quarrel ... and so ended, with a fittingly gay exit, Chaucer's role of love-poet, briefly revived in his old age for the entertainment of a royal child' (p 279).

102 Garbáty, Thomas J. 'The Degradation of Chaucer's "Geffrey".' *PMLA,* 89 (1974), 97–104.

'It appears to me that no narrator in Chaucer's works can be discussed in isolation from the others. There is a continuum of the pose in all the works that is too consistent to be disregarded' (p 97). (This would include the Geoffrey in *Scogan* as well as *PF.*) 'The narrator "Geffrey" ... is an individual whom law students meet daily in their case books, whom they know intimately as an omnipresent, faceless individual, the dull standard of common sense. He is the "reasonable (but not reasoning) man" in any situation of legal procedure. "What would the reasonable man do?" is the question always asked. To answer this we must remember that the man is "reasonable" but he is no more than that. Nothing more is expected of him, neither great intelligence, nor a refined sense of humour, sensitivity, imagination, nor sophistication. He has simply common sense, and reacts to any situation as reason dictates. After dealing with him, one begins to see the "reasonable man" as a rather dull, uninteresting pillar of social norms, ethics, and morality. He represents the average wit, the sense of right and wrong. He is the middle man' (pp 98–9). Garbáty draws on lyrics like *Scogan* and *Bukton* to illustrate Chaucer's posing.

103 Gardner, John. *The Poetry of Chaucer.* Carbondale: Southern Illinois University Press; London and Amsterdam: Feffer and Simons, 1977. Gardner comments on the lyrics in Ch 3, 'The Unfinished *Anelida and Arcite* and a Few of Chaucer's Short Poems, a Chapter Brief and Disorganized, but Rich in Curiosities (A Trinket Shop at the Foot of the Mountainous Chapter 4, on *Troilus and Criseyde*),' pp 65–95. He points out metrical experimentation and scans *Sted* to show metrical variety and effects of the 'rhythmic rush' (p 66), then notes the wit and 'Donne-like punning' in *Truth* (pp 67–8), the striking humour of *Ros* 'where conventional love-longing and Chaucer's love of food get comically mixed up' (p 69), and the amusing bravura of *Purse* where 'Chaucer merrily turns the high-minded conventions of courtly love to the purpose of comically outrageous begging' (pp 69–70). Taken as a whole the lyrics reveal the three ways in which Chaucer viewed the world – philosophically (*ABC*, *Truth*, etc), in a courtly manner (*Mars*, *WN*, etc), and with comic wit (*Ros*, *Scogan*, *Adam*). Gardner offers a cursory reading of *Mars* and *Venus* (see **342, 381**), noting Christian paradoxes in the language of each (he thinks they are related poems). He also comments on the richness of imagery in *FA* (pp 93–5; see **423**). The heart of the chapter is devoted to *AA*, with a detailed excursion into *Pity*. See **241** and **406**.

104 Getty, Agnes K. 'Chaucer's Changing Conceptions of the Humble Lover.' *PMLA*, 44 (1929), 202–16.

Getty sees a continuous development in Chaucer's treatment of the lover, which moves from the humble lover of French poetry in the early works to the satire and ironic poses in the late works. In the *Romaunt* 'Chaucer consistently follows the formal concept of the humble lover throughout. In Fragment A ... the theme and treatment are strictly those of conventional love, built about the French devices of the love vision and the court of love' (p 203). Neither *Pity* nor *Mars* deviates from French complaint. The lovers in *BD* are consistent with their sources too. But in *PF* Chaucer shows himself 'impatient with the precepts of the code' (p 206); similarly, though Troilus and Diomede are in keeping with *code d'amour* in *T&C*, Pandarus and Criseyde are not. The impatience continues through parody in *LGW* and *KnT*. In this regard, *SqT* is 'the most fascinating story never told' (p 212). After *LGW* and his mock romances, Chaucer's 'failure to conform to popular standards is frank and undissembled. *Merciles Beaute, Rosamound*, the *Envoy to Scogan*, and *The Compleint to His Empty Purse* are as satirical as his early poems are amorous; he frankly rebels, engaging in frequent poetic frolics with the romantics of the lover. We may conclude that, except for a temporary renewal of allegiance to formal love standards in the *Legend of Good Women*, Chaucer's rebellion against the conventional concept of the humble lover developed, and increased in intensity, after the writing of the *Hous of Fame*' (p 216).

105 Green, A. Wigfall. 'Chaucer's Complaints: Stanzaic Arrangement, Meter, and Rhyme.' *UMSE*, 3 (1962), 19–34.

Green lists stanzas according to line count and rhyme scheme, identifies the meters by the terminology of Latin scansion, and lists the rhymes for *CD, Mars, Venus, Lady, Pity*, and *Purse*, to conclude: 'If a poet may be evaluated in the light of his age and by the fecundity of his vocabulary, rhymes, and metrical forms, in English versification Chaucer is nonpareil' (p 34). Green excludes *BC* from his lists because its authorship is in doubt.

106 — 'Structure of Three Minor Poems by Chaucer.' *UMSE*, 4 (1963), 79–82.
Discusses tripartite structure, along with general comments on *Truth*, *Gent*, and *Sted*. See **550.**

107 Greene, Richard Leighton, ed. *The Early English Carols*. Oxford: Clarendon Press, 1935/rev and enlarged edn, 1977.
Introduction on the carol as genre, dance-song, and popular song, with discussion of Latin background and religious associations. The revised volume includes texts of nearly five hundred carols, with detailed notes on each. This distinguished volume provides an important part of the popular context surrounding art lyrics of the court.

108 Griffin, R.M. *Chaucer's Lyrics*. 1970. See **18.**
Griffin's first chapter defines 'lyric,' noting its occasional nature, formal versatility, specific audience, elaboration of a single theme, and, in Chaucer, its narrative elements which are subordinated to the lyric proper. The chapter also surveys criticism on Chaucer's lyrics. See individual entries for Griffin's views on specific lyrics.

109 Hales, John Wesley. 'Geoffrey Chaucer.' *Dictionary of National Biography*. Ed. Leslie Stephen and Sidney Lee. London: Oxford University Press, 1885/rev 1908. Rpt 1921–2. Volume 4, pp 154–67.
Hales notes that Chaucer wrote a few lyrics in his later years *(Mars, Venus, Scogan, Bukton, Fortune, Purse,* and perhaps *Truth)*, but 'credibly enough, the last few years of his life Chaucer, for one reason or another, wrote little, and his *magnum opus* was scarcely touched' (p 167). Hammond **37,** p 546, refers to Hales's Chaucer entry as 'inadequate.'

110 Haskell, Ann S. 'Lyric and Lyrical in the Works of Chaucer: The Poet and His Literary Context.' In *English Symposium Papers, III*. Ed. Douglas Shepard. Fredonia: SUNY College at Fredonia, 1972(1973), pp 1–45.
'There has been only a trickle of critical commentary on Chaucer's lyrics' (p 2). Haskell's contribution to the stream points to several common lyric types in Middle English and juxtaposes quotations from Chaucer with like kinds elsewhere. The types of lyric identified are: 1) religious (*ABC*); 2) Admonitions to forsake temporality ('O yonge fresshe folkes,' *T&C*); 3) Fortune as foe (*BD* 673–86); 4) Charms ('Jhesu Crist & seynt Benedight,' *MilT*); Love complaint (*BD* and *Ros* – 'a delightful satire' [p 26]); 6) Universal and Timeless Virtues (*Truth* and *Gent* – 'Considering the milieu of social stratification in which Chaucer lived, this poem is, indeed, curious. It is perhaps our surest statement that he was a citizen of all ages rather than of a single era' [p 28]); 7) Occasional lyrics (Complaint of fox in *NPT* and *Purse*); ubi sunt (*T&C*); 9) seasonal ('Now welcome somer,' *PF*, and the opening of *PF*). Chaucer's embedded lyrics provide 'textual contrast' to the surrounding narratives (p 34).

111 Hayes, Joseph John. *The Court Lyric in the Age of Chaucer. DAI,* 34 (1974), 4205A–4206A. Indiana University Dissertation, 1973. Director, Alfred David.

Hayes studies Machaut, Deschamps, Chaucer, Hoccleve, Lydgate, and Villon in relation to the particular audience, aristocratic patron, and court of each. 'The high point of the tradition initiated by Machaut and Deschamps is found in the lyrics of Chaucer, who first realized an ironic potential in the two-part structure of the framed complaint and the ballade-with-envoy. Although he did not abandon the generalizing manner and the respected authorities in his poems of 'good counsel,' Chaucer perceived that conventional poetry could have a fresh perspective by violating the expected norms with parody, and by drawing more attention to himself as persona.' 'Neither Hoccleve nor Lydgate, Chaucer's English successors, achieved his ironic subtleties. Hoccleve tended to reduce his ballades to the plain didactic level, and Lydgate's 'aureate' style tended toward sententiousness, except in the style *per antiphrasim.* Both poets, the first to provide us with examples of 'laureate' poetry, preferred the role of sober moralist to that of lover-poet' (p 4206A).

112 Hussey, S.S. 'The Minor Poems and the Prose.' In *The Middle Ages.* Ed. Whitney Frank Bolton. Sphere History of Literature in the English Language. London: Barrie and Jenkins, 1970, pp 229–62.

This general introduction concentrates mainly on Chaucer's dream visions. Hussey directs some comments toward the *Romaunt* as an early translation. Of the lyrics he finds least attractive those like *Lady,* which 'are allegorical in manner and heavily dependent on courtly love' (p 258). Set pieces in the longer narratives like the bird's rondeau in *PF* are 'more acceptable to us' (p 259). See **176, 394.**

113 Kane, George. *The Autobiographical Fallacy in Chaucer and Langland Studies.* The Chambers Memorial Lecture, 1965. London: H.K. Lewis, 1965.

Although Kane makes no specific mention of the lyrics, his remarks on the problem of reading autobiography into the poetry and of rereading public records in terms of what we want and know our poet to be have bearing on the many attempts to construe Chaucer biography out of the lyrics. 'Take Chaucer's references to his unsuccess as a lover; they might be autobiographical or they might not; without external information we could not conceivably know. As it turns out, someone discovers that the eight years of his hopeless passion verbally echo a love of equal length in his model Machaut, and those apparently melancholy lines in *The Parliament of Birds* where the dreamer, seeming to voice deep personal discontent, says *bothe I hadde thyng which that I nolde, and ek I nadde that thyng that I wolde,* prove to be a quotation from Boethius, in whose text it seems intended to describe the general human condition ... Thus particular speculations receive a check. But such corrections are fortuitous; they depend on external information. The process of free bio-graphical inference contains within itself no element to control its accu-racy, and therefore no means by which its logical necessity or even its probability can be checked. It has no rationale. It is essentially imagina-tive, affective, subjective, pure speculation' (pp 7–8). Pp 10–20 have some bearing on biographical interpretations of *Mars*.

114 Kean, Patricia. *Chaucer and the Making of English Poetry*. Vol 1: *Love Vision and Debate*. London: Routledge and Kegan Paul, 1972.

Ch 2, 'The Urbane Manner,' pp 31–66: 'Chaucer wrote poems of the kind he disowned in the *Retraction* as "worldly vanitees" throughout his working life, if we can judge from our scanty information about the dates of composition of "many a song and many a leccherous lay" ... Most of these poems are quite fairly to be called "minor" or "occasional"' (p 31). Kean stresses the urbanity of such verse – its shared intimacy and jokes, *divertissements* designed for a circle with definite expectations and accustomed to accepted literary forms and topics. Chaucer had no Eng-lish models to work from, but adapts English and Italian matter 'in a way which would be intelligible to an audience that knew only French or English poetry' (p 32). Chaucer always has the last word in his greater poems, 'but in the short, often experimental poems, we can sense poet and audience working together, so that an occasion or a personality must often have given life to a work which may seem to us less success-ful than those in which Chaucer comes a little nearer to the fifteenth-century conception of him as a "master" of poetry ... But it must have been, in part at any rate, through the existence of minor poetry of this sort that the milieu was created in which the major works could grow and flourish' (p 33). See also **346, 484.**

115 Kinney, Thomas L. 'The Temper of Fourteenth-Century English Verse of Complaint.' *AnM*, 7 (1966), 74–89.

Kinney reviews several features of the complaint as a vehicle of political reform. 'The verse of complaint reflects the basic bewilderment of fourteenth-century man in the face of change ... The temper of the verse of complaint, its lamentation, denunciation, its attempts at disinterested criticism, its exhortation, and other turbulent emotions reflect the insecu-rity of a changing world' (p 89). The essay does not deal with lover's complaints or Chaucer, though it provides background for some of the apocryphal works.

116 Kitchin, George. *A Survey of Burlesque and Parody in England*. Edinburgh: Oliver and Boyd, 1931. Pp 8–20.

'With Chaucer begins for us the true art of parody. His essentially comic genius was almost bound to indulge in this form of entertainment, see-ing that the rude beginnings of the art were to be found everywhere around him. But it is a difficult step from colloquial beginnings to finished art, and this is just Chaucer's supreme merit as a satirist' (p 8). Kitchin comments on *Thop* ('a tour de force,' p 9), *NPT* ('Chaucer's humorous masterpiece,' p 17), *MB, Ros,* and *Purse.* Also he comments on *Court of Love.* See **318.**

117 Legouis, Emile. *Geoffrey Chaucer.* Trans. L. Lailavoix. London: J. Dent and Sons, 1913; rpt New York: Russell and Russell, 1961. Originally published Paris, 1910. Pp 48–61.

Ch 2, 'The Making of Chaucer as a Poet': After discussing the state of the English Language ca 1360, Legouis turns to Chaucer at the school of the French trouvères (pp 48–61). 'The time was not altogether propitious to his aim, it would seem, for French poetry was never more wretched and destitute than during the period extending from Rutebeuf to Villon, or, if it be preferred, from the *Roman de la Rose* to Charles d'Orléans' (p 48). Legouis characterizes the qualities of Machaut which influenced Chaucer: his concern for art, his virtuoso experimentation with new groupings of verbs and fresh rhymes, his efforts at writing poems of definite length. Despite all his very great blemishes, 'Machaut presented an array of delicate qualities, which would render him attractive and valuable to his foreign disciple' (p 49). 'He sought rare poetical forms, capable of producing as such the emotions which his nature was too poor to arouse' (p 50). He could turn the commonplace image into a gem; 'that is why there are in his works small poems or passages of longer poems, which are not lacking in prettiness or brilliancy, and can still please for a moment' (p 50). 'Machaut is a refined versifier, not a great artist but nothing if not an artist' (p 51). The more one knows of Machaut, Granson, Deschamps, and Froissart, the more of Chaucer's debts one discerns. Chaucer demurs frequently to the French poets even when he is superior. 'The influence which the *Roman de la Rose* had on Chaucer should certainly not be reduced to a mere stylistic training. This romance ... was really the one poem which had the most constant hold on Chaucer'; it was 'a sort of poetic Bible' for him (p 54) which helped him but also hindered him: 'It led him to adopt and to retain for many years the allegorical style' (p 55). But *RR* is not the only French influence. Chaucer borrows from (and mocks) the degenerate romances; similarly curious bits from the trouvères crop up in some of his finest passages. 'He seems to have begun with lyric poetry, making known to his countrymen the learned new forms – ballad, virelai, rondeau – which Machaut had just brought into fashion in France ... It is in truth but a tiny stream of lyric which skirts the large fields of his narrative productions, and it is not by any means the most characteristic, nor curiously enough the most personal part of his work' (p 61). Regardless of subject 'his lyric poetry is always an imitation as regards form, and nearly always as regards subject.

He uses it less to express his feelings than to train his style and versification. That is why it should be studied, without any consideration of date, before passing to other forms, in which he left a deeper personal mark' (p 61). See also **181, 252, 354.**

118 Lewis, C.S. *The Allegory of Love.* Oxford: Oxford University Press, 1936.
Lewis devotes some attention to the lyrics in his chapter on Chaucer (pp 157–97). 'Perhaps none of our early poets has so little claim to be called the father of English poetry as the Chaucer of the *Canterbury Tales*' (p 163). But the Chaucer of the lyrics and dream visions was indeed influential. Even here, we need to be cautious in our assessment. 'Where we see a great comedian and a profound student of human character, they [ie, readers of the late fourteenth and fifteenth centuries] saw a master of noble sentiment and a source of poetic diction' (p 162). 'If they all took Chaucer's love poetry *au grand sérieux,* it is overwhelmingly probable that Chaucer himself did the same; and one of the advantages of keeping the *Canterbury Tales* out of sight ... will be that we may thus hope to rid ourselves of a false emphasis which is creeping into the criticism of Chaucer' (p 163). Lewis stresses the impact of Chaucer's love poetry and poetic forms on later generations; he was a technical source, 'a great model of poetical style' (p 164), and one who showed the way in uses of the *RR.* Lewis emphasizes the subtlety of Chaucer's tonal range – the sentiment as well as the mockery, the goose as well as the eagle. 'But Chaucer, whatever we may think of him, was not a "regular fellow", *un vrai businessman,* or a rotarian. He was a scholar, a courtier, and a poet, living in a highly subtle and sophisticated civilization' (p 173). See **253, 355, 532.**

119 Merrill, Rodney Harpster. 'Formal Elements in the Late Medieval Courtly Love Lyric.' *DAI,* 31 (1971), 4172A. Stanford Dissertation, 1970.
The study of medieval love lyrics is often hampered by 'too great a concern about poetic form in abstraction from meaning' or about codes of courtly love. 'These poems must not be considered as statements but as imitations of statements.' Merrill compares the love lyrics of Petrarch, which are Augustinian in attitude, with the works of northern poets, especially Chaucer and Wyatt, 'to suggest how Christian Aristotelianism conditions the northern lyrics.' Merrill interprets Chaucer's poems on three formal levels: 1) flux of sensitive experience; 2) coherence of rational apprehension; 3) eschatological directedness known by faith. The last chapter discusses extensively *The Broche of Thebes,* the poem modern editors regularly divide into *Mars* and *Venus.* See **359.**

120 Mitchell, Jerome, and William Provost, eds. *Chaucer the Love Poet*. Athens: University of Georgia Press, 1973.

Five symposium essays including Norman E. Eliason, 'Chaucer the Love Poet'; Edmund Reiss, 'Chaucer's Parodies of Love'; R.E. Kaske, 'Chaucer's Marriage Group'; James I. Wimsatt, 'Chaucer and the Canticle of Canticles'; and Edgar H. Duncan, 'Afterword.' It is perhaps notable that though the conference is on Chaucer the Love Poet no reference is made by any of the panelists to the lyrics. The closest anyone comes to the poems is Eliason's observation that 'Chaucer's mode, a product of the mind rather than the emotions, lacks the lyricism of later English poets, who sing love's praises and its joys and sorrows with an intensity of feeling that he rarely displays. He strikes a true lyric note now and again – as for example in the song Troilus sings just after being suddenly smitten ... Admirable as the note is, it is not sustained long enough nor sounded in such a way as to attract much notice. Indeed Chaucer seems to mute it quite deliberately, for instead of building up the lyric passages with suitable fanfare he plays them down, letting us enjoy them for what they are – delightful bits of decoration. Their omission would cause little serious damage to the poem and none whatever to the kind of love dealt with there' (pp 22–3). Eliason talks about 'ordinary love' in Chaucer; he mentions allegorical *(RR)*, philosophical (Boethius), and Christian love but gives them perfunctory treatment because they are not 'of vital significance in Chaucer's love poetry' (p 10).

121 Mogan, Joseph J., Jr. *Chaucer and the Theme of Mutability*. The Hague and Paris: Mouton, 1968.

Ch 3, 'The Shorter Poems,' pp 78–93: Chaucer is vitally concerned with the mutability theme in exactly half of his shorter poems (see esp. *Mars, Fortune, Truth, Sted, FA*). 'It is not enough to say that these ideas were "conventional" or "commonplace"; to Chaucer they were also intensely personal and he expressed them with sincerity and conviction' (p 93).

   – Review by Edmund Reiss, *Spec,* 46 (1971), 175–6: 'a resurrected thesis, which the author was apparently so tired of that he did not even care to revise in the light of subsequent scholarship' (p 175).

122 Moore, Arthur K. 'Chaucer's Lost Songs.' *JEGP,* 48 (1949), 196–208.

In the 'Retractation' and Prol. to *LGW* Chaucer refers to the many songs and lecherous lays, balades, roundels, and virelayes he composed; Gower refers to Chaucer's *ditees* and *songes* made for Venus' sake; and Lydgate recollects that Chaucer made 'ful many a fressh dite, / Compleyntis, baladis, roundelis, virelais.' Scholars have usually argued that these must refer to songs now lost. But it may be that the references include the many lyrics intercalated in the narrative poems. The French poets often interspersed lyrics in their longer poems and even had music for some of them. Thus, to the twenty short poems thought to be Chaucer's add the roundel (*PF* 680–92); the balade for Alceste in *LGW*; the Black Knight's two songs (*BD* 475–86 & 1175–80); and seven segments of *Troilus* including Antigone's song, Troilus' three songs, and the *aube* sections of Book III. This brings the total to over thirty. 'The question of indebtedness aside, some of these lyrics are excellent, and most of them achieve a level quite above the separate short poems, with the possible exceptions of *Merciles Beaute* and *To Rosemounde*' (p 199). Whether Chaucer composed music is uncertain; the strong debt to Machaut might suggest that he did. His poems are often referred to as 'songs,' but that does not necessarily mean that they were sung. Moore recalls Deschamps' distinction between natural and artificial music, whereby 'song' could simply refer to oral recitation. There may be no point to looking further for more lyrics by Chaucer; the thirty that we have are ample to justify the praise.

123 — 'Chaucer's Use of Lyric as an Ornament of Style.' *CL*, 3 (1951), 32–46. The essay concentrates on lyrics embedded in Chaucer's longer poems which 'unquestionably represent conscious employment of an ornament of style, which, if not explicitly sanctioned by formal rhetoric, had none the less ample warrant in the popular misconception of *poetica* as decoration and dilatation' (p 32). The ornament was abused as flagrantly as the formal *colores rhetorica* by French poets who used it in 'prolonging a thin book'; but Chaucer usually achieves 'artistic fusion of lyric with frame' (p 32). Moore discusses uses of embedded lyrics by Machaut and Froissart, and Chaucer's employment of them in *BD, PF, LGW, T&C,* and *CT*. Their scarcity in *CT* may be explained by the fact that in his later years Chaucer came 'to reject much French convention, developing a direct and vigorous narrative style which eschewed obtrusive ornament' (p 45). In the fifteenth century only Lydgate makes extensive use of the artifice (eg, his embedding of Chaucer's *ABC* in his *Pilgrimage of the Life of Man*). 'Chaucer alone in mediaeval England definitely understood the proper use of the lyric as an adornment of style, and like Shakespeare, who worked with a separate tradition, ultimately refined an artifice more often abused than artistically employed' (p 46).

124 — *The Secular Lyric in Middle English*. Lexington: University of Kentucky Press, 1951.
Ch 4, 'Art Lyric: A Preliminary,' pp 101–23: 'Coeval with the emergence of Chaucer a new chapter opens in the history of English lyric, taking its main impulse from artificial and restricted French forms and depending for its cultivation upon men of settled habits. The break with the singing past was hardly as abrupt as the meager remains suggest, although the naturalization of foreign techniques proceeded rapidly after the middle of the fourteenth century' (p 101). Moore discusses first efforts to write in metrical feet early in the century. Chaucer's position in the

transition from lyric song to art lyric is complicated by the fact that we do not know whether he composed songs for singing (p 105). His poems, which move away from the singing past, constitute the strongest influence on later generations at the court. Moore develops further ideas he began in **123** on the meaning of *song* and *chançon* and Deschamps' distinction between music *artificiele* and *naturele*, where *musique naturele* (the voice reciting poetry) is said to be the higher kind, higher than singing with notes and instruments (pp 105–16). Probably Chaucer considered oral recitation to be a division of music. Ch 5, 'The Chaucerian Lyric Mode,' pp 124–54: 'The lyric impulse in Chaucer and most of his disciples, acknowledged or otherwise, is admittedly weak, but the excess of defects in their shorter poems is partially owing to the decline of the trouvéres and to the fragmentation of the whole art in the practice of fourteenth-century French poets, who abandoned musical accompaniment and extirpated metrical and emotional licence ... Within this tradition, first given prominence by Machaut and confirmed by Deschamps, the lyric spirit could not thrive; in his short poems Chaucer's genius shines feebly' (p 125). Moore then discusses how 'anemic' Chaucer's love poetry is, based on its 'defective principle of objectification' (p 128). Exercises like *Truth, Gent,* and *Fortune* are 'in large part pious essays trimmed to fit the ballade framework and are lyrical only in a limited sense' (p 130). Chaucer's imitators are more feeble still.

  – Review by R.M. Wilson, *RES*, 3 (1952), 379–80: 'A remarkably full and scholarly piece of work' (p 379). 'Particularly valuable are his examination of and judgement on the art lyric' (p 380). The style is ponderous; 'The "aureate diction" of the art lyric seems to have infected the author' (p 380).

  – Review by R.J. Schoeck, *Spec,* 27 (1952), 114–6: Moore overemphasizes the French influences, thus underemphasizing 'the synthesis and real achievement of the English poets – hence a failure to do justice to such lyrics as Chaucer's "Merciles Beaute"' (p 115). But even so, the book is an important contribution.

125 Muscatine, Charles. *Chaucer and the French Tradition.* Berkeley and Los Angeles: University of California Press, 1960.
By French tradition Muscatine seems to mean romance tradition. He finds Chaucer 'less a kin of Machaut than of the great poets of the centuries previous' (p 5) and gives virtually no attention to the lyrics (two passing mentions of *ABC* and one reference to the pilgrimage figure in *Truth*). In Ch 2, 'The Courtly Tradition,' Muscatine discusses *RR* and Chrétien, where Chaucer in his mature work turns for narrative conventions. Discussion of 'lyric monologue' is restricted to set rhetorical pieces in *Iwain, Eneas,* and *RR*. Some attention is given to Machaut in connection with *BD* (pp 99–107).

126 Olson, Glending. 'Deschamps' *Art de dictier* and Chaucer's Literary Environment.' *Spec*, 48 (1973), 714–23.

Deschamps' *L'Art de dictier et de fere chançons, balades, virelais et rondeaulx* (1392) defines lyric poetry as a species of music and describes the formal requirements of various lyric types. It is a manual, with little theoretical examination of poetry, but 'the only critical document we have from a poet whose connections with Chaucer, both literary and personal, are demonstrable' (p 714). Olson roots Deschamps and Chaucer in the same poetic tradition and shows ways in which they think about poetry 'which differ from the familiar didactic and allegorical formulations of many medieval and modern commentators' (p 714). *L'Art* draws an analogy between music and medicine for their therapeutic value (cf Boethius and Cassiodorus); it sets music apart from the other arts in that music facilitates all study by assuaging man's weariness so that he may subsequently return to his work. Deschamps' precedent for classifying lyric poetry as music may be found in John of Garland's *musica instrumentalis* and Boethius' *De Musica*. Natural music is primarily pleasurable. *L'Art* is not concerned with underlying ideas. It 'shows no concern about proper *materia*' (p 718); its 'art' teaches one to make 'toutes maniers de balades, rondeaulx' etc by delineating simply 'the formal configurations of each ... It is a "maker's" view of poetry, for the essence of natural music is fabrication within tightly controlled formal restrictions' (p 721). On Deschamps' views on natural music see also Kenneth Varty, 'Deschamps' Art de Dictier,' *French Studies*, 19 (1965), 164–8; and I.S. Laurie, 'Deschamps and the Lyric as Natural Music,' *MLR*, 59 (1964), 561–70. There is no external proof that Chaucer ever saw *L'Art*, but 'the very existence of his short poems is testimony to his knowledge of the lyric forms advocated by Machaut and Deschamps. His favorite genres are the complaint and the balade, and within the latter form he deals with a variety of subjects which suggests something of Deschamps' range' (p 721). Olson stresses the variety of topics in Chaucer's lyrics to suggest that he wrote as the practitioners mentioned in *L'Art*, 'according to his "volunté et sentement," which included the desire to produce love lyrics and humourous occasional verse as well as balades of serious moral advice' (p 722). The point is that Chaucer works within this new tradition which makes reputable an attitude toward literature as a vehicle of pleasure as well as the moral tradition. 'That the maker's theory discussed here culminates in the excesses of the *grands rhétoriqueurs*, might not weigh against the attempt to understand as fully as possible the literary environment in which Chaucer wrote' (p 723).

127 Osgood, Charles Grosvenor. *The Voice of England*. New York and London: Harper and Brothers, 1935.

See Ch 5, 'Chaucer,' pp 100–17. Osgood gives some attention to the influence of Boethius, *RR*, and Boccaccio on Chaucer. 'Chaucer has touched the old conventions with the greatness that undates them' (p 110).

128 Pollard, Alfred William. 'Chaucer.' *Encyclopedia Britannica*. Eleventh edition. 1910.

'Chaucer's service to the English language lies in his decisive success in having made it impossible for any later English poet to attain fame, as Gower had done, by writing alternatively in Latin and English. The claim which should be made for him is that, at least as regards poetry, he proved that English was sufficient' (pp 16–7). Pollard discusses the *Romaunt*, the lost *Book of the Lyon, ABC*, and *Pity* in terms of Chaucer's French debt.

129 Prasad, Prajapati. 'The Order of Complaint: A Study in Medieval Tradition.' *DA*, 25 (1966), 3930. University of Wisconsin Dissertation, 1965. Director, Helen C. White.

Emphasizing the influence of Virgil on medieval love poetry, Prasad objects to the overemphasis in criticism on courtly love. 'We cannot appreciate the medieval English love complaints by being apologists of the code of courtly love, whose ideals are narrow and shallow and do not go deep enough in recognizing the complexities of the human heart.' Prasad illustrates 'a vigorous tradition of medieval English love poetry by discussing a number of Chaucerian and non-Chaucerian complaints, in which efforts were made to escape from the subversive influences of the values of Courtly Love.'

129a Preston, Raymond. 'Chaucer and the *Ballades Notées of Guillaume de Machaut*.' *Speculum*, 26 (1951), 615–23.

Readers of Machaut and Chaucer should devote more attention to the music of their poetry. Manly (*Canterbury Tales* [New York, 1940], p 503) had argued the likelihood of Chaucer's having composed 'the music as well as the words of his songs.' But it may be too much to expect 'the author of the *Canterbury Tales* to exhibit more than a squire's accomplishment in music,' especially in view of his active public life. 'Even in his early work, in which Chaucer is superficially closer to Guillaume, there is no poem with the inward emotion of the French music. Geoffrey Chaucer is never frigid or unsympathetic, but a line like that of a *Compleynt unto Pity* – "I fond her ded, and buried in an herte" – is characteristic neither of its context nor of the rest of his poetry' (p 615). Preston discusses the musical setting of Guillaume's Ballade 31, 'De toutes flours.' Historians generally agree that 'the music of Guillaume is more important than the poetry' (p 618). But Chaucer's music is of a different kind; his is *musique naturele*, the music in spoken language. Eg, the mellifluousness of *Romaunt*, lines 49–55 or 759–68, and *BD*, lines 848–54. The *Compleynt of Anelida* exemplifies 'lyrical virtuosity,' while *BD*, lines 475–86 reveals 'a lovely *cantabile* line'; 'has anything been written in English more singable than that cadence?' (p 620). Embedded lyrics in *T&C* reflect the singing voice too, though lyricism in the poem 'is not confined to, or even notably concentrated in, the set songs' (p 620). The beginning of *Mars* offers 'another kind of lyric altogether, a lyric of the speaking voice' (p 621). *Hyd Absolon* reflects a 'pure lyrical manner. The ballade to Rosemound was written by a court-poet of unsurpassed accomplishment; it gives authoritative expression to the vitality of an experience which, according to convention, ought to have been languishing; and so it does with frisky joy. The envoys to Scogan and Bukton may be regarded as free developments of the form: brilliant, witty, and not at all compliant to the musician. And possibly his last literary act was to parody the ballade of love in the *Compleynt to his Empty Purse*' (p 622). In this respect, he moves far beyond the French poetry of his time.

130 Reiss, Edmund. 'Dusting off the Cobwebs: A Look at Chaucer's Lyrics.' *ChauR*, 1 (1966), 55–65.

Chaucer's lyrics are to his longer poems what Shakespeare's sonnets are to the plays (p 55). 'Perhaps the most immediate virtue of Chaucer's short poems ... is that in them our eye rests on that which it can see wholly and clearly' (p 56). They provide a view of Chaucer not easily got in the longer works and in some cases reveal the younger Chaucer. 'No matter whether complaint, balade, moral-philosophical piece, or personal address to a friend; whether polished allegory or experimental *tour de force*; whether courtly, didactic, humourous, or satiric, they still reveal a Chaucer and an artistry we should know' (p 56). The lyrics need more careful attention. Reiss concentrates on Chaucer's use of language in *ABC* and *Ros* to show the rewards of such study. See **190** and **535**.

131 — 'Chaucer's Courtly Love.' In *The Learned and the Lewed: Studies in Chaucer and Medieval Literature*. Ed. Larry Dean Benson. Harvard English Studies, 5. Cambridge: Harvard University Press, 1974, pp 95–111.

Reiss shows the wide range of treatment of love topics in Chaucer, from Valerius to Apius, Sir Thopas and Don John to John and Aleyn and Dido, but he does not mention the lyrics or *Anelida and Arcite*. *BD* is 'Chaucer's only work to show the conventions of courtly love in a fully developed form' (p 101); Reiss contrasts its method and scope with *T&C* and *KnT*. 'Chaucer's method is to present earthly love as both good and bad. But, also as in these writings, his narratives bring out the ultimate destructiveness and folly of this love' (p 111).

132 — 'Chaucer's *fyn lovynge* and the Late Medieval Sense of *fin amor.*' In
Medieval Studies in Honor of Lillian Herlands Hornstein. Ed. Jess B. Bess-
inger, Jr., and Robert R. Raymo. New York: New York University Press,
1976, pp 181–91.

Chaucer's single reference to 'fyn lovinge' (Prol. *LGW*) seems to mean
'good love' as opposed to the usual kinds of objectionable love – amorous
love, folly love, etc. Reiss discusses other English usage of the phrase
and continental uses of the equivalent term, noting religious connotations of 'fyn amour' which imply divine love of God for man or charity.
'Pure love,' 'ideal love,' or 'married love' seem the more characteristic
glosses in the later Middle Ages, in contrast to the sensual or illicit associations with the term in twelfth-century Provençal or related French or
Italian poetry. In view of Alceste's treatment of Geffrey in *LGW* the
phrase 'fyn lovynge' seems to be ironic or at least ambiguous. Yet 'the
ideal itself remains to make us aware of the various inadequacies of love
detailed in this poem' (p 187).

133 — 'Chaucer's *deerne love* and the Medieval View of Secrecy in Love.' In
Chaucerian Problems and Perspectives: Essays Presented to Paul E. Beichner,
C.S.C. Ed. Edward Vasta and Zacharias P. Thundy. Notre Dame and Lon-
don: University of Notre Dame Press, 1979, pp 164–79.

Reiss provides a broad background for *deerne love* as it appears in
Chaucer, using Old and Middle English sources as well as French, classical, and patristic ones. 'The evidence would seem to indicate strikingly
that *deerne love* is not noble, not an expression of *fin amor*, but, rather, a
low love, one illicit and sinful, and more appropriate to fabliaux than to
accounts of noble and proper love' (pp 171–2).

134 Robbins, Rossell Hope, ed. *Secular Lyrics of the XIVth and XVth Centuries.*
Oxford: Clarendon Press, 1952/rev Oxford: Clarendon Press, 1955;
rpt 1961.

Includes 212 poems, notes, and glossary, including Popular Songs (min-
strel rhymes, drinking songs, love songs, popular songs); Practical Verse
(charms, almanack verse, verse on the body, gnomic tags, and alchemical
verse); Occasional Verse (book plates, presentations and prologues, verse
on the craft of writing, mummings and pageants, epitaphs); and Courtly
Love Lyrics (including descriptions, songs, envoys, love epistles, and
poems of mockery). Although Chaucer's poems are excluded, this
volume provides a context for them.

135 — ed. *Historical Poems of the XIVth and XVth Centuries.* New York: Columbia University Press, 1959.

Includes one hundred poems, notes, introduction, and glossary. Robbins
places the poems in the following categories: An outline of Dynastic History; Poems from Harley ms 2253; War Poems by Lawrence Minot from
Cotton ms Galba E.ix; Poems from Digby ms 102; Popular Struggles I: the

Great Revolt; Popular Struggles II: Later Discontent; Popular Ballads; Politics in Song; Commemoration of Kings; Political Prophecies; The First Utopia; The Wicked Age; Critics of the Lollards; Critics of the Friars; England's Commerce; The Falls of Princes; The Red Rose of Lancaster; The White Rose of York; The Well-Ordered Kingdom; and The Will for Peace. Although no Chaucer poems are included in this volume, it does provide historical context for Chaucer's poetry.

136 — 'The Lyrics.' In *Companion to Chaucer Studies.* Ed. Beryl Rowland. London: Oxford University Press, 1968, pp 313–31/rev 1979, pp 380–402. Robbins' essay is reprinted without revision in the 1979 edition, but with an afterword appended: 'The past decade has seen some twenty-two articles and notes on Chaucer's lyrics, but none, despite five papers on *The Complaint of Mars* and three on Scogan, has affected the conclusion originally presented in this chapter in 1967' (pp 395–6). The bibliography in the revised edition is brought up to date. (Subsequent annotations give page references to both editions.) 'Chaucer's lyrics are minor not only in comparison with his great works; they're just minor poems' (p 313/380), that is, they are occasional pieces, not significantly different from similar court poetry in the following century. Chaucer's lyrics are a major influence on subsequent poetry, however; 'as models, the least of the minor turns out major' (p 313/380). Only a few of Chaucer's lyrics survive, though Robbins identifies sixteen more that are embedded in longer poems, some of which have identifiable sources and some of which appear independently in mss, 'uprooted to make new poems' (p 316/383). English lyric collections prior to Chaucer had no influence on him. 'Chaucer started all over again, as if there had never been an English tradition. Chaucer's are – after 1340 – the *first* sophisticated lyrics in English, introducing from France new metrical and stanzaic forms and new themes that were to dominate court verse in the following centuries. Chaucer's lyrics are not only the pacemakers; they are the *only* specimens' (p 316/383). Robbins discusses French forms, conventions, and themes which Chaucer favours and devotes a paragraph or two to each of Chaucer's poems, noting, when possible, the occasions for which they were written. He also comments at some length on varieties of complaint. Of religious lyrics, besides *ABC*, he comments on the isolable prayers in *PriorT* and *SNT*. 'Chaucer's lyric reputation depends on his being "first with the mostest." Without Chaucer there could not have been a Hoccleve or a Lydgate, and – in that case – fifteenth-century court poets would have been imitating Gower's *Cinquante Balades* – in French!' (p 328/395).

137 — 'The Vintner's Son: French Wine in English Bottles.' In *Eleanor of Aquitaine: Patron and Politician.* Ed. William W. Kibler. Austin: University of Texas Press, 1976, pp 147–72.

This exploratory essay raises questions about the continuity of literature from the court of the famous *English* Queen Eleanor to the English Court of Chaucer's day and the generations following. One might quip that Eleanor and Chaucer were almost 'kissing cousins' (p 147) through the ten intervening generations and Chaucer's good marriage; but Robbins shows literary ties as well, as he divides the literature from 1100–1530 into seven broad areas. 1) 1100–1350: French Court Literature, during which period France and England were theoretically one political unit and 'actually one symbiotic literary unit' (p 150). Robbins emphasizes Anglo-Norman and Anglo-French contributions in the period, which included such literature as the *Song of Roland,* Chrétien's poetry, and that of Benoît de Sainte Maure, Marie de France, and the many French romances. 2) 1200–1350: Latin Literature, especially the writings of Geoffrey of Monmouth, Joseph of Exeter, Alexander Neckham, and Nigel Wirecker. 3) 1200–1350: English Noncourt Literature, during which time most English writers remained stubbornly indifferent to the sensibilities and sympathies of Chrétien. 'The Black Death marked the watershed for medieval literature in England, and the year 1350 introduced new trends' (p 154). 4) 1350–1500: French Court Literature (Continuing), where Anglo-Norman as a literary medium was disappearing and the dominant influence for poets like Machaut and Deschamps shifts from *Yvain* to *Le Roman de la Rose.* 5) 1350–1530: English Noncourt Literature (Continuing), with the popular romances: 'One could fill many pages with illustrations showing how changed social conditions affect artistic fashions' (p 156). 6) 1350–1400: English Court Literature – the Alliterative Revival, where the literature is more closely linked 'at least in the spirit of "fine lovynge" to Eleanor's court' (p 157); see especially *Sir Gawain and the Green Knight, Winner and Waster, Quatrefoil of Love,* and *Parlement of the Thre Ages.* 7) 1370–1530: English Court Literature: Chaucer and the Chaucerians, where Robbins outlines the influences of the leading French poets on Chaucer. 'This vintner's son was not the first to put French spirit into English bottles – that had been going on for nearly two centuries; but Chaucer was the first to establish "Chateau Geoffroi" as a mark of international excellence, as a recommended selection of Machaut et Deschamps et Compagnie, *importateurs*' (p 162). Robbins concludes by suggesting that Chaucer's earliest poetry may in fact have been written in French.

138 — 'Geoffroi Chaucier, Poète Français, Father of English Poetry.' *ChauR*, 13 (1978), 93–115.

If *BD* is as finished and graceful a poem as recent critics claim, 'where are all Chaucer's earlier poetic exercises that paved the way for that mature product?' (p 93) Robbins notes that the lyrics – even the so-called early ones like *WN* – were written when Chaucer was verging on forty, and many, like *Ros* and *MB*, are very late. Robbins' answer to his question takes the form of a fourfold hypothesis: 1) The courts of Edward III and Richard II were French-speaking; 2) Chaucer grew up in these courts, and if he were to prosper the first twenty or thirty years of his life had to be French-speaking; 3) If John of Gaunt commissioned the *Book of the Duchess*, Chaucer must already have had some reputation as a court poet. But why then did he not write the elegy in French? There may be two reasons: there was a small aristocratic audience developing for English (nb, Richard II's request that Gower write *CA* in English); moreover Blanche herself seems to have been interested in promoting English poetry, and *ABC* may have been made at her request. It is even possible that *BD* 'was composed for public recital at a small house gathering following the mass' (p 101). Certainly, it is with *BD* that Chaucer earned the right to be called 'father of English poetry,' rather than with *CT* and *T&C*, which had less effect upon the following generations than the standard French genres, the *salut* and *complaint*, which *BD* introduced. 4) 'The core of the whole hypothesis – that Chaucer's early poems, especially court love lyrics, were written in French – is probably the most debatable. Actually, it cannot be proved or disproved. I have found no French poem in any manuscript of English provenance inscribed "Quod Geoffroi le Chaucier" – yet!' (p 102) But we should acclimatize ourselves to think of Chaucer as a 'palace poet' rather than a 'court poet' (p 114, n 87). In searching for Chaucer's earliest poems perhaps we should be looking at the hundreds of anonymous French poems especially in mss of English provenance from the late fourteenth and early fifteenth centuries. Robbins cites several specimens of French court poems by Englishmen of the kind Chaucer might have written. 'Maybe the quest for Chaucer's lost lyrics is hopeless – after all, why should anyone want to preserve for posterity an ephemeral lyric by a young squire? Perhaps the later love lyrics attributed to Chaucer – *Merciles Beaute*, *Complaynt d'Amours*, *To Rosemunde* – were preserved only because by then Chaucer was famous as the author of *Troilus and Criseyde* and of the *Canterbury Tales*, so that any lines of his would be recorded' (pp 105–6). Robbins' notes in this essay are extensive and include excellent bibliography on the speaking, teaching and study of French in medieval England; see especially Helen Suggett, 'The Use of French in England in the later Middle Ages,' *Transactions Royal Historical Society*, 28 (1946), 61–83, which Robbins calls 'indispensable' (p 108, n 29).

139 — 'The Middle English Court Love Lyric.' In *The Interpretation of Medieval Lyric*. Ed. W.T.H. Jackson. London: Macmillan; New York: Columbia University Press, 1980, pp 205–32.

Chaucer was not just a civil servant writing the *CT* 'for a mixed audience in an increasingly mercantile milieu'; he was 'Chaucer the page and squire to the old King himself, to his sons, and finally to Richard II; Chaucer on the same royal payroll as the French court poet Froissart; Chaucer the translator of the *Roman de la Rose* and French court poets like Machaut and Oton de Graunson; and Chaucer the recipient of an accolade from the French court poet Deschamps' (p 205); Chaucer the brother-in-law of the Duke of Lancaster, ancestor of Henry VII and Edward IV and source of forty-five noble and even royal coats of arms. There are some three hundred short court love lyrics in English and some thirty longer love poems derived from French lyric forms like the *salut d'amours* and *complaint d'amours*; throughout both kinds Chaucer is the dominant influence. Robbins discusses several great books – Fairfax 16, Tanner 346, the Findern Anthology – which contain the poems and indicate the type of collectors who valued them in the following century. The fifteenth-century court love poems are 'probably the most neglected genre in English literature' (p 208). Ignorance of the genre obscures links between Chaucer and Spenser and other Renaissance writers. One problem is that the modern reader lacks useful guideposts to know what to expect; he needs to know *who* wrote the poems, *when* and *for whom* they were written. He needs to know *why* they were written and *where*. He then can consider what the poem says and how it says it. Robbins applies these criteria to several shorter lyrics. He suggests that the Cambridge ms 61 of Chaucer reading *T&C* is an accurate portrayal of the settings in which the poems were performed. 'Court poetry is indeed coterie poetry' (p 210), written for a close knit circle of upper-class people, an exclusive privileged group of one or two thousand out of a population of more than two million. 'When Chaucer in his *Retraction* abjured "many a song and many a leccherous lay", and all his poems of "worldly vanitees", which "sounen into synne", he was underlining their a-moral, even immoral, nature, for the aristocratic values they promote have no justification in the needs of any part of Christian society' (p 228, n 44).

140 Root, Robert Kilburn. *The Poetry of Chaucer: A Guide to its Study and Appreciation*. Boston: Houghton Mifflin, 1900/rev 1922.

Ch 4, 'The Minor Poems,' pp 57–79, includes separate discussions of *ABC*, *Pity*, *BD*, *Mars*, *PF*, *Lady*, *AA*, *Adam*, *FA*, *Fortune*, *MB*, *Ros*, *Truth*, *Gent*, *Sted*, *Scogan*, *Bukton*, *Venus*, *Purse*, *Prov*, *AWU*, *CD*, *BC*, *WN*. See **192, 217, 264, 285, 292, 365, 416, 428, 443, 459, 510, 539, 563, 573.**

141 Saintsbury, George. 'Chaucer.' In *The Cambridge History of English Literature*. Ed. A.W. Ward and A.R. Waller. Vol 2. Cambridge: Cambridge University Press; New York: G.P. Putnam's Sons, 1908, pp 179–224.
Of the minor verse Saintsbury observes: 'only *Truth* ... is unquestionably worthy of Chaucer ... It is quite evident that Chaucer required license of expatiation in order to show his genius. If the reference to "many a song and many a licorous lay" in the retraction is genuine and well-founded, it is doubtful whether we have lost very much by their loss' (pp 213–4). See **266**.

141a Saville, Jonathan. *The Medieval Erotic Alba: Structure as Meaning*. New York: Columbia University Press, 1972.
Saville defines the genre and traces its history from Southern France in the twelfth century into Northern Europe and the Renaissance, considering such general topics as the two worlds of love, enemies of love, the watchman and the lady, time, and distinctions between the alba and the chanson. He devotes considerable attention to *T&C* (pp 2, 28, 57, 84–6, 213–4, 249–53), with some commentary also on the alba in the *Reeve's Tale* (pp 226–7) and on its appearance at the beginning of *Mars*, where it is used to differentiate aspects of erotic grief produced by cupiditas. 'Such a love is doomed to failure' (p 238).

142 Schelling, Felix Emmanuel. *The English Lyric*. Boston: Houghton Mifflin, 1913. Pp 9–30.
'The polite poets of the fourteenth and fifteenth centuries were surprisingly unlyrical; even Chaucer ... with all his marvellous range of epic and dramatic art, is reflective and elegiac, ever musical, yet rarely quite lyrical' (p 28). Schelling finds *Truth, Gent, FA* to be 'admirably reflective'; *Ros* 'rings charming variations on its conventional and artificial themes. But when all has been said, there are few authentic lyrics in Chaucer' (p 28). 'Now welcom somer,' from *PF*, comes close. But 'it is not ... until we reach Henryson, Dunbar, and Skelton that the lyrical note breaks forth among these learned poets' (p 30).

143 Snell, F.J. *The Age of Chaucer*. London: Bell, 1901/rev 1906. Pp 121–236.
Snell devotes Chs. 6–8 to Chaucer. He relates *AA, Lady*, and *Mars* to Chaucer's Italian period. 'Chaucer had a much better chance of reproducing Dante's rhythm than later English bards, inasmuch as the final vowels were still sounded' (p 163). Snell favors the cheerful Chaucer of *Ros*: 'There is a glad song, and a humourous' (p 136). See **269, 418**.

143a Spencer, Theodore. 'Chaucer's Hell: A Study in Mediaeval Convention.' *Speculum*, 2 (1927), 177–200.
Chaucer's ideas on Hell came not only from Dante (whose influence on Chaucer Spencer minimizes), but also from Boethius, Claudian, Virgil, Ovid, and folk traditions. Spencer comments on the smoking hell in *Mars* 1. 120, hell fires in *ABC* 11. 95–6, and hellish stench in *ABC* 11. 54–6

(pp 189–91), as well as various references in *CT* and *HF* to torments in Hell.

144 Stainton, Albert Peter. 'The Time Motif in the Medieval Lyric.' *DAI*, 32 (1971), 3272A. Rutgers University Dissertation, 1971. Director, James J. Wilhelm.

The time-eternity dichotomy in medieval lyric poetry may be traced philosophically from Plato, Augustine, and Boethius into the hymns of Ambrose, Fortunatus and Abelard. The dichotomy is prominent in the *Carmina Burana* and the *Songs of Bernart de Ventadorn.* 'The English religious lyric shows little interest in the eternal as a philosophical idea. In the shorter lyrics of Chaucer, the time-eternity dichotomy remains only as background, as hollow rhetorical form, or as parody. The more creative aspect of Chaucer's time consciousness in these lyrics derives from his perception of cause and effect. His manipulation of this principle is particularly evident in his philosophical and political poems. The unifying theme of these poems is the temporal disorganization of the present. Chaucer employs the Aristotelian concept of rectilinear time as a basis for indictments of human behaviour.' See especially *PF*, which 'stands as a comprehensive embodiment of the metaphoric uses of the time-eternity dichotomy.'

145 Strohm, Paul. 'Jean of Angoulême: A Fifteenth Century Reader of Chaucer.' *NM*, 72 (1971), 69–76.

Jean, brother to Charles of Orléans, was hostage in England from 1412–1445. He died in 1467 and left a working library of some 150 volumes including a ms of *CT* (Paris, BN ms fonds anglais 39). The ms was written by Duxworth, but with over three hundred corrections in Jean's own hand. There are also many marginal comments in Duxworth's hand but presumably reflecting Jean's opinions (p 70). Jean refers to Chaucer as a compiler, maker, and compositor. Perhaps 'compilator' is a humiliating term, though Jean himself was one, so perhaps he is not being derisive. Many of the tales are fragmented – a few first lines and then omission. Eg, *Thop* is interrupted after 'semely nose'; the Monk after the introductory stanza on Samson. A marginal note calls *Thop* and *CYT* (also much abbreviated) 'extremely absurd' – 'valde absurda in terminis et ideo' (p 72). *MonkT* is 'extremely sad' – 'valde dolorosa,' while the *KnT* is 'valde bona.' 'Certainly, Jean does not represent the taste of the whole of Chaucer's circle. Chaucer needed and had Scogans and Buktons too. But even in his own day Chaucer must have had a mixed audience with mixed reasons for enjoying his work' (p 76).

146 Tatlock, J.S.P. *The Development and Chronology of Chaucer's Works.* Chaucer Society Ser. 2, no. 37. London: Paul, Trench, Trubner, 1907.
Pp x–xi list the dates for each work, including the *Romaunt, ABC, Pity, Mars, Boece,* and *AA,* according to the speculations of previous scholars (ten Brink, Koch, Kittredge, Mather, Skeat, Liddell, Pollard, Root, Furnivall, Heath, Lowes, and Hales). On Chaucer's development as a poet Tatlock observes: 'Till he went to Italy, what he lacked was a poetic form' (p 18). (See Maynard **67**, who challenges this view.) Tatlock's argument is concerned mainly with *T&C,* the dream visions, and *CT.*

147 — *The Mind and Art of Chaucer.* Syracuse: Syracuse University Press, 1950.
Ch 2, 'Chaucer and the French Tradition,' pp 21–32, explores the poet's kinship with *RR.* Ch 4 is devoted to *AA* (see **271**). Ch 8, 'Less Conspicuous Works,' pp 82–7, comments briefly on the lyrics and *Boece,* which Tatlock links to *T&C, Adam,* and the moral balades. *Ros* is 'light and delicious' (p 84); *Purse* is noted for its cleverness. *Lady* reveals technical experimentation with Dante's *terza rima:* 'Chaucer's genius is not greatly lyrical, and these poems mostly have little feeling' (p 85). *Mars* reveals that 'Chaucer's interest in astrology may have been enough to stimulate his imagination into "making"' (pp 85–6). Tatlock records a seventeenth-century response to Chaucer when Lady Anne Clifford, 'comforted by the excellent Chaucer's book,' writes: 'I were in a pitiable case, having as many troubles as I have, but when I read in that, I scorn and make light of them all, and a little part of his beauteous spirit infuses itself in me' (p 87).

148 Voretzsch, Karl. *Introduction to the Study of Old French Literature.* Trans. Francis M. DuMont. New York: G.E. Stechert, 1931.
Ch 5, 'Indigenous Song Writing in the Twelfth Century,' pp 131–56, discusses beginnings of different types of French lyrics. Ch 12, 'Traditional Literary Types in the Thirteenth Century,' pp 423–34, comments on the development of rhymed couplets as the vehicle for romance writing and discusses briefly lyric poetry in connection with 'poetic competitions in the so-called *puys*' (p 430). Ch 14, pp 474–6, deals with French lyric poetry in the fourteenth century.

149 Wimsatt, James I. 'Chaucer and French Poetry.' In *Writers and their Background: Geoffrey Chaucer.* Ed. Derek Brewer. London: G. Bell and Sons, 1974; Athens: Ohio University Press, 1975, pp 109–36.
Wimsatt discusses Chaucer's relationship to the French language and the French poets to stress his immersion in the French tradition of poetry; 'Chaucer had French sources for almost everything he wrote' (p 111). Most identifiably French are the chivalric romances he used, which make him throughout his career 'Worldly God of Love in Albion – poet of love par excellence' (p 112). Guillaume de Lorris influenced him especially in his garden descriptions; Machaut's influence was strongest in

the dream visions and *dits*. 'Probably Froissart's greatest service to
Chaucer' was to introduce him to Machaut. Machaut is more influential
on Chaucer than Froissart, Granson, Deschamps, and other lesser French
love poets combined (p 118). Wimsatt's discussion concentrates on *BD*,
LGW, *T&C*, *HF* and *PF*, with occasional mention of the lyrics.

150 — 'Guillaume de Machaut and Chaucer's Love Lyrics.' *MAE*, 47 (1978),
66–87.

Wimsatt argues that 'with the exception of the Granson-inspired *Complaint of Venus*, all of Chaucer's independent love lyrics are based on
poems of Guillaume de Machaut. The relationships postulated between
the French and English poems ... extend to all aspects of the works and
suggest that Chaucer's poetry participates to a degree not previously understood in the coherent and defineable tradition of French court poetry
which was originated by Machaut and for over a century dominated by
his model' (p 66). *Lady* and *AA* both use complex stanza forms from
Machaut. (The suggestion of Dantean influence, because of the terza
rima lines, 'has been overemphasized' – p 67.) Both have common
sources in two Machaut lyrics, the balade "Je suis aussi com cils qui est
ravis", and the chant royal "Amis, je t'ay tant amé et cheri" (p 67).
Chaucer makes use of Machaut's refrains, but beyond that 'the parallels
between *AA* and the chant are extensive and deeply grounded' (p 68).
CD and *Mars* are both lover's complaints on Valentine's day. The versification is again characteristic of Machaut's forms (p 71). Moreover, there
are counterparts in Machaut for the idea of seeking pain and even death
to give delight to the beloved (p 72). Wimsatt points to relationships
between *CD*, *Mars*, and the *Jugement dou Roy de Behaingne*. *Mars*, he notes,
also draws on three Machaut balades and possibly a fourth lyric. *Ros* and
WN share a common source, 'tout ensement com le monde enlumine,'
where there is a great likeness in the narrator's 'light-hearted, unqualified praise of the lady' (p 76). Also there is a congruence of rhyme
words, especially *–unde (–onde, –ounde)*, and gem imagery. The emphasis
in *WN* on enduring faithfulness relates to the virelay 'Foy porter.' *Pity*
and *MB* use abstract allegory. The opposition of Cruelty and Pity occurs
in *RR*, Deschamps, and *Thebaid*, but 'only Machaut ... presents the opposition clearly' (p 79). (See *Dit dou Vergier*). In *AWU* the colour symbolism
of blue (faith) and green (falseness) reflects Machaut's balade 'Se pour ce
muir, qu'Amours ay bien servi.' Chaucer 'borrows from his sources in
different ways: at times he translates them word for word; at others he
paraphrases them; and at still others he simply takes basic elements and
reconstitutes them with fresh diction and imagery. In *AWU* he
thoroughly reconstitutes a poem around central ideas of the Machaut
balade, though using its refrain word for word' (pp 83–4). In Chaucer's
day 'Machaut's influence in London doubtless overshadowed that of all

other poets' (p 85). And that is true from the beginning to the end of Chaucer's literary career. His 'French period' was lifelong (p 85).

❧ Individual Studies

An ABC – Prièr à Nostre Dame per Chaucer

FINE EDITIONS

151 *A Chaucer ABC. Being a Hymn to the Holy Virgin in an English Version. From the French of Guillaume de Deguilleville. Initial Letters designed and illuminated by Lucia Joyce.* Pref. by Louis Gillet. Obelisk Press, 1936.
A fine edition illuminated by the daughter of James Joyce, who also ornamented *Pomes Penyeach.* Gillet's introduction comments on her father's attraction to Chaucer and her decision to illustrate the poem; he also comments on the Abbey of Chaalis, where Guillaume dwelt.

152 *Geoffrey Chaucer's ABC called La Prière de Nostre Dame, Made, as some say, at the request of / Blanche, Duchess of Lancaster, as a / Prayer for her private use, being a / Woman in her Religion very devout.* San Francisco: Grabhorn-Hoyem, 1967.
A fine edition limited to 1000 copies. The abecedian letters were first printed in books issued in Ulm, in the last quarter of the fifteenth century, probably the work of Johan Zainer, woodcutter and printer. The text is taken from the Kelmscott edition of the *Works*; the type used is a nineteenth-century rendering of *lettre batarde.* A modern translation by Dave Haselwood faces the original text. Haselwood saw the work through the press.

CRITICISM AND HISTORICAL BACKGROUND

See also **49, 78, 340.**

153 Anderson, Marjorie. 'Blanche, Duchess of Lancaster.' *MP*, 45 (1948), 152–9.
Blanche, for whom the *ABC* is said to have been written, was praised by Chaucer and Froissart for her great beauty; but there is a paucity of material on her life (eg, no *DNB* entry). There are no life records before her marriage except for a 3 May 1347 childhood betrothal to John de Segrave,

which came to nothing. Second daughter of Henry, First Duke of Lancaster, and Isabel, daughter of Henry Lord Beaumont, she was married (age 19) on 19 May 1359 at Reading to John of Gaunt. Papal dispensation was necessary because they were third cousins, both directly descended from Henry III (John through Edward I – Edward III and Blanche through Edmund the Crouchback and the Earls of Lancaster). Anderson gives a full account of the wedding festivities, the gifts, and the brilliance of the occasion. Maud, the older sister, died of plague 10 April 1362 without issue. All of Henry of Lancaster's property then came to Gaunt – Leicester, Kenilworth, Pontrefract, Lancaster, Bolingbroke, Monmouth, and Carmarthen (p 154). During her ten years of marriage Blanche was mother of five children, two of whom (John and Edward) died in infancy. The three survivors were Phillippa (b 1360), who became Queen of Portugal; Elizabeth (b 1364), who married John Hastings, then eloped with John Holland (see *Mars*) and later had a third husband, John Cornwall; Henry (b 1366), who became Henry IV. Anderson suggests that if Blanche had lived 'possibly Elizabeth would not have had such a notorious career' (p 156). Blanche was noted for her piety. She died of plague (as did her father and sister) at the age of 29 (or possibly 27), on 12 Sept. 1369. (But see John H. Palmer, 'The Historical Context of the *Book of the Duchess:* A Revision,' *ChR*, 8 [1974], 253–61, which argues that the date of her death is 1368.) She was buried in St Paul's on the north side of the quire. The tomb bore an alabaster image of Blanche; beside the tomb an altar was erected, furnished with a missal and chalice, and two chaplains were paid £20 a year to sing masses for her soul. An anniversary was also sung on her behalf each Sept. 12, a custom continued by her son. The tomb was unfortunately destroyed in the time of Edward VI or Elizabeth. Blanche was remembered for her social brilliance, probity of character, goodness, beauty, and friendly spirit.

154 Boyd, Beverly. *Chaucer and the Liturgy.* Philadelphia: Dorrance, 1967.
Ch 2 discusses annotated calendars, mentioned in *ABC*, lines 73–4, and their use of colours to denote liturgical rank, etc (p 17). Cf Chaucer's 'Kalenderes enlumyned ben thei' and Deguilleville's 'Kalendier sont enlumine.'

155 Brewer, D.S. *Chaucer.* London: Longmans, 1953.
See p 31: 'It may be argued that Chaucer never completely assimilated directly religious poetry into his secular poetry, wide-embracing as that was. Chaucer tended to deal with his religion in terms of adapted pagan myth in order to adjust it to his secular inspiration. His excellent devotional verse stands a little apart in spirit from his other poetry. Only Dante seems to have been able to weld directly Christian love to other secular experience of love.' *ABC* is 'negligible as poetry, but it is important for reminding us that Chaucer's fundamental convictions were on the side of the Lady Reason, not of Cupid. It foreshadows the deep and

tender piety which later informed Chaucer's devotional verse, and which was always present, if in the background of his mind. There was a force in this piety which would ultimately be satisfied only by Chaucer's own condemnation of all his great secular works.'

156 Britt, Matthew. *The Hymns of the Breviary and the Missal.* New York, Cincinnati: Benziger Brothers, 1922/rev 1924.

'An introductory work on the hymns of the Roman Breviary and Missal,' including 'all the hymns in the Breviary since the Bull *Divino Afflatu* of Pope Pius X (1911), together with the five sequences of the missal, and a few other hymns' (p 13). 'The *Dies Irae*, the *Vexilla Regis*, the *Stabat Mater*, the *Lauda Sion*, and the *Pange Lingua* are of incomparably greater value to the Christian than the greatest of pagan odes. However, the study of the ancient classics and of Christian hymns may and should go hand in hand' (p 13). The Introduction discusses the history of the hymns, their meters, and the canonical hours. Texts of the hymns of the Psalter, with translation, are printed according to hour and day; also proper hymns of the season, proper of the saints, common of the saints, and *de contemptu mundi*. Britt includes notes on authors and translators, plates from various books of hours, English and Latin first line indexes, and bibliography.

157 Brown, Carleton. 'Prologue of Chaucer's *Lyf of Seint Cecile*.' MP, 9 (1911), 1–16.

Brown relates the *Invocacio ad Mariam* to Dante's prayer to the Virgin in *Paradiso* 33. If the prayer in *Paradiso* moved Chaucer he might have decided to add it to the *Lyf*. Brown thinks the interval between the *Invocatio* and *T&C* was not long (p 16). The phrase 'hauen of refut' is used in *ABC*, line 14, and *MLT*, line 852. Brown notes that the expression is common in Latin hymns to the Virgin (p 10). Some scholars date *ABC* and St Cecile together, ca 1373 (ie, after the first Italian journey); others push St Cecile back to 1366, the date generally assigned *ABC*. The choice turns on whether the *Invocacio* is a later insertion; Brown finds 'no obstacle to the theory that the *Invocation* is a later addition' (p 15).

158 — 'Chaucer and the Hours of the Blessed Virgin.' MLN, 30 (1915), 231–2.

Brown supports Tupper's thesis **(199)** that Chaucer made direct use of the Hours of BVM. He cites ms Ashmole 1288, an English text of *Mateyns of Oure Lady*, which supplies even closer parallels than the extract from Littlehales which Tupper reprints.

159 — *Religious Lyrics of the Fourteenth Century.* Oxford: Clarendon Press, 1924/rev by E.V. Smithers, Oxford: Clarendon Press, 1952; rpt 1957.

A selection of fourteenth-century lyrics including some from Harley 2253, William Herebert, John Grimestone's book, and Richard Rolle (135 poems in all). Brown includes a twenty-two page introduction on the genre and ms sources. None of Chaucer's poetry is included in the volume.

160 Brusendorff, Aage. *The Chaucer Tradition*. 1925. See **28**.

Mss provide running titles such as *Prière à Nostre Dame* and *Pryer A nostre Dame – per Chaucer*, which is certainly 'better, at any rate, than the hideous misnomer *Chaucer's ABC*' (p 238).

Fisher **23** follows Brusendorff's suggested title.

161 Chesterton, G.K. *Chaucer*. London: Faber, 1932; rpt 1965. Pp 116–9.

Chesterton uses *ABC* to show that Chaucer was the great 'translateur' Deschamps spoke of, not a translator of verses but of ideas, where Chaucer is 'more original than the original' (p 116). Chaucer deals 'with those profound intellectual passions that concern themselves with the ultimates of the universe; with the philosophy that is even prior to poetry. He was moved to translate the original, he was moved to make the translation greater than the original ... by what he himself would call the *primum mobile*, or Great Mover of all hearts and heads; by a direct appeal, not to the original, but to the origin. Those who do not happen to understand these emotions are at a disadvantage in the matter' (p 116). A French critic (ie, Legouis **181**, pp 58–65) pins the *ABC* to a single point, that it is a copy of a French prayer by a French priest, insinuating its 'artificial effect,' an example of 'ingenious form of verse,' and 'experiment in metre.' 'But this sort of technicality is not tenable in the presence of the poem itself. At least, it is not enough to satisfy anyone with a strong sense of poetry. The original French poem is an honest but somewhat bald statement in very short lines; the first line being "A toy du monde refui". Chaucer merely turns his mind to the same subject, and bursts out, "Almighty and all-merciable Queen!" You do not produce that sort of line by counting the syllables. Chaucer is not expanding his metre; he is expanding himself' (p 117). Of course the poet must sustain such an opening. Sometimes he becomes too ingenious, but the poem 'is not a piece of ingenuity, certainly not a piece of metrical ingenuity. It is an original poem, in the sense that the emotions have their origin in the poet, and not merely in the other poet whose work he had read' (pp 117–8). Ten Brink **78** mentions Chaucer's having passed through a period of intense devotion toward the Virgin Mary. 'I do not quite understand why Chaucer must have "passed through" this fit of devotion; as if he had Mariolatry like the measles. Even an amateur who has encountered the malady may be allowed to testify that it does not usually visit its victim for a brief "period"; it is generally chronic and (in some sad cases I have known) quite incurable' (p 118). In his *ABC* Chaucer is not singing out of admiration of Guillaume de Deguileville: 'He is singing to the singer of the Magnificat' (p 119).

162 Cipriani, Lisi. 'Studies in the Influence of the *Romance of the Rose* upon Chaucer.' *PMLA*, 22 (1907), 552–95.

Notes that the *ABC*, though not taken from Jean de Meun, harmonizes with the religious tendencies in *RR*, with its similar attitudes toward the Virgin Mary (pp 553–4).

163 Clemen. *Chaucer's Early Poetry*. 1963. See **92.**

Clemen considers 'Chaucer's vivid and graphic mode of expression' in the *ABC*; the 5-stress line 'lends the poem a deeper resonance, a more plangent, note' (p 175). The poem is 'an early and striking example of Chaucer's art of enhancing the expressive power and resonance of the English language by a varied and lavish use of words of romance origin' (p 176). Chaucer gives us far more epithets of the Virgin than Deguilleville to make her seem 'more present and alive in our minds' (p 177). Deguilleville tends to be more abstract. 'But it is when we read Chaucer's *ABC* aloud that its resonance, and intensity of feeling come home to us' (p 177).

164 Coghill, Nevill. *The Poet Chaucer*. London, 1949; rpt 1961. Pp 22–3.

On the *M*-stanza: 'The exquisite turning of the conceit (from one kind of fire to another) ... was an adornment of Chaucer's own, not in the original, and shows the true nature of a pun; namely, that it is, like allegory itself, a way of thinking two thoughts at once, whose double action opens the mind with surprise to something almost more than it can quickly hold, as do the best of Shakespeare's puns' (pp 22–3).

165 Coulter, Cornelia C. 'Latin Hymns of the Middle Ages.' *SP*, 21 (1924), 571–85.

A survey of origins, authors, and uses of the late Latin hymns, with some discussion of specific hymns like the *Stabat Mater* and *Dies Irae*. 'It is especially interesting to see how often the hymns run parallel to monuments of mediaeval art – as if the same emotion, the same creative impulse, found expression now in one and now in the other' (p 581).

166 Crampton, Georgia Ronan. 'Of Chaucer's *ABC.' Chaucer Newsletter*, 1 (Winter, 1979), 8–10.

'From its first line to its last, Chaucer's *ABC* voices an anxious politics of appeal,' an appeal for mercy culminating in the last line, which 'discloses the quickening reality of the whole, uncertainty within the soul about its status and fate' (p 8). In De Guileville the soul has been led astray; in Chaucer it seems to be 'hunted down.' 'The English poem's informing figure is the chase, with a desperate prey fleeing to cover, to Mary' (p 8). Crampton notes enclosure metaphors associated with Mary. The sinner flees over the poem's vague and contradictory landscape until he is exhausted (line 147) and begs Mary to convey him the rest of the way. 'Thus the poem traces a reciprocal choreography of two movements – the long flight to exhaustion, and a more uncertain one, sketched only in desire, when the "Queen of comfort" is to come and lead the sinner to the higher tower of Paradise ... Chaucer knew what he wanted his poems as a whole to be, however closely he might follow a model in segments' (p 8). Crampton relates the poem to other Marian prayers to provide insights into fourteenth-century intellectual style. The most interesting feature of the poem is the penitent speaker, 'self-described as quarry, lamed fugitive, invalid, guilty defendant, and child – stark faces of dependence' (p 9). With this insistent cry, 'help, *help me*,' the late medieval period offers many lyrics of devotion to Mary which are 'more gently amorous or more amply filial. But it had a place for this flight in panic, this needy cry' (p 10) as well.

167 Crosby, Ruth. 'Chaucer and Oral Delivery.' 1938. See **95**.
Crosby comments on Chaucer's use of religious formulas to begin or to end poems in lyric as well as narrative poems. Cf *ABC, Truth, Bukton*.

168 Donaldson, E.T. *Chaucer's Poetry*. 1958/1975. See **14**.
Donaldson finds *ABC* to be 'as superior to its original as it is independent of it' (p 960/p 1124).

169 Donahue, J.J. *Chaucer's Lesser Poems*. 1974. See **21**.
Donahue finds *ABC* much livelier than its original, 'a very creditable poem, and its piety should not be questioned' (p X).

170 Dunleavy, Gareth W. 'The Wound and the Comforter: the Consolations of Geoffrey Chaucer.' PLL, 3 (Summer Supplement, 1967), 14–27.
The wound-and-comforter motif of Boethius' *Consolatio* pervades Chaucer in works derivative and imitative, from *ABC* to *T&C* (p 14).

171 Gardner, John. *The Life and Times of Chaucer*. New York: Knopf, 1977, pp 116–7, 128.
'Chaucer's *ABC* is in effect a courtly-love poem to the Virgin, if not simultaneously (and only indirectly) to Lady Blanche herself ... The very act of Chaucer's translating the delicate *ABC* for Blanche shows that she was his friend long before the time of her death and his writing of the elegy' (pp 116–7).

172 Geissman, Erwin William. *The Style and Technique of Chaucer's Translations from French*. Yale University Dissertation, 1952. Director, Helge Kökeritz.
The *ABC* has not been properly appreciated; 'Chaucer's stanzas have more unity of sense than their French originals' (p 212). Sixty-eight of 1411 words are borrowed directly from De Guilleville, 'a large number for a rather free translation' (p 213). Twenty-two of the sixty-eight are rime words; eleven are initial words of the stanza providing the appropriate letter of the alphabet. Chaucer's longer lines, shorter stanzas, and vastly different rime scheme prevent his following the French literally. Even so, there is more direct translation in *ABC* than in *Venus* (p 216). Still, *ABC* is 'a skilful and ingenious piece of versification which deserves commendation if only as a minor exercise in technique' (p 219).

173 Griffin, R.M. *Chaucer's Lyrics*. 1970. See **18**.
ABC is unique among Chaucer's poems in that, like its model, its organization is essentially visual (p 15). Griffin compares the work to a musical composition – 'a series of imagistic chords, any two of which may contain the same imagistic note' (p 16). He also discusses the Mary-as-lawyer- and-doctor tropes.

174 Gripkey, Sister Mary Vincentine. *The Blessed Virgin Mary as Mediatrix in the Latin and Old French Legend Prior to the Fourteenth Century*. Baltimore: J.H. Furst, 1938. Published Catholic University of America Dissertation. Ch 1, 'Origins of the Marial Legend,' with discussion of Gregory of Tours, *Libri miraculorum*; Gregory the Great, *Dialogues*; Adamnan, *De locis sanctis*; Cixila, *Vita S. Ildefonsi*; Hatto, *Visio Westfini*; Paul the Deacon's account of Theophilus and Mary of Egypt; Flodoard, *De triumphis Christi et S.S. Palaestinae*; Hrotswitha; John and Nalgadus of Cluny, *Mater misericordiae*; Fulbert of Chartres in his sermons; Johannes Monachus, *Liber de miraculis*; Maurilius of Rouen, *Oratio 49* of St Anselm; Petrus Damian's various *opusculae*; Guaiferius Casinensis, *Carmina*; Lanfranc, *De nobili genere Crispenorum*; Radbod, *Sermo de Annuntiatione Beatae Mariae Virginis*; Sigebert of Gembloux, *Chronica*; Guibert of Nogent, *De vita sua*, etc; Hildebert of Tours, *Vita Beatae Mariae Aegyptiacae*; Honorius Augustodunensis, *Speculum Ecclesiae*; William of Malmesbury, various writings; Pseudo-Anselm, *Marienlegenden*; Peter the Venerable, *De Miraculis*; Radwin, *Gosta Fiderici*; Herbert of Torres, *De Miraculis*; Conrad Everbach, in *Exordium magnum Ordinis Cisterciensis*; and Helinand of Froidmont, *Chronicon*. Ch 2, 'Latin collections of the 12th- and 13th-Centuries,' with discussion of the theocentrism of the miracula and of Mary as merciful mediatrix. Ch 3, 'Local Collections in France,' with discussion of the optimism and theocentricity of the legends and their emphasis on Mary as mediatrix and operatrix. Ch 4, 'French vernacular collections.' Ch 5, 'Conclusion' and 'Bibliography.'

175 Hammond, E.P. *Bibliographical Manual*. 1908. See **37**.
Hammond lists mss, editions, and modernizations of *ABC*. In four of the mss 'the poem is inserted into a prose Englishing of De Guileville's *Pèlerinage de la Vie Humaine*,' and in Lydgate's verse translation of De Guileville (**183**) 'a space is left for the hymn, but it is not transcribed' (p 354). Hammond also discusses the title, authenticity, and date of the poem, and notes: 'For other ABC poems see Polit. Rel. and Love Poems 1866, p 244, and Jubinal's Nouveau Recueil, II: 245–90' (p 355).

176 Hussey, S.S. 'The Minor Poems and the Prose.' 1970. See **112**.
On the *ABC* Hussey observes: 'Although Chaucer's translation is more varied than its French source, it is hardly a remarkable poem. Its chief use may be to remind us that though his poetry is predominantly secular ... his wider view was fixed on Heaven'; and that helps prepare us for

the Retraction, which seems 'less strange in the light of an early poem like the *ABC*' (p 232).

177 Kean, Patricia Margaret. *Chaucer and the Making of English Poetry*. Vol II: *The Art of Narrative*. London: Routledge and Kegan Paul, 1972.

Ch 5, 'The Religious Poetry,' pp 186–209, concentrates on *SNT* and *PriorT* but makes use of *ABC* throughout. Kean finds the *ABC* diffuse in the handling of its material and contrasts the M-stanza with the intensity of treatment of similar material in the prologues to the two nuns' tales (pp 194–7). Kean notes the 'heartfelt satisfaction' with which Chaucer speaks of his religious writings in the Retraction (p 186) and reminds us that the religious sensibility of the fourteenth century was different from our own: The *PriorT* is 'a perfect *exemplum* of the statement in its prologue that the Blessed Virgin sometimes anticipates men's prayers'; the pathos and tenderness of the Prioress' feelings 'are hardly to be equated with her tears over trapped mice and little dogs ... If we feel that the tale is too soft or its contrasts too crude, we are, I think, merely demonstrating the difference between fourteenth- and twentieth-century sensibility. We cannot share the tears which "trikled doun as reyn" when the little clergoun finally gives up the ghost any more than we can weep with Petrarch over Griselda, but we need not therefore doubt the genuineness of these displays of emotion or try to read an extreme of subtlety into a moment in which the fourteenth century was probably at its simplest and most sincere' (p 209).

178 Klinefelter, Ralph A. 'Chaucer's *An ABC*, 25–32.' *Expl*, 24 (September, 1965), item 5.

The D-stanza beginning 'Dowte is ther noon, thou queen of misericorde,' which discusses the participation of 'Crystes blisful mooder deere' in man's redemption, refers to the allegory of the Four Daughters of God, a theme otherwise known as 'The Reconciliation of the Heavenly Virtues,' or 'The Parliament of Heaven.' It is an extension of Ps. 84.11: 'Misericordia et veritas obviaverunt sibi; justicia et pax osculatae sunt.' Klinefelter reviews the quarrel between the daughters before God's throne, which leads to the Son of God offering Himself as a redeeming sacrifice and the dispatching of Gabriel to break the news of the Incarnation to Mary. 'This legend accounts for Chaucer's allusions in these lines to God's vouchsafing "with us to accorde" and Mary's being the "cause of grace and merci". It accounts also for the reference in line 31: that God would not *hear* of mercy because of "justice and of ire" until the redemption through the Incarnation. There is an echo also of the allegory later in the poem at line 115: "Whan Gabrielles vois cam to thin ere".' (See also 183 on this motif in Lydgate's *Life of Our Lady*.)

179 Landrum, Grace W. 'Chaucer's Use of the Vulgate.' *PMLA*, 39 (1924), 75–100.
There are approximately 730 biblical references, quotations and allusions in Chaucer. Many of these could be derived second hand, especially when Chaucer is translating works like *ABC, Mel, SNT, MonkT,* and *MLT*, which are more or less saturated with the Bible. Jean de Meun's knowledge of scripture was extensive; so too Gower's. Nonetheless, Chaucer's translations reveal independent knowledge of scripture: eg, in *ABC*, line 109, the *ancille* introduces scriptural reference from Luke not found in Deguilleville; so too, lines 97–8: 'When he twined into Deguileville's *A.B.C.* the quotation from Colossians, he showed at times a liking for texts by no means well-worn, as we count them to-day' (pp 97–8). Landrum concludes that Chaucer's knowledge of the Vulgate is intimate: 'After the subtraction of second-hand borrowings there remain unquestionably to Chaucer's credit about 275 cases of direct dependence upon the Vulgate' (p 99).

180 Langhans, Viktor. *Untersuchungen zu Chaucer.* Halle: Niemeyer, 1914.
Langhans argues against Speght's suggestion that *ABC* might have been written at the request of Blanche, either for her prayers or for her pleasure (pp 302–3).

181 Legouis, E. *Geoffrey Chaucer.* 1910/1913. See **117**.
Legouis refers to Guillaume's *Pèlèrinage* as 'a puerile devotional composition' which Chaucer follows stanza after stanza 'as if the subject mattered little to him' (p 63). 'He does not always understand the French very well and he does not care' (pp 63–4). It is an exercise in meter. Occasionally Chaucer aims at artistic effect and succeeds. 'Clair' is one of those 'gems of the French language' which Chaucer hung 'at the end of the most lovely line of his prayer to the Virgin Mary – "Continue on us thy piteous eyen clere"' (p 58; *ABC* line 88). And 'by means of an improved stanza, a more ample rhythm and a more dramatic tone, especially at the end [of the T-stanza], Chaucer attains a fervour of which his model was incapable' (pp 64–5). See **161** for Chesterton's response to Legouis' assessment of *ABC*.

182 Lydgate, John. *The pilgrimage of the life of man, Englisht by John Lydgate. A.D. 1426, from the French of Guillaume de Deguileville A.D. 1330, 1355.* Ed. F.J. Furnival, with Intro., notes, glossary and indexes by Katherine B. Locock. EETS e.s. 77, 83, 92. London: Paul, Trench, Trubner, 1899–1904.
The Lydgate ms left space to incorporate Chaucer's translation of the *ABC* into Lydgate's translation of Deguileville; the editors include *ABC* in their edition (lines 19734–974, pp 526–33). In the notes Locock quotes ten Brink's assessment **(78)** of the *ABC* as an imitation rather than a translation and gives two stanzas of Deguileville's poem 'for purposes of comparison' (pp 689–70). The introduction to the edition discusses the

relationship of Deguileville's poem to *RR*; different versions of the poem; Lydgate's meter, language, and style; and the influence of Lydgate's poem on Bunyan.

183 — *Life of Our Lady.* Ed. Joseph A. Lauritis, Ralph A. Klinefelter, and Vernon F. Gallagher. Duquesne Studies: Philological Series 2. Pittsburgh: Duquesne University, 1961.

Life of Our Lady reflects the attitudes toward the Mary legend of an Englishman nearly contemporary with Chaucer, who borrowed Chaucer's translation of the *ABC* for his own translation of the *Pilgrimage of the life of Man.* Lydgate wrote the poem in rime royal perhaps as early as 1409–11, though 1421–2 is the more likely date. The poem survives in 42 mss. Lydgate uses the Marian epithets of the *ABC* throughout his long poem, though his principal sources are varied: Bks. 1–2 derive mainly from the Apocryphal Gospel of Pseudo-Matthew. The opening 350 lines of Bk. 2 comprise Lydgate's version of the Four Daughters of God story (an extension of Ps. 84.11). Hope Traver, *The Four Daughters of God* (Philadelphia, 1907), thinks this portion of Lydgate's poem is modelled on St Bernard, though the story was very popular in Medieval and Renaissance literature (cf versions in Grosseteste's *Le Chateau d'Amour*, the *Cursor Mundi*, and *Gesta Romanorum*; the *Piers Plowman* version bears little resemblance to Lydgate). Bks. 3–4 follow Pseudo-Matthew, *Legenda Aurea*, Bonaventure's *Meditationes Vitae Christi*, and the Vulgate, though there also are evidences of St Augustine and St Bernard. Bks. 5–6 are drawn mainly from the *Legenda Aurea*. These would be the same principal sources for Chaucer's knowledge of the Virgin. Lydgate includes, after a stanza praising Petrarch, a four-stanza commendation of Chaucer in II.1628–55 (pp 426–7), who is praised as the 'firste to distille and rayne / The golde dewe, dropes, of speche and eloquence / Into our tunge, thurgh his excellence.' Lydgate laments the want of him and his support to 'amende eke and corecte / The wronge tracez, of my rude penne / There as I erre, and goo not lyne Right' [cf the language of *Adam* and *Truth*], but since he is dead and cannot help, Lydgate can at least 'with all my myght / With all myne hert, and myne Inwarde sight / Pray for hym, that liethe nowe in his cheste / To god above, to yeve his saule goode reste.'

184 Madeleva, Sister Mary, C.S.C. *A Lost Language and Other Essays on Chaucer.* New York: Russell and Russell, 1951.

In the *ABC* Chaucer's 'business with Mary is pardon and praise' (p 13). 'A very litany one could make of epithets with which he takes his singing way to tell of God's wonders in Mary and the world's deep need of her. "Kalenderes enlumyned ben thei," he says to her in delicate employment of figure, "that in this world ben lighted with thi name"' (p 15). Chaucer's task was threefold: to translate, to introduce the

inherent formality of prayer, and to manipulate the conventional
formality of the vocabulary of title and belief. 'No one pretends that it is
great poetry. On the other hand, most readers do not realize how extraordinarily good it really is' (p 16). The tone of the poem might be
compared to that of the Hoccleve portrait of Chaucer saying his beads –
a thoughtful, quiet man. Chaucer's first and last works were prayers.
'This practice of prayer was something of a habit with Chaucer' (p 17).

185 Maynard, Theodore. *Connection Between the Ballade*. 1934. See **67**.
Chaucer wrote the *ABC* in eight-line stanzas long before he came across
ottava rima. Its stanza 'is nothing but the ballade octave removed from
the restrictions of the ballade' (pp 72–3). Though we associate his use of
the decasyllabic line with his later work, it first appears in his first work
(pp 79–80).

186 McNabb, Vincent Joseph, O.P., S.T.M. *Geoffrey Chaucer: A Study in Genius
and Ethics*. London: Pepler and Sewell. 1934. [Unpaginated]
McNabb's fervent eulogy to Chaucer and his piety begins with the texts
of the *Retractation* and the *ABC*. McNabb imagines how a book like the
ABC might have been used: 'When a child had to be shown its letters it
was taken to Church, to the Altar of Our Lady. Before the image of its
mother in heaven it knelt down whilst a Primer or Book of Our Lady's
Hours was opened before its wondering eyes. Then on the page, bright
with the blues and red and golds of medieval art, the little finger was
directed to the letters of the alphabet, A.B.C. Chaucer was poet and
catholic enough to see in that an epic of the nursery.' Yet although he a-
dored Our Lady throughout his life and was buried in a nook near Our
Lady of Westminster, perhaps the poem was written 'in deep love and
contrition by and for Chaucer the Child.' Regardless, it remains 'a
master-poet's masterpiece.' Yet, McNabb is troubled by the other side of
Chaucer, which would require that he write penitential literature and a
Retraction. 'I will at once confess to you that I have never had the heart
to read those verses and tales which the poet himself meekly confessed
that he should never have written. Life is too short to spend on what
comes into the poet's work only as an incongruity and perhaps as
bathos.' McNabb contrasts Chaucer with the saints, like St John of the
Cross, who did not waste their genius to amuse a court and had no need
for retractions, yet wrote with a realism of great power. 'It is not the
Chaucer of the coarse or bawdy tale that is the supreme poet of Our
Lady's Dowry, it is the singer of Our Lady's praise whose chaste and
courtly language approves him a younger brother of Gabriel of the An-
nunciation.'

187 O'Brien, Joseph. 'An Ave-Marie or Tweye.' *Columbia*, 26 (May 1947), 2.

In the *ABC* Chaucer speaks like a child to his 'ladi deere,' who asks of him only 'an Ave-Marie or tweye.' O'Brien emphasizes the sincerity of the poem, despite detracting scholars who would see it as a literary curiosity as they 'mull over the technicalities of his rhetoric' and heap up evidence 'to show that he was worldly, obscene, and skeptical.' 'If Bunyan is to be looked upon as deeply religious because of his "Pilgrim's Progress", then Chaucer is to be regarded as just as sincere in his effusion of love for Mary through his *ABC* ... This *ABC*, filled with such true devotion to Mary, does not deserve to be lost, or to become a mere plaything in the hands of unsympathetic scholars who are interested only in dating it or in working out its metrical pattern. Because it is one of the best and sweetest of Marian poems in our language, we must take care that it is not lost to our Catholic tradition.' O'Brien's essay is illuminated by a picture of Jesus under an olive tree on a hill overlooking a town in Palestine. To the left is a picture of a car running on an 'empty' gas tank, advertising Payroll Savings Bonds.

188 Pace, George B. 'The Adorned Initials in Chaucer's *ABC*.' *Manuscripta*, 23 (1979), 88–98.

After citing various responses to *ABC* by modern readers, Pace adds a new dimension to the poem's interpretation: 'Chaucer could think of publication only in terms of the medieval manuscript book and that publication included the adorned or illuminated initial' (p 88). The adorned page was almost the rule for religious literature and though we may think such matter to be extraliterary, neither Chaucer nor the Middle Ages would have done so. To the medieval reader, 'the very alphabet carried religious connotations' (p 89). In the mss, the *ABC* is a different poem from that of modern editions, with a different potential. Fourteen of the seventeen ms copies have special initials. Pace classifies the mss in three groups: a) those with two alphabets (ie, an illustrated letter in the margin beside the stanza, which begins with its appropriate letter); b) those with only stanza initials which are adorned; c) the three late mss without decoration. He also discusses the kinds of lettering used in the different mss. Chaucer could count on a hand-lettered text, a poem recognized by its alphabet structure, and one using probably two alphabets with some decoration and colour. 'He could be virtually sure that the *A* of his first stanza would be quite large, be given special adornment, and might employ gold' (p 95). That is, Chaucer 'had a set of *reasonable expectations* for his poem, some ... deriving from the character of the poem but many simply because of the nature of the medieval book' (p 95). Pace includes a plate of Bodleian ms Bodley 638, f 204r, with two alphabets; he notes that *ABC* is the only poem in this ms which has its own particular kind of decoration.

189 Patterson, Frank A. *The Middle English Penitential Lyric: A Study and Collection of Early Religious Verse.* New York: Columbia University Press, 1911.

Text and notes for sixty-nine penitential poems. Does not include *ABC*. Comment is made on its source and kind of poetry in the introduction, however: 'In the fourteenth century and before, there also flourished in France another kind of religious poetry. In style this was very ornate; it employed long words, and delighted especially in placing an adjective of many syllables in the rhyme; it abounded in allusions and in all kinds of ornaments and embellishments. A single line will illustrate admirably the nature of these lyrics: – O femme resplendissans, roïne glorieuse! – This literary affectation soon spread to England. Chaucer in translating his ABC poem from De Guileville's *Pèlèrinage de la vie humaine,* managed to preserve the spirit and manner of the original, thereby inaugurating a new school of English lyric poetry. He was followed by Gower, Occleve, Lydgate, and some anonymous poets' (pp 44–5).

190 Reiss, Edmund. 'Dusting off the Cobwebs.' 1966. See **130**.

Reiss discusses in detail *ABC* and *Ros* to illustrate the range and skill of Chaucer's lyrics. The *ABC* is a problem for modern readers in that it seems an exercise. 'Its basic structural principle, the letters of the alphabet, offends our sense of the dignity of literature' (p 57). It does not appear to go anywhere but is 'in essence a series of variations on the merits of the Virgin' (p 57). Chaucer's variations seem static rather than dramatic: 'Rather than be "Twenty-three ways of looking at the Virgin," the various stanzas tend to be repetitious, saying essentially the same thing several times in many of the same words and phrases; and the only way the reader knows he has come to the end of the poem is that the letter z begins the last stanza' (p 57). Perhaps it is best to think of the stanzas as twenty-three different poems, each a complete praise to and of Mary, each complementing the other. 'The construction is a coordinate one with stanzas coexisting as equals' (p 62). Chaucer makes use of two characters, Mary and the narrator, who interact despite the static framework with a 'surprising amount of movement, vitality, even drama – much more than in Deguilleville's original' (p 58). One character is restless, apprehensive, full of a sense of urgency; the other is calm, at peace with herself, God, and the world. Though the one is uncertain of himself, he is sure of the other (p 59). 'Chaucer's accomplishment at least in certain parts is due ... to his creating an interplay of sound, movement and meaning in which no element seems to be wasted. The result of the interplay is an intensity of a sort not usually found in the later narratives where Chaucer is primarily concerned with such matters as character creation and plot development' (p 62).

191 Rogers, William Elford. *Image and Abstraction: Six Middle English Religious Lyrics.* Anglistica 18. Copenhagen: Rosenkilde and Bagger, 1972, pp 1–128. The works considered in Rogers' study are Thomas of Hales, 'Luue-Ron,' before 1272; 'Edi beo thu, heuene quene,' ca 1300; 'Mon in the mone, stond and strit,' ca 1320; Richard Rolle, 'Jhesu, God sonn,' after 1343; Chaucer, 'An ABC,' ca 1369; and Richard Maidstone's version of Psalm 51. 'The most sensible approach to the *ABC*, at least initially, is comparative. If we can determine whether Chaucer's revisions of Deguileville are significant or merely haphazard, we will have come a long way toward understanding and evaluating the *ABC* according to its own assumptions and on its own merits' (p 96). Rogers notes that many of Chaucer's added images are drawn from the liturgy and compel the reader to consider fully the theological position of Mary. He uses the same technique in *SNT* and *PriorT*, where the liturgical epithets likewise reveal Chaucer's consciousness of the Virgin's unique theological position (pp 96–105). 'Deguileville's images serve as Chaucer's raw material,' but by adding additional liturgical material 'Chaucer frequently controls the abstract meaning of a particular image so that it points in a different direction entirely from its apparent use in the French original' (p 96). Eg, Mary's queenliness, the uniqueness of her position, her pity, her role as mediator, her bounty, her role as intercessor, as the devil's foe and man's protectress at the hour of death and his advocate after death. Often Chaucer introduces legal metaphors not found in the original (p 104) and makes the idea of penitence explicit (pp 105–6). 'It seems fair to conclude that Chaucer focuses attention to a greater extent on doctrine ... thus compelling an intellectual activity of a type not necessarily belonging to the appreciation of Deguileville's affective prayer' (p 106). Chaucer's use of liturgical imagery imposes 'a certain imagistic consistency' which is 'to a large extent lacking in Deguileville' (p 106).

192 Root, R.K. *Poetry of Chaucer.* 1900/1922. See **140.**
Root calls the poem 'merely a translation, as literal as the exigencies of rime and rhythm would permit'; among the poet's earliest works, it is 'merely a meritorious essay in verse composition' (p 57).

193 Saintsbury, George. *A History of English Prosody.* 1906. See **72.**
The *ABC* innovates its own prosody, using decasyllabic lines. 'This instinctive and early striking out for the great staple line of English poetry is a prosodic fact, the importance of which cannot be overrated. ... Chaucer, as to the manner born, seems to have hardly the slightest difficulty with it' (I, 148).

194 Severs, J. Burke. 'Two Irregular Chaucerian Stanzas.' *MLN*, 64 (1949), 306–9.

Most mss of *ABC* read 'That but thou er that day correcte me' rather than 'That, but thou er that day me well chastyse' (line 39, in Skeat **1**, Robinson **12**, Pollard **3**). The editors reject the ms reading because it destroys the rhyme scheme, turning the regular *ababbcbc* into *ababbcac*. But ten mss of group A all give the rejected variant; one other has 'me chastyse' written over an erasure of 'correcte me.' 'Since, then, "correcte me" is the reading of one of the two main groups, and of one of the two subgroups in the other main group, it must have been the reading of the archetype. Readings ending in "folise" or "chastyse" must be regarded as merely scribal efforts to regularize the rhyme scheme. A critical text demands the irregular reading "correcte me"' (p 308). The sense favours 'correcte me' as well. 'Chaucer is praying the Virgin for mercy against the day of judgment; on that day his works will be found so unacceptable (unless before then the Virgin *corrects* him) that he will be lost. Correction (improvement) is what is needed, not chastizement' (p 308). Chaucer uses the same irregular rhyme in line 47 of *FA*, written in the same meter and rhyme scheme (ababbcac); 'There can be no doubt that the irregularity here is genuinely Chaucerian, for the manuscripts are unanimous' (p 309). Why Chaucer fell into the irregularities can only be conjectured (two times in 135 stanzas). Had he noticed the irregularities and cared to correct them he could have done so with ease. 'Anyone capable of such *tours de force* as *Fortune*, the *Complaint of Venus*, the balade *To Rosemounde*, and the envoy of the *Clerk's Tale* could not have suffered too great "penaunce" in the comparatively easy rhyming of *An ABC* and *The Former Age*' (p 309). Fisher **23** follows the ms reading in his edition.

195 Skeat, W.W. *Oxford Chaucer.* 1894/1899. See **1**.
Skeat prints Deguilleville's *ABC* beneath Chaucer's text (I, 261–71), along with Deguilleville's last two stanzas, which Chaucer did not translate (I, 60).

196 Thiébaux, Marcelle. *The Stag of Love: The Chase in Medieval Literature.* Ithaca: Cornell University Press, 1974, pp 44–5.
Thiébaux uses *ABC* in discussing the iconography of the hunt, especially the allegory of man's life being like that of a driven animal (pp 44–5).

197 Thomas, Mary Edith. *Medieval Skepticism and Chaucer: An Evaluation of the Skepticism of the 13th and 14th Centuries of Geoffrey Chaucer and his Immediate Predecessors – An Era that looked Back on an Age of Faith and Forward to an Age of Reason.* New York: William-Frederick Press, 1950, pp 84–131.
Thomas uses *ABC* and *Truth* as poems indicative of the sincerity of Chaucer's Catholic spirit. 'An early work, the *ABC*, is a translation, and was undertaken perhaps by request; so we cannot accept it as conclusive evidence of the poet's piety. Yet even his translations, conscientious though they might be, were never artificial or wanting in a spirit of spontaneity. In this early piece which was scarcely more than "a poetic

exercise," he exceeds his source in religious fervor; and the expression of devotion to the Virgin is notable for its sincerity and genuine religious spirit, which we may call Chaucer's own' (p 98).

198 Tuggle, Thomas Terry. 'Medieval Rhetoric and Chaucer's "An ABC," *Book of the Duchess, and Parliament of Fowls.*' Iowa Dissertation, 1974. Director, John C. McGalliard. See *DAI*, 35 (1975), 7882A–3A.

Ch 2 surveys comments on the *ABC* then considers rhetorical devices in the poem. Tuggle compares the *adnominatio* at the beginning of Deguileville's poem with Chaucer's to show that even though Chaucer cannot salvage Deguileville's pun (*refui – fui*) in English, he does use *adnominatio* for comparable rhetorical colour (*almighty – al merciable*). Deguileville frequently uses the device. Chaucer mainly restricts it to end rhymes at the beginning and end of his poem (cf *tente – entente*, in stanza 2; *Adam merciable – merci able*, at the end). 'Chaucer's *adnominatio* is an effective means of tying together two notions which are doctrinally interdependent: the mercy of the Virgin is available only to those who actively seek it and who are spiritually fit to receive it' (p 18). Chaucer also uses *exclamatio, repetitio, compar, traductio*. 'Although Deguileville's lines are not dramatic, Chaucer's *exclamatio*, "*O freshe flour!*" provides a more spontaneous and moving sense of the speaker's feelings for the Virgin than anything in the French passage' (p 21). The *P* and *Q* stanzas are organized by *subjectio*, 'in which the speaker directs a question to himself and then answers it' (p 23). One result of Chaucer's rhetorical changes is that *ABC* is more compact than its French source. He uses *commoratio* (the device of elaboration which gives Deguileville's poem its sprawling quality) more selectively. 'In conclusion, Chaucer displays in this early poem an awareness of rhetorical devices as well as skill in their use. He is not content always to leave them intact when translating a poem, but modifies or omits them altogether to achieve his artistic purpose. As a result of Chaucer's virtuosity, *An ABC* possesses a dramatic quality and a conciseness which Deguileville's prayer to the Virgin does not have' (p 25).

199 Tupper, Frederick. 'Chaucer's Bed's Head.' *MLN*, 30 (1915), 5–12.

Tupper considers the *Prymer* or Lay Folks Prayer Book to be a source for the *Invocacio ad Mariam* in *SNT*. 'It is significant that the anthem for Sext (Mid day), "*Rubum quem,-Bi* the busch that moises si unbrent, we knowen that thi preisable maidenhede is kept," corresponds to Chaucer's figure both in the Prologue of the Prioress and in the *ABC*' (p 10). It seems not only natural that such images go back to the Prymer but inevitable. Tupper cites Patterson **189**, p 22, who notes that 'the many poems that celebrate the joys of the Virgin go back ultimately to certain antiphons in the *Horae.*' In drawing upon the universally familiar Hours, 'Chaucer was but following the tradition of the religious lyric' (p 10).

200 Tuve, Rosemond. *Allegorical Imagery: Some Mediaeval Books and their Posterity*. Princeton: Princeton University Press, 1966.

Deguileville's *Pèlèrinage de la vie Humaine* is given prominent treatment throughout this book; Ch III is devoted entirely to it (pp 145–218). Tuve emphasizes the *Pèlèrinage*'s popularity and its use by fifteenth-century Book of Hours makers to enhance the firm iconographic tradition they share.

201 Wolpers, Theodore. 'Geschichte der englischen Marienlyrik im Mittelalter.' *Anglia* 69 (1950), 3–88.

The tendency to present the Virgin as powerful queen of heaven derives from thirteenth-century lyrics on the Feast of the Assumption. The diction is borrowed from the same courtly traditions which provided Chaucer his vocabulary in translating the *Romaunt* (pp 29–32). In view of the conventional vocabulary and the fact that it is a translation, Wolpers suspects the religious sincerity of the *ABC* (p 32). He comments on the regal vocabulary in the poem and rhetorical features of Chaucer's style.

202 — *Die Englische Heiligenlegende des Mittelalters: Eine Formgeschichte des Legendenzählens von der spätantiken lateinischen Tradition bis zur Mitte des 16. Jahrhunderts*. Tübingen: Max Niemeyer, 1964.

Wolpers makes no mention of *ABC* or Deguileville, but does include extensive discussion of Chaucer and Lydgate's use of saints' legends, especially of St Cecile.

203 Woolf, Rosemary. *The English Religious Lyric in the Middle Ages*. Oxford: Clarendon Press, 1968. Pp 239–308.

Woolf uses *ABC* as an example of Marian lyrics in which 'typology is treated in a strictly theological way and is never developed into emotionally evocative imagery.' She chooses the M-stanza to illustrate the burning bush as 'a type of the virgin birth' (cf various carols). 'Chaucer here catches some of the wonder inherent in the type, and the beauty and marvel of the flaming bush appropriately illuminates the quality of the Virgin's "unwemmed maidenhede". This literary development of the aesthetic potentiality of the type can be compared with the painting of Nicholas Froment, where the Virgin and Child appear at the top of a burning rose-bush: in this, similarly, the effect produced by the abundance of rich and precise detail is that the two ideas match each other in beauty rather than in theological correspondence' (p 286).

204 Young, Sir George. *An English Prosody on Inductive Lines*. Cambridge: The University Press, 1928.

'For the purpose of an English Prosody it is best to start with Chaucer' (p 10). Young cites *ABC* for its decasyllabic lines, 'the first lines of this sort ever published in English' (p 16). He quotes *ABC*, line 25, 'Dowte is ther noon, thou queene of misericorde,' and *AA*, line 18, 'Singest with vois memorial in the shade,' for their singular beauty (p 17).

205 Zbozny, Frank T. 'The Metrical Structure of Chaucer's *ABC.*' University of Pittsburgh Dissertation, 1970. *DAI,* 31 (1970), 2359A.
Zbozny rejects the approaches of Jakob Schipper and James Southworth for metrical analysis. He uses the typology of Haller-Keyser to discover that Chaucer deliberately erected a pattern of heavy stresses in the initial syllables of twenty-one of *ABC*'s twenty-three stanzas. 'Since these unusual stress variants coincide with illuminated or rubricated initials in the abecedarian structure of the poem ... the pattern "illuminates" the poem aurally.'

Chaucers Wordes Unto Adam, His Own Scriveyn

See also **52**.

ON THE IDENTITY OF ADAM

206 Bressie, Ramona. 'Chaucer's Scrivener.' *TLS,* May 9, 1929, p 383.
Bressie thinks 'Adam scryven' is 'undoubtedly' a real name, for Chaucer 'habitually addresses his contemporaries by their real names.' After surveying records of scriveners and scribes of the fourteenth and fifteenth centuries Bressie finds only one who might qualify – Adam Stedeman, who was a bit of a hustler, found guilty of falsifying the intent of the man for whom he was working by slipping in a clause appointing himself executor of the will he was writing in 1384.

207 Manly, John M. 'Chaucer's Scrivener.' *TLS,* May 16, 1929, p 403.
Adam Acton (not a scrivener but a limner, according to ms records of the Collegiate Church of St George at Windsor, ca 1379–85) might also be a candidate to be added to Bressie's Adam Stedeman. See **206**.

208 Wagner, Bernard M. 'Chaucer's Scrivener.' *TLS,* June 13, 1929, p 474.
Add to the list Adam Pinckhurst, from the records of the Scrivener's Company preserved in Bodleian ms Rawl D 51. f 23r, a list of forty men who belonged to the brotherhood between 1392–1404. If he was a member in 1392 he would have been at least an apprentice in 1385 when *T&C* was being written. Brusendorff **28** p 57 also suggests Pinckhurst.

CRITICISM

209 Donahue, J.J. *Chaucer's Lesser Poems.* 1974. See **21**.
'This lampoon is the easiest to understand of anything left by Chaucer. We cannot disbelieve that the well-directed dart was also well-deserved, but it has kept some memory of Adam alive where a better scribe might have been long since forgotten' (p 173).

210 Donaldson, E.T. *Chaucer's Poetry*. 1958/1975. See **14**.
'While medieval scribes have always enjoyed a reputation for supreme inefficiency, it might be said in Adam's defence that since none of Chaucer's works have come to us in the poet's handwriting, we cannot be sure that there was not some excuse for Adam's errors' (p 961/p 1125).

211 Flügel, Ewald. 'Chaucers Kleinere Gedichte.' *Anglia*, 23 (1901), 195–224.
Flügel discusses *scalle* or 'scabies' as a clerkish ailment (p 209).

212 Hammond, E.P. *Bibliographical Manual*. 1908. See **37**.
One authoritative ms survives (Shirley's codex Trin. Coll. Cambr. R.3.20), although a later copy is found in ms Gg.4.27. In the margin Shirley writes 'lacheres,' possibly 'a miswriting of *lachesce*, sloth, or intended as a proper name?' (p 405). (Cf Hammond, *MLN* 19 [1904], 36).

213 Kaske, R.E. '*Clericus Adam* and Chaucer's *Adam Scriveyn*.' In *Chaucerian Problems and Perspectives: Essays Presented to Paul E. Beichner*. Ed. Edward Vasta and Zacharias P. Thundy. Notre Dame: Notre Dame University Press, 1979, pp 114–8.
Kaske sees figurative overtones of the old Adam in the poem, citing a short antifeminist poem sometimes entitled *Versus de femina*, which juxtaposes *clericus Adam* with the first Adam. Kaske's gloss becomes: 'Look here, *clericus Adam*, you little bungler, don't you disfigure *my* handiwork the way your namesake disfigured that of God' (p 115). Kaske cites medieval sources which draw parallels between the artist as creator and God as creator and sees possible links between 'the scalle' and leprosy, the sin 'bequeathed by the first Adam'; he notes also the tradition of Adam as the inventor of letters. Such a reading 'produces still another example of Chaucer's comic tension between the actual and the typical or even symbolic, seen at its finest in the portraits of the General Prologue' (p 117).

214 Kuhl, Ernest P. 'A Note on Chaucer's Adam.' *MLN*, 29 (1914), 263–4.
In light of Chaucer and Petrarch's complaints against scribes it is important to know that there was concern for professional standards among the copyists themselves. Wardens were selected among scriveners in 1403 '"diligently to oversee, that good rule and governance is had and exercised by all folks of the same trades, ... and *to the shame and blame of the bad and disloyal men of the same*." ... Unfortunately Chaucer did not live to enjoy this new lease of honesty' (p 263). Kuhl discusses the will of Geoffrey Patrik, a scryveyn who apparently did very well for himself by his trade.

215 Peck, Russell A. 'Public Dreams and Private Myths: Perspective in Middle English Literature.' *PMLA*, 90 (1975), 461–7.
Peck explores ways in which medieval poetry enjoys a common mythology which enables its language to shift meaning abruptly from the private connotations of an immediate context into the resonances of the culture

at large. He cites *Adam* at the conclusion to his argument to show how 'words and images turn upon themselves' as the reader, having been amused by Geoffrey's spirited scolding and sentencing of the clerk to hard labor scratching his head, instantly discovers another poem within the same words when he recalls that other Adam Scriveyn, who gave the names to all the creatures and wrote the first chapter of the book in which all men are characters, whose careless act of negligence and rape left all men, through that inborn human propensity for error, to labor and scrape out a living correcting mistakes. Because of his old errors it becomes mankind's job to renew the work 'ofte a-daye' (p 467).

216 Robinson, F.N. *Works.* 1957. See **12.**

'The lines to Adam Scriveyn, which read like one of the personal epigrams of the ancients, reveal some of the anxieties which beset an author before the invention of printing' (p 521).

217 Root, R.K. *Poetry of Chaucer.* 1900/1922. See **140.**

To illustrate the 'half-serious, half-playful' tone of Chaucer's poem Root quotes an amusing letter by Petrarch to a friend criticising the incompetence of scribes: 'These fellows are verily the plague of noble minds ... Such is the ignorance, laziness, or arrogance of these fellows, that ... they do not reproduce what you give them, but write out something quite different' (p 70).

218 — 'Publication before Printing.' 1913. See **52.**

Root discusses the fears authors had of releasing their works to scribes because of the irrevocableness of publication. He speaks of *Adam* in connection with problems of proofreading, noting that proofreading often led to revision rather than simple correction (pp 430–1).

Anelida and Arcite

See also **24c, 58, 71, 78, 150.**

SEPARATE EDITIONS

219 *The Story of Queen Anelida and the false Arcite: by Geoffrey Chaucer. Printed by William Caxton about the year 1477.* Ed. F. Jenkinson. Cambridge: The University Press, 1905. [A limited edition of 250.]

A facsimile of the only known copy of Caxton's original in the Library of the University of Cambridge. *AA* was probably one of the first pieces printed by Caxton in England. 'The group of small quarto pamphlets to which it belongs are likely to have preceded such large works as the Canterbury Tales; and in this group the Anelida, the Temple of Brass and the Book of Courtesy may probably, on account of the narrowness of the page, be placed earlier than the others' (p 2).

220 Spehar, Elizabeth Marie. 'Chaucer's *Anelida and Arcite*: A New Edition.' University of Colorado Dissertation, 1962. Director, Harold Kane. *DA*, 23, 1010.

The edition is based upon collation of the twelve extant mss. It includes an introduction, typed transcript, textual notes, explanatory notes, and bibliography. Fairfax 16 was selected as the base text. 'The copy text has been faithfully reproduced, without emendations, and all variants carefully recorded. Silent corrections such as expansion of abbreviations and omission of meaningless stops and flourishes have been made.' Spehar modifies mss relationships in Butterworth's schema which Robinson relied on by establishing 'a new A^2 sub-group and a consequent regrouping under A^3.'

CRITICISM

221 Baugh, Albert C. 'The Middle English Period: Chaucer.' In *A Literary History of England*. Ed. A.C. Baugh. New York: Appleton-Century-Crofts, 1948, pp 249–63.

'It is a pity that it [*AA*] remains such a fragment, if for no other reason than that it keeps from the full recognition of its worth the beautiful "Complaint" of Anelida, which with its perfect balance of strophe and antistrophe is one of the most finished and charming examples of the type in medieval literature' (p 254).

222 Baum, P.F. *Chaucer's Verse*. 1961. See **58**.

Though Chaucer was first of all a narrative poet, *AA* is a primary example of his attempts at 'art poetical.' Baum discusses Chaucer's experiments with sound (pp 92–3); he finds Anelida's complaint to be 'a veritable studio piece of *art poetical* and *maistrye*' (p 99). 'There are many examples of fancy riming in Froissart, Machaut, and Deschamps, and many examples of internal rime in mediaeval Latin verse, but nothing which can be regarded as a model of Anelida's Compleynt has ever been found. There was nothing like it before; one would be hard pressed to find anything like it since' (p 101).

222a Bennett, H.S. *English Books and Readers, 1475 to 1557, being a Study in the History of the Book Trade from Caxton to the Incorporation of the Stationer's Company*. Cambridge: The University Press, 1952.

Considers Caxton's early printing of *Anelida* (p 13).

223 Bilderbeck, J.B. 'Chaucer's "Anelida and Arcite".' *NQ*, 9 (1896), 301–2.

Bilderbeck links the situation of false love in *AA* to the notorious infidelity of Robert de Vere, Earl of Oxford, who repudiated his wife Philippa de Coucy in 1387. The scandal is mentioned in the chronicles of Walsingham and Froissart.

224 Brookhouse, Christopher. 'Chaucer's *Impossibilia.' MAE*, 34 (1965), 40–2.
Despite numerous examples of the *Impossibilia* device in classical and
medieval literature the rhetoricians of those periods did not comment at
any length upon the figure. Curtius notes that by the Middle Ages it
had become a topos of the upsidedown world. Nowhere does Chaucer
use series of *impossibilia* for overtly critical or satiric purposes. Instead
his usage is classical (especially Virgilian) 'to convey the deep sincerity
or profound longing of characters who are involved in personal trials,
not in situations which are primarily political or in which mainly the
moral order of society is under attack' (p 40). Cf Anelida's lament, lines
308–10; *T&C* III.1495–8 and V.507–8; *BD* 1054–74; and *FrankT* 467–9.

225 Brusendorff. *Chaucer Tradition.* 1925. See **28**.
In his discussion of Shirley mss Brusendorff notes that some titles to
poems contain instructions or admonitions to the reader. Eg, 'takethe
heed sirs I prey yowe of this compleynt of Anelyda Qweene of Cartage.
Roote of trouthe and stedfastnesse that pytously compleyneth vpon the
varyance of Daun Arcyte lord borne of the blood Royal of Thebes . en-
glisshed by Geffrey Chaucier In the best wyse . and moost Rettoricyous
the moost unkouthe metre . coloures and Rymes . that euer was sayde .
tofore this day – redethe and prevethe the soothe' (p 219).

226 Bush, Douglas. 'Chaucer's "Corinne".' *Spec*, 4 (1929), 106–7.
Bush challenges Shannon's notion (**267**) that Corinne is a confused reference to Ovid's *Amores*, which was known in some mss as *Corinna.*
Tupper **273** suggested that Chaucer might be alluding to the Theban poetess Corinna whom Chaucer somehow found associated with Thebes and
its legends. Bush notes a list in Lydgate's Troy book which mentions
Statius and 'Corrynne.' 'Could Chaucer have met the name of Corinna in
some such list and simply taken it over as suitable authority for a complaint?' (p 107)

227 Cherniss, Michael D. 'Chaucer's *Anelida and Arcite:* Some Conjectures.'
ChauR, 5 (1970), 9–21.
Cherniss rejects the theory that *AA* was to be a 'framed complaint' or a
chivalric romance with epic pretentions. 'The introductory material leads
one to expect a more elaborate and expansive poem' (p 11). Perhaps what
we have was to be the beginning of a dream vision (p 14); eg, Anelida
becomes the central figure of a Boethian philosophical dilemma. Is
suffering the result of man's nature? Has it been planned by some su-
pernatural power, or is it the result of a capricious Fortune? Why do the
innocent suffer at the hands of an apparently malevolent Fortune? 'Her
situation cries out for some sort of visionary experience which will help
her to understand and overcome her dilemma' (pp 16–7). Cherniss cau-
tions against too quick a linking of *AA* to *KnT*. Neither *KnT* nor the
Teseida has an Anelida, and in neither is Arcite 'fals.' 'In general, the

story of Anelida and Arcite appears to have almost nothing to do with that of Palamon and Arcite' (p 18). Even so, it may be that Chaucer intended his story to be tied to the *Teseida*. Perhaps Arcite is false after being captured by Theseus; his death trying to win Emily would be punishment for his falseness. The philosophical meaning of the poem would then turn out to be like the Boethian ideas in the *KnT* (p 20). Perhaps Chaucer left the poem incomplete not simply because it was going badly or that it got displaced by *KnT* and was put aside: 'The possibility that he encountered serious difficulties in attempting to integrate the Anelida story and the story of Palamon and Arcite seems to me to be more acceptable' (p 21). How could he keep Anelida before his reader as he unfolded the story of Palamon and Arcite? And ultimately what would her fate be? 'It is easy to see how Chaucer would become disenchanted with such an approach to the *Teseida* story and abandon Anelida altogether, until at a later time he took up the *Teseida* once more as the model for the poem we know as the *Knight's Tale*' (p 21).

228 Cipriani, Lisi. 'Studies in the Influence of the *Romance of the Rose* upon Chaucer.' 1907. See **162**.

Suggests that *AA* owes something to *Rom* for its treatment of the false lover (p 554).

229 Clemen, Wolfgang. *Chaucer's Early Poetry*. 1963. See **92**.

Clemen emphasizes the 'experimental, tentative, and unequal stamp' of *AA* (p 198). In the *Complaint* he finds 'some very beautiful and impressive passages ... unsurpassed indeed anywhere in Chaucer's work' (p 200). 'The chief reason why Anelida's expression of her grief is so convincing is that she is not content simply to lament and to describe her woe ... She considers every possibility arising out of her situation and searches for some way out; but she finds none' (p 208). As the story breaks off after a single stanza 'the whole poem may be said to end without solution or reconciliation' (p 209). There is much in Chaucer's later poetry that is prepared by the earlier; in *T&C* 'Anelida's helpless despair has become the self-knowledge of a Troilus schooled by grief' (p 209).

230 Clogan, Paul M. 'Chaucer and the *Thebaid* Scholia.' *SP*, 61 (1964), 599–615.

Having examined eighteen of approximately seventy-five extant mss Clogan attempts to determine whether Chaucer knew or used the extensive glosses and commentaries found in most *Thebaid* mss of Chaucer's time. In the Invocation to *AA* Chaucer confuses Bellona and Pallas. In the *Thebaid* Mars, Bellona, and Pallas play important roles in shaping the destiny of Thebes. 'Statius tends to syncretize the different divinities and to consider them various manifestations of the same power. Although he keeps Bellona and Pallas distinct, I find the two being confused in several glosses on the *Thebaid*' (p 606). Later, in Chaucer's paraphrase of

Theseus' victory over the Amazons, numerous details in the imagery
indicate use of a glossed manuscript of *Thebaid*. The influence of *Thebaid*
glosses appears in *HF*, *T&C*, and *KnT*, as well as in *AA*. 'Chaucer's relationship to the *Thebaid* was less pretentious and more natural than has
sometimes been supposed. The various touches of the *Thebaid* in
Chaucer's poetry show an intimate acquaintance, familiarity, and fond-
ness. They reveal not only his continual interest in the story of Thebes
but also his perpetual admiration of "The Tholosan that highte Stace"'
(p 615).

231 — 'Chaucer's Use of the *Thebaid*.' *EM*, 18 (1967), 9–31.
Statius was 'the perfect counterpart of the Silver Age ... which in spite of
its ban against Stoic philosophers and astrologers really did encourage
the pursuit of literature and music' (p 12). 'The rhetorical influence [of
the period] is seen in the systematic use of figures of speech, exclama-
tion, apostrophe, interrogation, and the frequent use of hyperbole, epi-
gram, word–play, and antithesis' (pp 112–3). Clogan traces the great popularity of the *Thebaid* in the Middle Ages and discusses its influence on
Pity, *BD*, *Mars*, *HF*, *AA*, *T&C*, and *KnT*. He compares the combining of
Mars, Bellona, and the Muses in the Invocation with corresponding passages from Statius (p 17) and observes: 'Although the plot of *Anelida and
Arcite* is slightly developed and lacks the artistry of the *Knight's Tale* ...
the fragment does reveal Chaucer's increasing interest in poetics and his
ability to combine and rearrange material from the *Teseida*, the *Thebaid*,
Dante's *Paradiso*, and probably Boethius' *De Consolatione Philosophiae*'
(p 18). Chaucer seems to regard Statius as 'an ancient font of epic material that could be used as a check and commentary on the *Teseida* and as a
model of narrative skill' (p 18). The *Thebaid* provided Chaucer with a
rich source of epic material and classical mythology; it provided narrative models; and its legend of Thebes gave Chaucer an example of the
struggle of individuals against fate and destiny. 'Next to Ovid and
perhaps Virgil, Statius was Chaucer's most familiar Roman poet' (p 29).
Perhaps he studied him in school; or perhaps he was introduced to him
through Boccaccio and Dante. The period of 1380–5 shows Statius'
greatest literary influence on Chaucer.

232 Cook, Albert S. 'Two Notes on Chaucer.' *MLN*, 31 (1916), 441–2.
Cook repudiates Koeppel's proposed reading of *Emony* for *Ermony* (*ESt*, 20
[1895], 156–8); Armenia poses no difficulty since 'le rei d'Ermine' is found
in *Roman de Thebes*, lines 3871–2.

233 Crosby, Ruth. 'Chaucer and Oral Delivery.' 1938. See **95**.
Chaucer 'clearly imagines himself before an audience in *Anelida and Arcite*' (p 419).

234 Cummings, Hubertis M. *The Indebtedness of Chaucer's Works to the Italian Works of Boccacio (A Review and Summary)*. University of Cincinnati Studies, n 10, pt 2. Cincinnati: University of Cincinnati, 1916.

Ch 6, 'Chaucer's Use of the *Teseide*,' pp 123–46, notes that the *Teseide* 'exerted a general influence over the *Anelida and Arcite*' (p 123), but develops the point no further.

235 Dodd, W.G. *Courtly Love.* 1913. See **96.**

Dodd includes *AA* with Chaucer's more mature works which reveal the 'poet's personality' (p 101). 'On the whole, students and critics have underrated the merit of this remarkable poem' (p 108).

236 Donahue, J.J. *Chaucer's Lesser Poems.* 1974. See **21.**

The fragmented *AA* appears to be of 'almost epic pretension. Perhaps the grand Italianate design broke down under the contrasting demands of the elaborate French Complaint and was abandoned ... The Complaint portion remains the most aspiring and highly contrived of Chaucer's lyrics' (p 120).

237 Eliason, Norman. *Language of Chaucer's Poetry.* 1972. See **60.**

Only rarely does Chaucer attempt anything elaborate; *AA* is the most notable instance where 'he rings almost all the possible changes ... The poem remains a mystery to critics, who can make nothing of it except as a dazzling display of technical virtuosity. Very likely its unfinished state indicates Chaucer's feeling that such displays were not worth his time or effort' (p 38). Eliason comments on the formal parallelisms in the poem (p 142) and on its 'pretentiousness' (p 196).

238 Fabin, Madeleine. 'On Chaucer's *Anelida and Arcite.*' MLN, 34 (1919), 266–72.

Some have thought that the *singing-crying* metaphor of 'I fere as doth the song of "chaunte-pleur"' refers to Chaucer's earlier lyrics, but more likely the allusion is to Machaut's 'Le lai de Plour' or 'Le Lai de la Souscie.' Fabin stresses the genuineness and pathos of the latter poem. But 'feelings and sentiments alone in Machaut did not appeal to Chaucer. The great charm of Machaut's short poems lies in his love of form, in the graceful, richly-varied rhythm of his stanzas, and to this charm Chaucer was alive' (p 270). Of all Chaucer's complaints Anelida's, unique in form and rich in metre, compares well with those of Machaut. Moreover it reveals verbal parallels with Machaut, an actual translation in one place, similarities in versification, and parallels in situation, all of which 'indicate that Chaucer knew Machaut's lays, especially *Le Lai de la Souscie*, that he had felt the charm of their form and had tried to vie with his master in the "Compleynt" of Anelida' (p 272).

239 Galway, Margaret. 'Chaucer's Sovereign Lady.' 1938. See **101.**
The love situation in the poem may derive from Thomas Holland's
desertion of Joan of Kent in their youth. One of Joan's titles was Lady
Wake of Liddel, which leads Galway to discover the 'remarkable resemblance' of Joh-*ann-a Lidd-el* and *An-el-id-a* (p 180). Galway suggests that
the same affair is alluded to in *SqT*, where Canacee, like Anelida, is
played false.

240 Gardner, John. *Life and Times of Chaucer.* 1977. See **171.**
Edward III was a godlike man who in his prime thrilled all who came
into his presence the way Theseus does in *KnT* and *AA* (p 105). The image of Ipolita, 'faire in a chair of gold' that, enhanced by the bright beauty of her face, filled 'with brightnesse' all the ground around her (*AA*,
lines 36–42), may perhaps be based on a great procession in the early
1370s, when Alice Perrers was carried through Aldersgate and London as
the Lady of the Sun (p 185).

241 — *The Poetry of Chaucer.* 1977. See **103.**
See Ch 3, 'The Unfinished *Anelida and Arcite* and a Few of Chaucer's
Short Poems,' pp 65–95. Gardner views *AA* as 'a crucial experiment in
[the] technique of counterpoise' (p 72), a sort of turning point in
Chaucer's development between *PF* and *T&C*. Gardner summarizes
Wimsatt's theory of the poem's structure (**277**), which is 'far superior to
any other yet advanced' (p 73), emphasizing numerological patterns like
those found in *PF,* which must have been written about the same time.
'The whole cause of the poem's failure' (p 73) lies in the absence of a
narrator. Chaucer is experimenting and is in a transitional phase
between the 'omni-present narrators in the early poems and his skillful
handling of an unobtrusive but sharply characterized narrator who can
fade his voice in and out as Chaucer does in the *Troilus* and *Canterbury
Tales*' (p 73). The poem's attempt at high style may reflect overconfidence
after Chaucer's success with *PF* (p 74). The character of Theseus makes
Anelida seem trivial and silly; perhaps 'a narrator-voice could have
saved this' (p 74). In *T&C*, on the other hand, one suspects that Chaucer
learned from his failure in Anelida. The invocation to *AA* is 'as memorable and as perfect, in its own way, as anything in the classical epics'
(pp 74–5). The poem begins with a sure hand – a solemn epitaph; then
shifts to 'melodrama' with the story of Anelida. Gardner praises Chaucer
for line 171 on Anelida's convulsively cramped limbs. 'In studying the
failure he had on his hands and in thinking back to the technique of
counterpoise more successfully worked out in his dream visions,
Chaucer realized that henceforth he must choose between ... the use of a
narrative voice implying a real man speaking and ... a use of artifice that
keeps all concrete reality at arm's length. Either he must keep the two
separate or he must combine them in such a way as to make one a

comment on the other or, better yet, each a comment on the other. From this point on, Chaucer was a poet sure of his grounds' (p 79).

242 Gaylord, Alan. 'Scanning the Prosodists.' 1976. See **61**.

Gaylord discusses the limitations in methodology of four recent prosodists as they attempt to deal with *AA*.

243 'Green, A. Wigfall. 'Meter and Rhyme in Chaucer's *Anelida and Arcite.' UMSE*, 2 (1961), 55–63.

Though tragic in essence, *AA* 'becomes something of a mock-heroic poem, largely because Chaucer cannot repress the humour that wells up in him' (p 55). Green compares the metrical and rhyme versatility to that of *Thop*, pointing out intricacies of internal rhymes, alliterative devices, repetitions, end-rhymes and tail rhymes to show that 'the rhymes are appropriate when serious, and delightful when humourous' (p 60). Chaucer uses an extra foot in every fourth verse of the complaynt to vary his general pattern (p 62). 'In "Anelida and Arcite" there are five distinct types of stanza. There is merit, therefore, in the statement of Lounsbury that the poem contains "unusual metrical forms" and "daring experiments in versification." In skill of versification, poetry has not excelled that of stanzas 36, 37, 40, 42, and 43' (p 63).

244 Hammond, E.P. *Bibliographical Manual*. 1908. See **37**.

Lists mss; discusses genealogy of texts and printed editions; records mss headings, explicits, and colophons; summarizes discussions of the poem's date and sources; and reviews critical opinions on the names *Anelida* and *Ermony* (pp 355–8). 'The relation between this poem and the Knight's Tale is an enduring Chaucer-crux' (p 358).

245 Hulbert, James R. 'Chaucer and the Earl of Oxford.' *MP*, 10 (1912–3), 433–7.

Was the Earl of Oxford Chaucer's sponsor in his petition for permission to appoint a permanent deputy in his office of the customs? Tatlock and others used the event in dating *LGW* and *AA*. 'Yet I think it can be shown that this indorsement by the Earl of Oxford indicates no connection with Chaucer at all, but is merely a piece of official business' (p 433). Endorsement by some member of Privy Council was essential before a warrant could be issued by Chancery (p 434); and the duty of signing petitions from early times was a special part of the function of the King's Chamberlain. Thus 'Oxford, in indorsing Chaucer's position as he did, was merely performing a secretarial act' (p 436).

246 Ker, William Paton. *Essays on Medieval Literature*. London: Macmillan, 1905. Pp 76–100.

AA is the culmination of the whole French school, 'the perfection of everything that had been tried,' and Anelida's lament 'that most exquisite deliverance of Chaucer's finest poetical sense' (p 199). *AA* is 'the finest work of Chaucer in the more abstract and delicate kind of poetry' (p 82). It is a poem 'too often and too rashly passed over. It has a good deal of the artificial and exquisite qualities of the court poetry; it appears to be wanting in substance. Yet for that very reason the fineness of the style in this unfinished poetical essay gives it rank among the greater poems, to prove what elegance might be attained by the strong hand of the artist, when he chose to work in a small scale. Further, and apart from the elaboration of the style, the poem is Chaucer's example of the abstract way of story-telling. It is the light ghost of a story, the antenatal soul of a substantial poem. The characters are merely types, the situation is a mathematical theorem; yet this abstract drama, of the faithless knight who leaves his true love for the sake of a wanton shrew, is played as admirable ... as the history of the two Noble Kinsmen, or the still nobler Troilus' (p 83).

247 Kittredge, George Lyman. 'Chauceriana.' *MP*, 7 (1910), 465–83.

Item 5: 'Chaucer and L'Intelligenza': Koeppel's argument on Chaucer's knowledge (*ESt*, 20 [1895], 156–8) has 'no force' (p 478); it is based on the 'name *Analida* (which proves nothing)' (pp 477–8).

248 Knight, Stephen. *Rymyng Craftily*. 1973. See **63**.

See Ch 1, '*Anelida and Arcite* and *the Parlement of Foules*' pp 1–48. 'From this comparison it becomes clear that the stylistic pattern of *Anelida and Arcite* is on the whole unsatisfactory and that in *The Parlement of Foules* Chaucer has perfected the subtle and various style typical of the poems that are commonly thought to be his greatest' (p 1). Knight presents a stanza by stanza analysis to demonstrate that *AA* is a poem of mixed style. 'One of Chaucer's subtlest skills is his ability to make the movement of his poetry seem at times dense and slow and at other times open and swift' (p 7). But in *AA* there is an unevenness within the adopted styles. For example, at Anelida's entrance (lines 71–7) there is 'a flatness ... that would not be surprising in Gower, where we expect a smooth unvarying line (though he can sometimes startle us), but compared with other Chaucerian poetry where so much is done with variation of pause and rhythm, the stanza is poor' (p 9). Perhaps his writing is a dull, plain style here 'to highlight the Complaint to come ... but I cannot believe that ... Chaucer meant to write badly in this sequence. Rather it seems that at this stage he was unable to master the delicate variations of rhythm and pause that can make a plain style interesting; quite often his syntax becomes awkward, rather than plain, in order to fit the stanza form and, while a simple diction is obviously appropriate, he too often creates a clumsy effect by repeating words' (p 11). In the Complaint Anelida has suddenly 'become a mouthpiece for metrical virtuosity, and the evolving "real" character disappears' so that 'the reader is now confused about the very nature of the poem' (p 20). The poem wavers between two genres and three styles: 'such a confusion must be a major flaw' (p 20), a flaw 'intrinsic to the poem as it stands, not the result of its being incomplete' (p 23). 'The invocation promises a mixed style and segments of the poem do seem to follow this, though rather crudely ... But the poverty of the plain style and the infelicities that appear in the middle style damage the poem's effect badly, and the contradictions of tone and genre which become overt in the Complaint only confirm this failure. Above all, as we read the poem we lack that essential confidence that the narrator and poet ... knows where he is going; the poetic infelicities shake our faith ... and no clear directions come to restore our confidence' (p 24).

249 Koch, John. 'Ein neues Datum für Chaucers Quene Anelida and Fals Arcite.' *ESt*, 56 (1922), 28–35.
A detailed review of Tupper's allegorical reading of the poem (**273**) as a commentary on events surrounding the Countess of Ormonde.

250 Langhans, Viktor. 'Chaucers Anelida and Arcite.' *Anglia*, 44 (1920), 226–44.
Langhans challenges ten Brink's theory that *AA* is earlier than *Palamon and Arcite*. There is no mention of it in Chaucer's catalog of earlier writings in *LGW*, though *Pal. & Arc.* is mentioned. He also questions ten Brink's second thesis, that a redaction of the *Teseida* preceded any of the works we now know. He relates *AA* to other unfinished works. 'Ist meine Erklärung des so genannten Fragmentes vom Winter 1373–4 richtig, so haben wir in ihm, so verfehlt und unbedeutend as an sich ist, einen Markstein in der Entwicklung des Dichters, und es ist uns dadurch von Wert' (p 244). This 'Markstein' of the poet's development must have preceded the *KnT*, however.

251 Lawlor, John. 'The Earlier Poems.' In *Chaucer and Chaucerians: Critical Studies in Middle English Literature*. Ed. D.S. Brewer. University, Alabama: University of Alabama Press, 1966, pp 39–64.
Lawlor praises the 'decasyllabic line and stately stanzaic pattern [which] give full scope for the use of high-sounding polysyllables' (p 60), but concludes that 'in its essential nature' *AA* is not 'a piece of fine writing' (p 61). Nonetheless, with its mixed style and the 'plangent simplicity' of some parts it is 'highly-skilled work; here is a poet whose control over his medium is virtually complete' (p 61).

252 Legouis, Emile. *Geoffrey Chaucer*. 1913. See **117**.
On *AA*: 'Here the tender soul of the poet, easily moved by human woes, especially if they be feminine, successfully expresses in a variety of complicated and marvellously difficult rhythms, the sincere effusions of a bruised heart, still amorous and ready to forgive in the height of its undeserved sorrow' (pp 66–7). 'The sustained pathos of the complaint of Anelida was never repeated in Chaucer's lyrical work' (p 68).

253 Lewis, C.S. *Allegory of Love.* 1936. See **118.**
Lewis passes quickly over 'the ambitious and soon abandoned *Anelida*'
(p 171), though he does praise line 18 – 'Singest with vois memorial in
the shade' – for its 'heights of a newly discovered diction' which 'seems
to contain within itself the germ of the whole central tradition of high
poetical language in England' (p 201).

254 Lockhart, Adrienne Rosemary. 'The Draf of Storyes: Chaucer as Non-
Narrative Poet.' Penn State Dissertation, 1972. *DAI*, 33 (1973), 3592A.
Lockhart examines different kinds of non-narrative structures in
Chaucer's poetry to reveal a range in his art which has been largely ignored. A close study of *AA* 'shows that the narrative section is not an
unfinished story, intended to be completed, but that it is functionally
complete; when it is placed in a parallel relationship to the lyric "Complaint," the poem can be seen as structured according to a principle of
non-progressive parallelism. The same material is covered in both the
"Story" and the "Complaint," the differences between the two sections
lying in the mode of approach and emphasis. Since the assumptions as
to the date of *Anelida and Arcite* have been based on a misunderstanding
of the nature of the "Story" and its relation to Chaucer's sources, it is
suggested that *Anelida* may have been composed more contiguously to
the *Legend of Good Women* than has usually been supposed.' Attention is
given also to *Fortune, FA, Truth, Gent, Sted, Purse,* and *Scogan* in terms of
their 'consistent use of contrast as a structural principle.'

255 Lowes, John Livingston. 'Chaucer and Dante.' *MP*, 14 (1917), 705–35.
Lowes comments on Dantean influence on passages in *PF, T&C, LGW,
KnT, HF, Pity, Lady,* and *AA.* The first three stanzas of the proem to *AA*
are based on the first three in reverse of *Teseida.* (There is also some influence of *Teseida* on st 63 of Bk 11.) But Boccaccio is not alone as a
source. The immediate suggestion for *Cirrea (AA,* line 17) is *Paradiso* I.36;
other allusions come from *Par., XXIII,* and 'the poynte of remembraunce'
(AA, lines 211, 350) corresponds to Dante's 'la puntura della rimembran-
za' – *Purg.,* XII.20 (p 731).

256 Manly, John M. 'Chaucer and the Rhetoricians.' *Proceedings of the British
Academy,* 12 (1926), 95–113.
'The much discussed and little understood *Anelida and the False Arcite*
seems also purely an experiment in versification and is of interest, chiefly if not solely, because the formal Complaint is an even more remarkable *tour de force* in rhyming than the famous translations from Sir Otes
de Granson' (p 98).

257 McCall, John P. *Chaucer Among the Gods.* University Park and London:
Penn State University Press, 1979.

Ch 4, 'The Classical Scene,' notes Chaucer's lack of concern for details of real settings and real geography. The Scythia of *KnT* and *AA* is an ill-defined region north of the Black Sea with cold climate, cruel behaviour and barbarous culture (pp 87–9).

258 Owen, Charles A. 'Thy Drasty Rymin⸎ ... ' 1966. See **69**.

'*Anelida and Arcite*, though a failure in it⸰ combination of disparate genres, furnishes us with Chaucer's one attempt to rival his French models in "ryming craftily"' (p 536). 'Chaucer must himself have real-ized that the attempt to convey emotional intensity through manipula-tion of rhyme and stanza pattern was a very much qualified success' (p 538).

259 Pratt, Robert A. 'Chaucer's Use of the *Teseida*.' *PMLA*, 62 (1947), 598–621.

Pratt traces influences of the *Teseida* in *HF*, *AA*, *PF*, *T&C*, *KnT*, *LGW*, and *FrankT*. In *AA* the *Teseida* seems to have inspired Chaucer to try for the first time 'a high style,' 'to attempt a kind of pseudo-epic of his own,' for all the passages he borrowed for *AA* possess '"epic" qualities' (p 604). Even though the poem is fragmentary, it is apparent that Chaucer 'ap-proved of and tried to imitate Boccaccio's incongruous juxtaposition of epic solemnity and medieval love complaint' (p 605). But the characters and situation of *AA* are stock; the poem has almost no unity or plot. 'Indeed, one may question whether Chaucer had given much thought to the possible outcome of the slight fragment of narrative he had com-menced' (p 605).

260 Preston, Raymond. *Chaucer*. 1952. See **70**.

'For the first half of his career Chaucer experimented, in the troubadour manner, with many forms, and reached the utmost virtuosity in the *com-pleynt* of Anelida, which in its sheer brilliance has something more than the technical exercise of *Womanly Noblesse*, of the *Compleynt to his Lady*, or the mistitled *Compleynt of Venus*. By the second half of his career he had found two forms that were most flexible and effective for what he wanted to do' [ie, couplets and Chaucerian stanzas] (pp 24–5).

261 Reed, Gail Helen Vieth. 'Chaucer's Women: Commitment and Submis-sion.' University of Nebraska Dissertation, 1973. *DAI*, 34 (1974), 4215A–6A. Director, Robert S. Haller.

Chaucer's women are 'consistently portrayed as seeking out a niche in the social (or religious) hierarchy which will permit them to serve in the subordinate position designated for them by the Middle Ages.' Ch 1 in-cludes discussion of *AA*, along with *BD*, *HF*, *PF*, and *LGW*.

262 Reeves, James. *Chaucer: Lyric and Allegory*. 1970. See **19**.

The reader will recognize in lines from *AA* 'a tone which had never be-fore been heard in English poetry and which was to become permanent' (p 21).

263 Robbins, Rossell Hope. *Companion to Chaucer Studies.* 1968/1979. See **136.**
'None of Chaucer's virelais has survived. Robinson's suggestion [12,
p 790] that the rhymes in Anelida's strophe (*AA*, lines 256–71) "approach
the arrangement of a virelai" lacks precision – no interlocking rhymes
(as correctly in stanzas 8 and 18 of *The Lay of Sorrow*). Stanza 6 shows a
closer virelai pattern, and should be printed as short lines' (p 317/p 384).
The metrical virtuosity is inspired by Machaut's *Le lai de la souscie.* 'The
major reason for the success of Anelida's complaint is that Chaucer created a character reacting spontaneously and colloquially to her grief; she is
not a talking doll with three inches of pre-recorded tape in her sawdust'
(pp 322–3/pp 389–90).

264 Root, R. *The Poetry of Chaucer.* 1934. See **140.**
'Who "Corinne" may be, we do not know, – very likely the name is one
of Chaucer's sheer inventions' (p 68). Since stanzas from the *Teseide* are
also found in *PF* and *T&C* it is likely that the three poems were written
at about the same time, when Chaucer was also busy with Palamon and
Arcite (ie, soon after 1380). Perhaps the poem celebrates some love story
of the English court, with Corinne invented 'to increase the obscurity of
his allegory. Fragment as it is, the piece gives unquestioned proof of
Chaucer's power' (p 69).

265 Saintsbury, George. *A History of English Prosody.* 1906. See **72.**
On *Annelida and Arcite* Saintsbury remarks, 'The double *n* is prettier and
there is ms authority for it' (I, 153–4). It is 'a beautiful poem' with remarkable variations in prosody, including 'Chaucer's only attempt at the
ringing internally rhymed carol arrangement' (I, 154).

266 — 'Chaucer.' In *CHEL*, 1908. See **141.**
Concerning *AA:* 'The poem acquires that full-blooded pulse of verse, the
absence of which is the fault of so much medieval poetry' (II, 196).

267 Shannon, Edgar F. 'The Source of Chaucer's *Anelida and Arcite.'* *PMLA,* 27
(1914), 461–85.
Parts of *AA* come from Boccaccio's *Teseide* and parts from Statius. 'If
Chaucer had been following a definite source, he would no doubt have
finished the story' (p 462). But two questions arise: Why should Chaucer
give Corinne as authority; and why is this complaint so different from
ordinary complaints of the period? 1) The Theban poetess Corinne was
little known in the Middle Ages, even as a reputed author. Statius mentions her in *Silvae* Lib. V, eclogue III, line 158, but though that work was
mentioned in the age of Charlemagne it was apparently lost thereafter
until rediscovered in a ms at St Gallen, in 1416. A Corinna is Ovid's mistress in *Amores,* however, and this work was occasionally referred to as
Eligae and Corinne (p 467). 2) The Complaint of Anelida differs from those
of *Venus, Lady,* and *Pity,* in that it is woven into a story. In this respect it
is most similar to *Mars* (p 477). But, even so, Anelida's is more personal:

'There is genuine feeling and passion in it. We are made to feel that
Anelida is an individual and our sympathies are aroused in her behalf'
(pp 477–8). Chaucer may have conceived of his idea from Ovid's
Heroides, especially the stories of Ariadne, Medea, Brisius, and Dido.
Perhaps Chaucer's copy of Ovid his 'owne booke' began with *Amores,*
called *Corinna,* which was followed by *Heroides.* 'We may reasonably conclude that Chaucer intends to indicate his indebtedness to Ovid under
the name *Corinna* when he says, "First folow I Stace and after him
Corinne"' (p 485).

268 — *Chaucer and the Roman Poets.* Cambridge, Mass.: Harvard University
Press, 1929.
Part I, 'Chaucer, Ovid and Virgil,' pp 3–47, deals with *BD, Mars, PF, AA,*
and *FA.* The discussion of *AA* is an adaptation of **267**, discussing Corinne
and the *Amores,* the uniquely genuine feeling of the complaint which
differs from those of Froissart, Deschamps and Machaut (it is 'more concrete and personal throughout' p 35), and the Epistles of the *Heroides,* a
'fertile field' for Chaucer, which 'fired Chaucer's imagination to attempt
something of his own upon a similar theme' (p 37). But Chaucer is more
refined. 'Earthly as Chaucer sometimes is in his treatment of love, in
drawing from Ovid he always elevates the theme' (p 37). Anelide's complaint is like the *Heroides* in general theme, in situation, and in details,
'for almost every idea expressed in *Anelide* has a parallel in some one of
the *Heroides*' (p 44).

269 Snell, F.J. *The Age of Chaucer.* 1901. See **143**.
Snell places *AA* in Chaucer's Italian Period. 'Chaucer had a much better
chance of reproducing Dante's rhythm than later English bards,
inasmuch as the final vowels were still sounded' (p 163). He discusses
AA's sources and gives a synopsis.

270 Tatlock, J.S.P. *The Development and Chronology.* 1907. See **146**.
Tatlock notes and discusses datings for *AA* by the following scholars:
Furnivall (1374–84); Koch (1383); ten Brink (before recasting *Pal.;* he
thinks the opening of *AA* draws from *Pal.*); Pollard (1380, Chaucer's first
study of *Teseide* before turning to the *Filostrato*); Skeat (after 1373 and
after *Pal*: 'Chaucer's thoughts may have been turned towards Armenia by
the curious fact that, in 1384, the King of Armenia came to England' [1, I,
p 83]); Lowes (1380–2); Mather (the necessary middle stage between *T&C*
and *KnT*); Bilderbeck (1387, an allegory on a court scandal of that year).
Tatlock concludes that 1383–4 seems the most likely date – sometime
between *T&C* (1377) on the one hand and *Pal. & Arcite* (1385) on the other. The origin of Anelida as a lover probably lies in some voluminous
Arthurian romance (p 86, n 1).

271 — *The Mind and Art of Chaucer*. 1950. See **147**.

'No feature of Chaucer's literary life is more noticeable than the number of works he left unfinished. Writing for him was pure avocation, though doubtless essential to him; he made his living otherwise, and no doubt many people did not think of him as a writer at all ... The fact that the plots of all of the unfinished poems seem to be original favors the view that their incompleteness is not due to any loss of endings early in the manuscript tradition, especially since there are a considerable number of independent early authorities for the texts of all of them' (p 52). Tatlock sees *AA* as the antithesis of *T&C*; it is probably the earliest of the four poems which show influence of *Teseide* (ie, before *PF*, *KnT*, and *T&C*). Corinna is 'probably no more authentic ... than Lollius' (p 54).

272 Ten Brink, Bernhard. *Chaucer: Studien zu Geschichte Seiner Entwicklung und zur Chronologie Seiner Schriften*. Münster, 1870.

Ten Brink argues that *AA* was once to have been the beginning of an epic (p 48). The reference to the love of Palamon and Arcite mentioned in *LGW* refers to an early redaction of the *Teseide*, probably written in the Chaucerian stanza. Later, Chaucer rewrote the redaction as the *KnT*, but saved the opening stanzas for *AA* (pp 40–70). John Koch, *Essays on Chaucer* (London, 1877), pp 357–411, supports ten Brink's view. Tatlock **270** vigorously attacks the view. So too does Langhans **250**.

273 Tupper, Frederick. 'Chaucer's Tale of Ireland.' *PMLA*, 36 (1921), 186–222.

Perhaps some court event rather than books is responsible for the 'violent reversal of character' as Chaucer makes 'that paragon among lovers, the Theban Arcite ... in this little poem, the weakest of philanderers' (p 186). Rejects Bilderbeck's suggestion (**223**) in favour of 'a contemporary example of man's inhumanity to woman' (p 187) in Ireland. The key lies in wordplay in the names, a device Chaucer favoured elsewhere in his poetry as well. Ermony=variant on Ormond, the title of the great Irish house of Butler. Anelida 'is a happy play upon the name of Anne Welle, who was the young Countesse of Ormonde' (p 190). And Arcite puns on the name of a noble man of royal blood who was a d'Arcy on his mother's side (James Boteller, 3rd earl of Ormonde, who, had he resembled his father, 'the chaste Earl,' could never have provoked the tale). Tupper links events of the poem to the *SqT*, as Skeat had done, which supplies details in the Ormonde affair as well. 'Chaucer, after his desultory wont, left the story of *Anelida and Arcite* incomplete. Life finished the tale very happily. Whatever the lapses of youth, the third Earl wore his manhood hale and green' (p 199). Tupper praises Chaucer for the subtlety with which he deals with sensitive events: 'he treads most meticulously on delicate and dangerous ground' (p 202). Tupper then goes on to relate his interpretation to *KnT* as well, where Scythia is Ireland, which is being tamed. 'In *Anelida and Arcite*, uneven and fragmentary though it is, we come very close to Chaucer – as close as anywhere else in his poetry ... We share his very real indignation, as he scourges a false lover not of an old fable of Greece, but of a modern family of Ireland' (p 221).

Robinson **12** summarizes Tupper's argument, but concludes that Chaucer follows Boccaccio, which makes 'the whole allegorical explanation as unnecessary as it is unlikely' (p 788).

274 Vallese, Tarquinis. *Goffredo Chaucer visto da un Italiano*. Milan: Società anonima editrice Dante Alighieri, 1930.

Vallese argues that the real source of *AA* is Boccaccio's *Fiametta*.

275 Williams, George. *A New View of Chaucer*. Durham: Duke University Press, 1965. Pp 154–63.

In *AA* the returning Duke Theseus, as in the *KnT*, is reminiscent of Gaunt's coming home from Spain in 1371 with a new-wedded queen and her sister (pp 154–63). The plot is essentially the same as that of the *SqT*, in which a trusting damsel gives her love to one who betrays her for another interest. Perhaps Gaunt had another mistress besides Katharine Swynford. Chaucer writes poems in a critical vein, fearing Katharine's a-bandonment. 'Perhaps the return of Gaunt to Katharine after his three years' Spanish adventure influenced Chaucer not to finish these two ill-tempered poems, or, if he did finish them, to destroy their endings' (p 163).

276 Wimsatt, James I. *Chaucer and the French Love Poets: The Literary Background of the Book of the Duchess*. Chapel Hill: University of North Carolina Press, 1968. Pp 103–6, 151, 173.

The eleven-line complaint in *BD* with its different rhyme scheme 'shows that Chaucer did think of the complaint as a distinctive entity. Anelida's complaint likewise interrupts the rhyme-royal form of *Anelida and Arcite*' (p 105).

277 — '*Anelida and Arcite*: A Narrative of Complaint and Comfort.' *ChauR*, 5 (1970), 1–8.

Wimsatt discusses the poem in terms of long French love narratives (*dits amoureux*) with their stylized emotional histories – the desertion motif in Machaut's *Jugement dou Roy de Behaingne*, and the set complaints and laments of Froissart's *Paradys d'Amours* and Machaut's *Dit de la Fonteinne Amoureuse* and *Remede de Fortune*. Wimsatt suggests that a completed *AA* might have ended with a consolation, a 140-line 'comfort' at the end to balance the 'complaint' at the beginning. The completed poem would perhaps have had another 350 lines (ie, five more 70-line stanzas), making the finished poem 700 lines long altogether.

278 Wise, Boyd Ashby. *The Influence of Statius upon Chaucer.* Baltimore: J.H. Furst, 1911.

Wise includes chapters on the *Thebaid*'s direct influence on Chaucer, its indirect influence through Boccaccio and *Le Roman de Thèbes,* and the possible influences of the *Achilleis* and *Silvae.* He relates Statius to *T&C, HF, LGW, Pity, BD, Mars, AA,* and *CT.* In *AA* he sees lines 22–42 to be based directly on the *Thebaid,* and notes 'how freely Chaucer rearranges the material given by his original' (p 45). There is some indirect influence of Boccaccio, too, though Chaucer 'follows Statius much more closely here than in the *Knight's Tale*' (p 67). Wise suggests that Boccaccio is *Corinne* (cf It. *corina,* wry face). 'It is probable that Chaucer understood the import of the name *Boccaccio* and that he has here used an exact and euphonius synonym' (pp 67–8). 'When Chaucer wrote *thy Bellona,* he may have had in mind Statius' lines immediately following the description of the temple, where Bellona is mentioned as Mars' charioteer (VII.69).' Though Chaucer is working with Boccaccio here he 'would not have adapted Boccaccio's statement had he not been familiar with the old story to which Boccaccio refers' (p 73). Chaucer's notion that Helicon was a well on Parnassus seems also to come through Boccaccio. 'It was Chaucer's way to consult all available sources and to make up the most authentic story consistent with his artistic purpose.' But it is evident that with the *Thebaid* he maintained an 'intimate acquaintance extending over almost the entire period of his literary activity' (pp 141–2).

279 Witlieb, Bernard L. 'Chaucer and *Ovide Moralisé.*' *NQ,* 17 (1970), 202–7.

Perhaps the Bellona-Pallas confusion at the beginning of *AA* is influenced by the *Ovide Moralisé.* In *OM* XIII, 1–383 (but especially lines 284–7) Bellona is mentioned twice and linked to 'arms' and 'temple'; 'knowing that Pallas and Minerva were equivalent goddesses, Chaucer could easily consider Bellona as another name for the same deity' (p 204).

280 — 'Chaucer and a French Story of Thèbes.' *ELN,* 11 (1973), 5–9.

Witlieb would add *Ovide Moralisé* IX, 1437–1838 to Statius' *Thebaid,* Boccaccio's *Teseida,* and the *Roman de Thèbes* as possible sources for Chaucer's Theban matter.

Against Women Unconstant
Also called Newfangleness

Robinson includes *AWU* under 'Short poems of Doubtful Authorship'; Fisher includes it under 'Poems Not Attributed to Chaucer in the Manuscripts.'

See also **73, 150.**

281 Birney, Earle. 'The Beginnings of Chaucer's Irony.' 1939. See **83**.
Birney finds *AWU* 'more pedestrian' than Chaucer's other courtly lyrics, but with 'glimpses of the sly, cryptic, "later" Chaucer' (p 641).

282 Dodd, W.G. *Courtly Love*. 1913. See **96**.
Dodd relates the poem to Deschamps and also compares it to one of Gower's *Cinkante Balades* (p 98).

283 Donahue, J.J. *Chaucer's Lesser Poems*. 1974. See **21**.
'Scholars approach the piece with interest rather than admiration, though they esteem it highly enough. They might devote more words to saying so' (p 134).

284 Hammond, E.P. *Bibliographical Manual*. 1908. See **37**.
No mark of authorship in the mss. Stow gives it the title 'A balade which Chaucer made agaynst women unconstaunt'; the source of his information is not known. Tyrwhitt 'did not exclude this poem from the sweeping condemnation which he passed upon Stow's "heap of rubbish"' (p 440) and other editors followed him and did not reprint it. Skeat (*Minor Poems*, p lxxvii) and Koch (*Chronology*, p 41) favour its genuineness. Furnivall rejected it and gave it the title 'Newfanglenesse' (p 441).

285 Root. R.K. *Poetry of Chaucer*. 1900/1922. See **140**.
'Though there is no sufficient external evidence to prove this poem one of Chaucer's, it is so thoroughly Chaucerian in manner, and withal so charming and graceful, that one is strongly inclined to think that the manuscripts and the early editions are right in associating it with his genuine work' (p 78).

286 Salomon, Louis B. *The Devil Take Her. A Study of the Rebellious Lover in English Poetry*. Philadelphia: University of Pennsylvania Press, 1931.
Under the chapter entitled 'Personal Revolts' Salomon comments briefly on *AWU*: Chaucer 'is saying what scores of poets will say after him, for of all the various complaints which we shall find lodged against forsaking mistresses, none occurs so frequently as this of "new-fangleness," or "unsteadfastness," which was one of the few unforgivable sins. It should be noted, as a doubtful tribute to Chaucer's mistress, that her fickleness surpassed that of most, for it affected even her color' (p 117).
In an appendix Salomon lists poems of the English anthology according to the following love motifs: Farewells to love (and advice); Personal Revolts (and advice); Equal rights; Against Women; Light Love; Reminders of Mortality (with persuasions to joy); Miscellaneous (sophistry, egotism, disillusionment, pseudo-revolts, ungallant choice).

287 Skeat, W.W. *Oxford Chaucer*. 1894/1899. See **1**.
'For the genuineness of this Balade, we have chiefly the internal evidence to trust to; but this seems to me to be sufficiently strong. The Balade is perfect in construction, having but three rimes ... and a refrain.'

The "mood" ... strongly resembles that of Lak of Stedfastnesse; the lines run with perfect smoothness, and the rimes are all Chaucerian. It is difficult to suppose that Lydgate, or even Hoccleve, who was a better metrician, could have produced so good an imitation of Chaucer's style' (I, p 88). There is external evidence too. The poem draws on Machaut, Chaucer's favourite author, and it is found only (and frequently) with other Chaucer poems. In Cotton, Cleo. D.7 it is found with just four poems in the same hand: *Gent, Sted, Truth,* and *AWU;* and in Harl. 7579 it appears exclusively with *Gent* and *Sted.* In his notes Skeat points out several verbal ties in *AWU* with other Chaucerian poems (I, pp 565–6).

A Balade of Complaynt

Printed as doubtful by Skeat **1**, Heath **3** and Robinson **12**. Fisher **23** places it with poems not designated as Chaucer's in the mss.

See also **73**.

288 Donahue, J.J. *Chaucer's Lesser Poems.* 1974. See **21**.
BC is 'not highly esteemed' by most critics but their verdicts are 'too harsh. The little "poor ditty" is not poor within its class, and its limitations are more those of its class than of itself' (p 58).

289 Hammond, E.P. *Bibliographical Manual.* 1908. See **37**.
BC was discovered and printed by Skeat in *Academy,* 33 (1888), 292. Pollard, *Academy,* 34 (1889), 178–9, 'says that Prof. Skeat is "laying down a new and very dangerous canon" by claiming these and other poems for Chaucer because of metrical smoothness. The poems are in a Shirley ms but not by him attributed to Chaucer; "a fact alone almost sufficient to condemn them." Skeat himself ... now rejects this poem from the list of Chaucer's works' (p 410). Hammond notes that Furnivall and Koch also reject *BC.*

290 Robbins, R.H. *Companion to Chaucer.* 1968/79. See **136**.
BC may have started as a strict ballade (*–ere* rhymes in all stanzas) without refrain. Like *CD, BC* 'is a series of simple apostrophes to "my hertes lady," "my worldes joy," "myn heven hool, and al my suffisaunce"' (pp 319/386).

291 Robinson, F.N. *Works.* 1957. See **12**.
BC must be regarded as very doubtful. 'Though smooth and correct in language and meter, it is loose in structure and wholly without distinction.' Skeat's resemblances of phrasing between *BC* and genuine poems 'are not particularly significant' (pp 866–7).

292 Root, R.K. *Poetry of Chaucer.* 1900/1922. See **140.**
The accidental recurrence of the *c*-rhyme in the first stanza as the *a*-rime of the second is 'a metrical blemish which may be taken as an argument against its Chaucerian authorship' (p 79).

293 Skeat, W.W. *Oxford Chaucer.* 1894/1899. See **1.**
Skeat discovered the poem in Shirley's ms Addit. 16165, f 256r. 'I had not read more than four lines of it before I at once recognised the well-known melodious flow which Chaucer's imitators (except sometimes Hoccleve) so seldom succeed in reproducing. And when I had only finished reading the first stanza, I decided at once to copy it out, not doubting that it would fulfil all the usual tests of metre, rime, and language; which it certainly does. It is far more correct in wording than the preceding poem [*CD*], and does not require that we should either omit or supply a single word ... Altogether, it is a beautiful poem, and its recovery is a clear gain' (I, 90). But see *Chaucer Canon 1* **73**, p 64), where Skeat rejects the piece.

Complaynt d'Amours
An Amorous Complaint, Made at Windsor

Printed as doubtful by Skeat **1**, Heath **3**, and Robinson **12**; placed by Fisher **23** with poems not designated as Chaucer's in the mss.

See also **150.**

294 Birney, Earle. 'The Beginnings of Chaucer's Irony.' 1939. See **83.**
In *CD* 'the lady herself enjoys the irony and laughs like Fortuna at those who pine for her ... If the *Complaint d'Amours* be not Chaucer's, it is the most remarkable imitation of his early style which has ever been written' (pp 640–1).

295 Braddy, Haldeen. *Chaucer and the French Poet Graunson.* 1947. See **84.**
Relates *CD* to Graunson's *Complainte Amoureuse*, which is also a Valentine poem. Perhaps they should be regarded as companion pieces. Braddy thinks Chaucerian authorship of *CD* has 'strong foundations' (pp 55–7).

296 Bright, James W. 'Minor Notes on Chaucer.' *MLN,* 17 (1902), 278–80.
CD, v 12: Bright objects to Skeat's restricting of the 'spitous yle' to Naxos. *CD*, vv 15–8: the middle lines 16–7 should be an apologetic parenthesis which would translate: 'The truth is (I can't deny it), when I compare myself with you, – if indeed it were possible to measure your beauty and goodness, – I am not surprised that you cause me distress' (p 279). *CD*, v 81: emend *sterre* to *sterres.* The poet is employing, by metaphor, the figure of *micat inter omnes*, which, by simile, occurs in *BD*, vv 817–29 and

in *PF*, vv 298–301. The same figure is heightened into the extravagant contrast of *AA*, vv 71–3 (pp 279–80).

297 Dodd, W.G. *Courtly Love.* 1913. See **96**.

Of *CD* Dodd observes: 'No analysis is necessary. The piece does not contain an idea or a sentiment that was not thoroughly conventional' (p 99).

298 Donahue, J.J. *Chaucer's Lesser Poems.* 1974. See **21**.

'Critics who deem [the poem] inferior naturally dismiss it as an imitation' (p 54).

299 French, Robert Dudley. *Chaucer Handbook.* 1927. See **99**.

French does not find sufficient merit in *CD* to justify its admission to the Chaucer canon. The likenesses Skeat finds with other Chaucer poems, including the striking similarity of the first lines of the last stanza and *PF*, lines 309–10, are best explained as 'a natural tendency on the part of an inferior writer to imitate the works of the greatest poet of the age' (p 116).

300 Griffin, R. *Chaucer's Lyrics.* 1970. See **18**.

This early work is 'a consolidation of what Chaucer had learned in the earlier complaints' (p 53). It is not an experimental piece, but rather is 'a *tour de force* in the courtly model,' polished, formal, and ceremonial (p 54).

301 Hammond, E.P. *Bibliographical Manual.* 1908. See **37**.

'In all three mss [Harl. 7333, Fairfax 16, Bodley 638] this poem is preceded by one markedly similar in tone, headed in the Fairfax "Complaynt ageyne hope", 15 stanzas of eight lines' (p 416). Hammond reviews arguments for and against authenticity; the title; and the date.

302 Robbins, R.H. *Companion to Chaucer.* 1968/1979. See **136**.

CD (ca 1374) consists of 'a proem introducing "the sorwefulleste man," two terns of direct address to his lady (stanzas 2–4, 10–2), and five parenthetic stanzas generalizing on her lack of pity. This theme, "It is hir pley to laughen when men syketh," is thrice repeated (10, 48–9, 61). A final envoy-like stanza, paralleling the proem, brings the complaint into the valentine tradition' (p 319/386).

303 Skeat, W.W. *Oxford Chaucer.* 1894/1899. See **1**.

'Whilst searching through the various mss containing Minor Poems by Chaucer in the British Museum, my attention was arrested by this piece [in Harl. 7333], which, as far as I know, has never before been printed. It is in Shirley's handwriting, but he does not claim it for Chaucer. However, the internal evidence seems to me irresistible; the melody is Chaucer's, and his peculiar touches appear in it over and over again. There is, moreover, in the last stanza, a direct reference to the Parliament of Foules' (I, p 89). Skeat comments on the ms heading, '"and next folowyng begynnith an amerowse compleynte made at wyndesore in the laste May tofore Nouembre,"' with its apparent contradiction of the

St Valentine date; he notes that Chaucer, as valet of the King's chamber, must often have been at Windsor. Skeat compares the complaint to Dorigen's in *CT*, f 1311–25, 'which is little else than the same thing in compressed form' (I, p 89). He also notes similarities with *T&C*. The subsequent discovery of the poem in two more mss (Fairfax 16 and Bodley 638) considerably strengthens the argument for genuineness.

The Complaint of Chaucer to his Empty Purse

See also **44, 93, 102, 334.**

304 Benham, Allen Rogers. *English Literature from Widsith to the Death of Chaucer: A Source Book.* New Haven: Yale University Press; London: Oxford University Press, 1916.
Benham traces moments in Chaucer's life by examples from his writings. *Purse* is included to indicate the poet's need in old age. Benham also includes a translation of King Henry's reply, Oct. 18, 1399, granting Chaucer's request (pp 610–1).

305 Braddy, Haldeen. 'Chaucer's Comic Valentine.' *MLN*, 68 (1953), 232–4.
Braddy relates *PF* to the negotiating of the betrothal of Richard and Marie in February, 1377. *PF* is a comic valentine, but also a begging poem, like *Purse*, from which he hopes to 'mete som thyng for to fare / the bet.' Like *Purse*, *PF* is successful as Chaucer gets a 'special gift' of £40. The roundel at the end of *PF* is a complementary allusion to the betrothal, whose 'note imaked was in France' (p 234). That Chaucer should deal in so comic a manner with such serious matters is comparable to his envoy to Vache in *Truth*, or the witty but earnest request in *Purse*, or the good-humoured reference to Graunson's versification in *Venus* (p 233).

306 Brusendorff, A. *Chaucer Tradition.* 1925. See **28.**
Brusendorff prefers the French title: *La Complainte de Chaucer à sa Bourse Voide* (p 253).

307 Bühler, Curt F. 'A New Lydgate-Chaucer Manuscript.' *MLN*, 52 (1937), 1–9.
Pierpont Morgan ms 54 (mid-fifteenth century) includes *Purse* in three stanzas without the Envoy. (Other mss lack the envoy as well.) The ms seems to be associated with Humphrey, Duke of Gloucester. Bühler thinks that the envoy is probably of a later date, as it could only have been written after Henry IV had been declared king. But the rest of the poem originally must have been written earlier, in which case 'out of this toune' (line 17) might refer to Chaucer's desire to retire from London. On May 4, 1398, Richard took Chaucer into his special protection, 'forbidding him for two whole years to be arrested or sued by anybody

except on a plea connected with land.' Bühler thinks the poem must have preceded May 4, 1398.

308 Cohen, H.L. *The Ballade.* 1915. See **93.**
Cohen contrasts *Purse* with French begging poems (pp 244–5).

309 Cook, Albert S. 'Chaucerian Papers.' *Transactions Connecticut Academy of Arts and Science,* 23. New Haven: Yale University Press, 1919, pp 33–8.
Cook finds Skeat's tying of the poem to Deschamps (1, I, pp 562–3) to be unconvincing. Not only is the envoy different, but the tone and diction throughout are quite unlike Deschamps. 'Chaucer's ballade has the air of being a genial parody of a love-lyric' (p 34). Cook suggests a better model in Guy de Cousy's ballade beginning 'A vos, amant, plus qu'a nule altre gent.' Cook notes several verbal echoes. Chaucer's envoy is more in the vein of such demands as Deschamps sometimes made on his patrons. The phrase 'Brutes Albioun' also seems reminiscent of Deschamps. But the envoy may be a late addition, as Root suggests (**140,** p 78).

310 Donahue, J.J. *Chaucer's Lesser Poems.* 1974. See **21.**
Donahue praises Chaucer for his 'deft use of the conventions' and sees pathos in the envoy's simple formula – this song to you I send – 'because it will never be repeated' (p 266).

311 Eliason, Norman. *The Language of Chaucer's Poetry.* 1972. See **60.**
'Although Chaucer's carelessness about facts is largely a pose, I suspect that he may actually have been not overcareful about them and even prided himself on it. As a writer, he got some things astoundingly wrong ... If he carried the habit over into his work as a civil servant, God knows what the budget bureau made of his accounts! Perhaps his straitened and tangled financial circumstances in the last decade of his life are less illusory than is commonly supposed, and his charming little begging poem addressed to Henry IV ... was not intended solely to amuse the king. But whatever Chaucer's personal indifference to strict accuracy, as a poet he usually took care that anything factually wrong would be artistically right' (p 94).

312 Ferris, Sumner J. 'The Date of Chaucer's Final Annuity and of the *Complaint to his Empty Purse.'* MP, 65 (1967), 45–52.
Ferris disagrees with Scott **325** that Chaucer was well enough off in his late years. Since the document in which Henry renews and increases Chaucer's annuity has been back-dated from Feb. 1400 to Oct. 1399, the poet may have been five months without income. 'Alle our harmes' (line 25) refers not just to troubles of the kingdom but to the poet's own troubles. The 'have mynde upon my supplication' leaves little room to doubt that 'Chaucer is making a pretty desperate "supplicacioun" for money' (p 46). The tenor of the complaint 'seems unmistakable. It is courtly, jocular, and probably comically exaggerated in tone, but it is still

essentially a begging letter' (p 46). The cause for the delay in Chaucer's receiving his annuity may have been the turmoil that arose when the government passed from Richard to Henry, but Ferris is doubtful. 'The last payment had been due on what was, technically, the last day of Richard's reign, and Henry was not obliged to meet such commitments of his predecessor' (p 50). Chaucer did not feel threatened as he might have felt from Gloucester's faction in 1387–99; but still his resources must have been strained since the annuity was his chief source of income. If the complaint came to the immediate attention of Henry IV the poem with its envoy could be dated early February 1400, though it might possibly have been written any time after September 30, 1399.

312a — 'Chaucer, Richard II, Henry IV, and 13 October.' In *Chaucer and Middle English Studies in Honour of Rossell Hope Robbins.* Ed. Beryl Rowland. London: Unwin; Kent, Ohio: Kent State University Press, 1974. Pp 210–7. Chaucer was 'a shrewder courtier than we usually imagine him to have been' (p 210). Richard II promised him a tun of wine on Christmas 1397. The grant was not awarded, however, until October 13 of the following year. October 13 is St Edward the Confessor's feast day. Sumner argues that it was a feast day special to Richard as it had been to his ancestors. Chaucer waited to petition for the promised gift at a time when the king was 'likely to be generous' (p 214). In the following year, when Henry usurped the throne he forced Richard to renounce the throne on Michaelmas, then was himself crowned on Richard's feastday. Chaucer's barrel of wine, due that day, was not awarded until he petitioned Henry for it, perhaps as late as February of 1400, with his witty *Purse.* The award was then made, but back-dated to 13 October. In dealing with both kings, Chaucer showed great tact. The 'tone of the *Complaint to His Purse* is matched by the aptness of his choice of 13 October to present a petition to Richard II. In both cases he flattered his King, in both cases he allowed them to show largesse, and in both cases he was successful' (p 216).

313 Finnel, Andrew J. 'The Poet as Sunday Man: "The Complaint of Chaucer to his Purse".' *ChauR,* 8 (1973–4), 147–58.
In explicating 'Oute of this toune helpe me thurgh your myght' (line 17) Finnel suggests that Chaucer really was poor and had taken refuge at Westminster Abbey against debtors (24 Dec., 1399). 'Toune' means 'walled enclosure'; Westminster Abbey was in Chaucer's day quite literally a walled monastery, a royally chartered sanctuary. Chaucer is asking: 'By your power as King help me out of debt – help me so that I can once more walk the streets of London, help me so that I can leave this enclosure, this monastery' (p 153). The poem must have been written between Dec. 24, 1399, and Feb. 16, 1400, when the annuity was awarded.

314 Giffin, Mary. *Studies on Chaucer and His Audience.* Hull, Quebec: Les Editions l'Eclair, 1956.

Ch 5, 'O Conquerour of Brutes Albyon,' pp 89–106, discusses the political implications of three phrases in the opening formula of the envoy: Henry claimed descent from Henry III through his mother Blanche of Lancaster. His ascension to the crown in no way was to set precedent for a change in liberties, franchises, rights, or customs. The 'Conqueror's' claim is 'by lyne' as well as 'free eleccion.' Still in view of the Mortimer claim 'the striking contrast to the slender claim of Henry IV is obvious' (p 95). Giffin prints in colour the four-age genealogy of the Mortimer family, which traces the line back to Brutus, found in University of Chicago ms 224, fols 51v–52r (pl 6–7). She also presents Adam Usk's defence of the Mortimer claim and the prophesies of Bridlington. 'Chaucer must have been well aware of the strength of the Mortimer family, and of the importance of their legendary ancestry for the control of Wales and Ireland' (p 104). The first line of the Envoy reads like a poetic cliché, 'but it carries a weight of meaning out of all proportion to the familiar words, and a special meaning for the king, lately triumphant over an adversary descended from Brutus. The salutation leads swiftly to the legal formula, "by lyne," which is more than a formula in its context. Each of the two phrases in its own way points directly to the "free eleccion," which could not have taken place without Henry's victory over Richard II and the commission's determination of the royal line. The three parts of the apostrophe ... are closely linked, each in its own way recalling events of twenty years as Chaucer refers to the happenings of the weeks which immediately preceded the writing' (pp 104–5).

315 Hammond, E.P. *Bibliographical Manual.* 1908. See **37.**

Purse occurs in three mss forms: 'as three seven-line stanzas with a five-line envoy; similarly without the envoy; without the envoy and having continuous with it a series of seven-line stanzas on imprisonment' (p 392). The 'continuation' appears separately in one ms. See **316.**

316 — 'Lament of a Prisoner Against Fortune.' *Anglia*, 32 (1909), 481–90.

Purse appears among the Shirley group of mss with a continuation, a prisoner's lament against fortune. The poem got assigned to Hoccleve, and in Speght's editions of 1602 and in the 1687 reprint *Purse* appears, with its envoy, as Hoccleve's poem. The authorship of the *Lament* is not known; it was never printed with the work of Chaucer. Hammond presents the text in print for the first time. One attempt was made to assign the poem to Lydgate, but Hammond warns: 'We who are compelled to restrain ourselves from assigning to Lydgate every anonymous piece of work existing in fifteenth-century manuscripts may find consolation in the thought that even Chaucer scrupled to send an idea out into the world unless he could bind upon it a name' (p 483).

317 Kellogg, Alfred L. 'Amatory Psychology and Amatory Frustration in the Interpretation of the *Book of the Duchess.*' In *Chaucer, Langland, Arthur: Essays in Middle English Literature.* New Brunswick: Rutgers University Press, 1972, pp 59–107.

Kellogg suggests that the opulent scene of the glorious room with its 'magnificent vitreous creation' (p 86) of uncracked windows at the beginning of the dream in *BD* 'is something of an inverted version of the later Chaucer's *Complaint to His Purse*' (p 106, n 79).

318 Kitchin, George. *A Survey of Burlesque and Parody in England.* 1931. See **116.**

That Chaucer could make a burlesque of the Complaint, the most characteristic of love modes, as he does in *Purse,* reinforces the argument for burlesque in *Ros* and 'makes us often suspect a smile in a serious context' (p 15).

319 Legge, M. Dominica. 'The Gracious Conqueror.' *MLN,* 68 (1953), 18–21.

In response to Smith **327,** Legge argues that 'conqueror' is neither ironical nor flattering but an appropriate designation for Henry (p 18). It is simply a synonym for 'victor.' The case Chaucer presents is cumulative: Henry is king by conquest, by inheritance, and by elections. Conquest here means 'the acquisition by peaceful means of inheritance vacant through the misconduct and ineptitude of his predecessor. Richard, by contrast, had been a bloody tyrant' – the first to take a view of royal prerogative which pushed toward a doctrine of divine right; 'Henry stood for law and order, for something which in time to come would be parliamentary government' (p 20).

320 Ludlum, Charles D. 'Heavenly Word-Play in Chaucer's "Complaint to His Purse".' *N&Q,* 23 (1976), 391–2.

The language of 'Chaucer's playful apostrophe works up to a third level beyond the crassly material and courtly: that is, the heavenly' (p 391). Cf *hertes stere, Quene of comfort, lyves lyght, saveour, tresorere* – all terms shared with religious poetry, like the *ABC.*

321 MacCracken, Henry H. 'An Odd Text of Chaucer's *Purse.*' *MLN,* 27 (1912), 228–9.

MacCracken prints two stanzas of *Purse* as they appear in ms Caius College 176, fol 23, a mid-fifteenth-century text which 'has hitherto escaped notice' (p 228).

321a Mitchell, P. Beattie. 'A Chaucer Allusion in a 1644 Pamphlet.' *MLN,* 51 (1936), 435–7.

Purse, attributed to 'Ocleve in Chaucere,' is included in a pamphlet by Thomas Jordan which endeavors 'to prove that the state of a debtor is good both for his friends and himself' (p 435).

322 Rickert, Edith. 'Chaucer's Debt to Walter Bukholt.' *MP*, 24 (1926), 503–5.
The suit against Chaucer, often cited as proof of his poverty, proves little.
Walter Bukholt (Bukworthe) was a supplier and purveyor of wood, stone,
timber, tiles, shingles, etc while Chaucer was Clerk of the Works. The
suit of £14.1s.11d in 1398 pertains to official business and was brought not
by Bukholt but by Isabella, administratrix of Bukholt. She also sued a
John Goodale for £12.8s. 'It is clear that the Bukholt suit and the king's
letters of protection cannot safely be cited ... to prove Chaucer's poverty'
(p 505).

323 Robbins, R.H. *Companion to Chaucer Studies*. 1968/1979. See **136**.
Purse, 'a bouleversement of the love complaint,' may have been modeled
on Deschamps' ballade no. 247, or Froissart's ballade no. 31, or Hoccleve's
rondel 'Lady Moneye,' but these 'all forgo the witty money-mistress personification' (p 327/394).

324 Robinson, F.N. *Works*, 1957. See **12**.
'It is interesting to see the elderly Chaucer reverting to the type of poem
which he wrote in his youth, the lover's complaint, here skillfully
travestied in the appeal to his new lady, his empty purse' (p 523).

325 Scott, Florence R. 'New Look at "The Complaint of Chaucer to His Empty Purse".' *ELN*, 2 (1964), 81–7.
Scott challenges the hypothesis that Chaucer was light-hearted in his
new allegiance to Henry or that he was sad because of poverty.
Chaucer's family connections with the king lie behind Henry's generosity. Scott reviews Chaucer's and Phillipa's closeness to Gaunt's household, noting that Thomas Chaucer was made Constable of Wallingford
Castle on the day of Richard's deposition and thus was guardian of the
deposed queen. His cousin Sir Thomas Swinford (son of Katharine by
Gaunt) was put in charge of Richard (Usk's *Chronicon* says he was
Richard's tormenter). *Purse* is more than a humourous adaptation of a
lover's appeal to his mistress, or a tribute to a new King, or a lament for
poverty. 'It is rather a document offered by an astute courtier reminding
a highly esteemed master that a little generosity to an old and tried civil
servant would be gratefully received – indeed might even be a matter of
noblesse oblige' (pp 86–7). Henry was deeply in debt both to Thomas
Chaucer and Thomas Swynford. 'Loyalty such as these men had
displayed was a rare quality then as always, and their loyalty was based
on kinship as well as long service' (p 87). The king's gift to Chaucer was
not just recognition for the poet's skill but gratitude for services performed by his nephew and son – 'services which even a king in those
troubled days might hesitate to reward more openly' (p 87).

326 Skeat, W.W. *Oxford Chaucer.* 1894/1899. See **1.**

'I do not know on what grounds Speght removed Chaucer's name, and substituted that of T. Occleve' (I, pp 87–8). It is highly probable that the poem is older than the envoy. One ms entitles the poem 'a supplicacioun to King Richard by Chaucer' (I, p 563). 'The Envoy is almost certainly Chaucer's latest extant composition' (I, p 88). Skeat cites Bell's note on line 23: '"In Henry IV's proclamation to the people of England he founds his title on *conquest, hereditary right,* and *election*; and from this inconsistent and absurd document Chaucer no doubt took his cue"; Bell' (I, p 564).

327 Smith, Roland M. 'Five Notes on Chaucer and Froissart.' *MLN,* 66 (1951), 27–32.

Chaucer is perhaps indebted in *Purse,* line 22, to Froissart's Ballade no. 32, whose refrain explains the prosperity of 'Brutes Albyon' as the fulfilment of Diana's prophecy to Brutus. She promises that he and his descendants 'moult conquerront soit à droit, soit à tort.' With characteristic irony Chaucer expresses 'his secret opinion of the usurper Bolingbroke, who had "conquered *soit à droit, soit à tort*" (probably the latter) the Albion of Brutus' (p 32).

The Complaint of Mars
Also called The Brooch of Thèbes

See also **55, 80, 89, 150, 575.**

328 Baskervill, Charles R. 'English Songs on the Night Visit.' *PMLA,* 36 (1921), 565–614.

Baskervill relates the poem's opening stanzas, the parting of the lovers, and the complaint of Mars to the aube tradition (pp 593–5).

329 Braddy, Haldeen. *Chaucer and the French Poet Graunson.* 1947. See **84.**

Ch 5, 'Personal Allegory in the Valentine Poems,' focuses on *PF* and *Mars.* In *Le Songe Sainct Valentin* Graunson leaves no doubt that the bird allegory is linked to human affairs (p 72). In several of his poems Graunson alludes to his own life; two poems bear acrostics on ISABEL of York, who may have requested poems from Chaucer (viz *Venus*), as well as Graunson. Braddy discusses ms addenda which connect *Mars* and *Venus* to Isabel. *Mars* probably reflects Gaunt's hostility toward Holland. Shirley linked the poem to Gaunt and to a different situation involving a different woman and a different Holland; it may be that he simply 'misremembered,' but was essentially right, at least, in perceiving the kind of poem it is. In discussing Shirley and the fifteenth-century court Braddy makes interesting observations on Suffolk and Charles of

Orléans. For a more thorough explanation of Braddy's theories on historical allusion in Chaucer's poetry, especially events pertaining to *PF*, see his *Chaucer's Parlement of Foules in its Relation to Contemporary Events* (London: Oxford University Press, 1932/rev with additional material, New York: Octagon Books, 1969). The revised edition includes an extensive bibliography, some of which is annotated, on works pertaining to *PF*, historical allegory, and occasional genres (pp 94–108).

330 Brewer, Derek S. 'Chaucer's "Complaint of Mars".' *N&Q*, n.s. 1 (1954), 462–3.

Chaucer's source is usually said to be Ovid's account of the lovers being surprised by Vulcan. But the story is also treated by the astrologising mythographers. Hyginus (Poet. Astron. II.42 in the *Mythographi Latini*), speaking of the amour, calls Mars the third planet, 'which may have suggested Chaucer's reference to Mars as "the thridde hevenes lord" (line 29)' (p 462). It would be rash to assert that Hyginus was certainly Chaucer's source; 'but no other mythographer takes quite the line that both Chaucer and Hyginus take. It is at least a curious coincidence' (p 462). The characteristics of Venus (lines 171–81) are likewise essentially those of the planet, as developed in the fourteenth century. The most useful compendium of astrology and mythology open to the literary men of the day is Boccaccio's *De Genealogia Deorum*. It is not known for certain whether Chaucer knew the work, but 'Chaucer's stanza is in fact a fair summary and selection of the characteristic traits attributed to the planet [in Boccaccio]' (p 426; cf *De Genealogia*, III.22). In view of possible ties with Hyginus and Boccaccio 'it becomes more than ever difficult to accept the theory that Chaucer was writing an allegorical account of a courtier's *amour*, and not a traditionally allegorical account of certain astronomical movements' (p 463).

331 Browne, William Hand. 'Notes on Chaucer's Astrology.' *MLN*, 23 (1908), 53–4.

Browne discusses astrological references in *MLT*, *KnT*, and *Mars*. After commenting on 'Cylenius tour' (*Mars*, line 113) and 'Venus valence' (*Mars*, line 145) Browne repunctuates Skeat's text to read: 'Cylenius, riding in his chevauche / Fro Venus valance, mighte his paleys see' (lines 144–5), with the sense being: 'Mercury, coming in his swift course from Pisces, the "exaltation" and place of power of Venus, enters Aries, whence he can see his own palace in Gemini, where Venus is' (p 54).

332 Brusendorff, A. *Chaucer Tradition*. 1925. See **28**

Brusendorff records Shirley's endnote to *Mars* in Trin.R.3.20: 'Loo yee louers gladethe and comfortethe you . of thallyaunce etrayted bytwene the hardy and furyous Mars . the god of Armes and Venus the double goddesse of loue made by Geffrey Chaucier . at the comandement of the renommed and excellent prynce my lord the duc John of Lancastre'; and also the endnote to *Venus:* 'thus eondethe here this complaint whiche some men sayne was made . by my lady of York doughter to the Kyng of Spaygne and my lord of huntyngdon . some tyme duc of Excestre and filowyng begynnethe . a balade translated out of frenshe . in to englisshe by Chaucier Geffrey the frenshe made sir Otes de Grauntsomme . knight. Savosyen. Hit is sayde that Graunsome made this last balade for venus resembled to my lady of york . aunswering the complaynt of Mars' (pp 263–4). Brusendorff discusses Isabel and John Holland's 'unsavoury' reputations: 'The whole episode certainly throws a curious light on the relations between the poet and his patrons, and this is perhaps the most important result for the Chaucer student' (p 268). Nb, ms Fairfax 16, f 14b, has a splendid drawing of the chief persons of Chaucer's *Brooch of Thebes* – ie, Phoebus, Mars, and Venus, which Brusendorff reproduces in black and white (pl 3). See also the colour frontispiece in Norton-Smith 24a.

333 Carter, Thomas. 'The Shorter Poems of Geoffrey Chaucer.' *Shenandoah*, 11 (1960), 48–60.
Mars is 'an exercise' which 'reeks with cleverness' (p 53).

334 Clemen, Wolfgang. *Chaucer's Early Poetry.* 1963. See **92**.
Clemen considers *Mars* to be an early poem in which Chaucer transforms Valentine and aubade matter to new effects as he blends lyric devices with narrative techniques: 'It was inevitable that Chaucer should find the traditional "complainte d'amour" too narrow and too rigid a form' (p 188). 'His artistry reveals the consummate knowledge of astronomy and astrology possessed by the author of the *Treatise on the Astrolabe*, a knowledge which enabled him to manipulate his material with such ease and skill' (p 192). The poem does not fulfill the promise of the bird or expected Valentine gift: rather, Chaucer ' "disillusions" us, setting the sober disenchantment of reality side by side with what corresponds to an idealized view of things' (p 194). The breaking of the conventional with unconventional touches shatters the dignity of the lovers. The result is 'a significant expansion of the genre and a skilful blend of contrasting attitudes and features' (p 197). In its use of irony it points to later works like *Purse,* with the 'disintegration of genre as such' (p 197). In its treatment of faith amidst transience and inconstancy *Mars* approaches 'the very threshold of the profoundly moving analysis which was to make *Troilus* one of the most serious medieval poems in English' (p 197).

335 Clogan, Paul M. 'Chaucer's Use of the *Thebaid.*' *EM*, 18 (1967), 9–31.
Clogan traces to Statius several features of the poem surrounding the Brooch of Thebes fashioned by Vulcan for Harmonia against her wedding day.

336 Cowling, G.H. 'Chaucer's *Complaintes of Mars and of Venus.*' *RES*, 2, (1926), 405–10.

Cowling reviews Shirley's assertion that *Mars* is an allegory of a liaison of Isabella of York and John Holland (see **332**); Chaucer was too much a gentleman for such gossip and wrote instead a fanciful poem about planetary motions. Cowling notes that no liaison of Sir John Holland stains the good name of Isabella of York. It must be that Shirley misnamed the lady. Besides, 'If one thinks of the affair in terms of human life, would Chaucer have dared to make a jest of it? With Gaunt and Holland absent in Spain, would Edward Langley have exacted no retribution from Chaucer for such a reflection upon his honour and the honour of his wife? To me, the supposition that Chaucer intended to mock John Holland and the Duchess of York is incredible' (p 407). Perhaps the point is not to mock but to congratulate – to apologize for the sin. Shirley may be right in naming Holland. Cowling compares Mars' 'crueltee, and bost and tyrannye' with the acts of a gentleman 'almost capable of any crime,' several of which Cowling lists. But the woman must be Gaunt's second daughter Elizabeth, who had an affair with Holland, which was exposed just before Gaunt's departure for the second expedition to Castile in 1386. Elizabeth's betrothal to the Earl of Pembroke was annulled, and she was married to Holland to save her honour. Holland was appointed Constable of Gaunt's Spanish expedition and the pair sailed together for Corunna. If the circumstances of the poem are based on these events, then Phoebus would be Gaunt. Chaucer, recalling the conjunction of Mars and Venus in 1385, 'turned the romantic love of the daughter of his patron into something poetic, dignified, and apologetic, by the astronomical fancy with which he invested it. Possibly "the broche of Thebes" is a cryptic allusion to Eli*sebeth* of Pen*broche*. I imagine that the poem was written in 1386 as an apology for the match ... The "broche of Thebes" brought woe, but the cause was not the fault of the brooch (Elizabeth), but of its maker (Gaunt) and its "covetour" (Holland) (line 261). Chaucer in the last stanza urges pity, and begs his readers not to condemn' (p 409). *Venus* refers to the same marriage, which Shirley connected with Isabel of York also. But if he remembered wrong in the first instance, 'may he not have erred twice?' The Lady must be 'Elizabeth, Countess of Huntingdon, and the poem, intended to represent her feelings towards her husband ... Sir John Holland, afterwards Earl of Huntingdon' (p 409).

337 Dean, Nancy. 'Chaucer's *Complaint*, A Genre Descended from the *Heroides.*' *CL*, 19 (1967), 1–27.

'The Latin *planctus* is not the *fons et origo* of all "complaints," but the ancestor of the public lament; ... the personal love lament may be descended from Ovid's *Heroides*, those individual letters of complaint by

miserable heroines' (p 1). In the fourteenth century it is not a clearly
defined genre. To Deschamps the term 'seems to have referred to content, not form' (p 2). The term is not discussed in his *L'Art de Dictier; lai*
is the closest equivalent. *Compleynt* and *lai* merge as terms in Chaucer,
perhaps under the influence of Machaut. Dean differentiates between
salut, chanson, and *complaint.* 'Unlike Ovid in his writing of the Heroide-
an complaints, Chaucer could not count on his audience's knowledge of
the story; therefore he told it himself as he did in *Anelida* and *Mars.* But
he could learn many techniques to add depth, verisimilitude, wit, and
irony to his writing of "complaints" by observing Ovid's *Heroides'* (p 16).
(Eg, selecting an important moment from a well-known story and treat-
ing the heroic in a non-heroic fashion by slanting it towards the pathos
of the lover, as in *Mars.*) In *Mars* Chaucer uses a non-Christian context,
placing Mars within the known astrological situation in which Venus,
the planet, must be unfaithful to him. 'The astrology gives the wider
perspective of destiny to the Ovidian story which caused laughter in
heaven' (p 19). The main subject of the poem is not Mars or Venus but
the nature of love, 'turning by necessity in destined paths at destined
rates' (p 19). The poem is a *tour de force* in shifts of tone. In placing the
complaint within the narrative 'Chaucer does not choose the obvious
dramatic moment at which the two are startled by discovery; he elects to
tell the story through and then have Mars, who is made to appear foolish in Chaucer's account, give his "compleynt" after the events of the
story are concluded and Venus has left him. Mars' "compleynt" is not
for what he should complain, Venus' infidelity to him, but for her necessary departure. That is, Chaucer exploits the ironic possibilities as Ovid
did ... Chaucer's astonishing delicacy of treatment gains seriousness and
dignity for Mars at the end, despite his folly and his ignorance. Mars'
ambivalent situation is seen at the close as itself one of the "aventures"
of love' (p 20). Commenting on the intricacies of the poem (three
changes in narrators, two changes in rhyme scheme, four divisions of
poetic material), Dean suggests that Chaucer's purpose is 'to gain a combination of perspective and intensity of the moment' (p 20). The bird
sees the alternations of joy and woe in love; Mars shows the universality
of the principle. Dean discusses possible sources besides Ovid, namely
Statius. What is original in Chaucer is 'the *sustained* astrological treatment blended with human terms for wit and humour, and then the reversal, the serious treatment in human terms which extends the human
significance by the earlier astrological application' (p 23). 'For Chaucer
the "complaint" needed to include a convincing cause for lament, a cause
all men would grasp as "real," hence the biographical settings of the majority of his complaints' (p 24). Dean concludes with a detailed reading
of the comical progress of the complaint, the burlesque effects once the
sun enters the story, and the farce of Mars' ineptitude.

338 Donahue, J.J. *Chaucer's Lesser Poems*. 1974. See **21.**
Donahue lists four possible scandalous affairs which might have provoked the poem: John Holland and Isabel of York; John Holland and Elizabeth, daughter of Gaunt; John of Gaunt and Katharine Swynford; Thomas Holland and Joan of Kent. 'The piece has values which many
modern readers will not stay for' (p 162).

339 Emerson, O.F. 'Some Notes on Chaucer and Some Conjectures.' *PQ*, 2
(1923), 81–96. Reprinted in Emerson, *Chaucer Essays and Studies*. Cleve-
land: Western Reserve University Press, 1929, pp 378–404.
Note 2, on 'voide cours' in *Mars*, line 114: Skeat glosses *voide* as 'solitary'
(1, I, p 499); Manly says it is 'a technical phrase meaning that after
separating from conjunction, Venus passed through the rest of the sign
without coming into familiarity with any planet' (**358**, p 120.) Emerson
thinks both go too far in finding a special astrological sense for *voide*. Of
voide "sachant, fin, rusé" (ie, cunning, artful) would be a better gloss.
Such usage 'is not otherwise found in Chaucer, but in its origin is not an
unnatural development of *voide* "empty, vacant, vacated for the purpose
of eluding." Compare *avoid*, "make empty, shun, elude"; and *voidance* "act
of emptying," then "evasion, subterfuge," the latter older meanings'
(p 83).

340 Furnivall, F.J. *Trial-forewards to my parallel-text Edition of Chaucer's Minor
Poems*. Chaucer Society, 2nd Ser. no 6. London: N. Trübner, 1871.
Of nineteenth-century discussions of Chaucer's lyrics Furnivall's is
among the most important and is still cited by scholars. The opening
discussion considers the chronology of Chaucer's works, with special attention to the *Romaunt, Pite,* and *ABC*; Pt. 4, *Complaynt of Mars*, pp 78–92,
discusses Shirley's colophon and the affairs of Isabel of York. 'But people
were not of old so particular in love-matters as we are now, and we must
not judge Chaucer by our own modern standard for glorifying the adultery of his patron's sister-in-law with even more power than the memory
of that peerless patron's wife' (p 80). After a brief discussion of the astronomical matter in the poem Furnivall introduces Sandras' observations
on the amalgamation of *Venus* with *Mars* (*Etude sur Chaucer considéré
comme Imitateur des Trouvères*, Paris, 1859), to note his emphasis on Granson in *Venus* which must then extend also to *Mars*, thus bringing both
'into his wide drag-net of French imitations. Scratch a Russian, and you
find a Tartar, said Voltaire: Scratch Chaucer, and you find a Frenchman,
says M. Sandras. Well, well, it pleases him, and doesn't hurt us or our
bright old English soul' (p 91).

341 Galway, Margaret. 'Chaucer's Sovereign Lady.' 1938. See **101.**
Mars is 'in allegorical form' the story of the liaison between Thomas Holland (Mars) and Joan of Kent (Venus) before their official marriage, the
departure of Holland with Edward III (Phoebus) and the flight of Joan to

Salisbury (Cilenius). Shirley was close in his note on the poem but had the parties wrong (pp 183–4).

342 Gardner, John. *The Poetry of Chaucer.* 1977. See **103**.

The 'use of astrological phenomena for the plot of a love poem inevitably urged for the poet's immediate audience an ironic view of love,' which, for rational creatures, is more or less comic. But Chaucer goes beyond the easy joke as 'Mars nonetheless sees his way, at last – as any lover can – to rise, through love into freedom' (p 82). Gardner draws several comparisons from *Boece* to illustrate, in the *complaint* itself, Mars's progress as, in his suffering, he happens onto the fish (lover)-fisherman (God) metaphor 'and so unwittingly anticipates the idea of Christ as fisher of men ... Unaided by revelation Mars sees the Maker as cruel, not loving, and so inverts the scriptural signs, confounding the wages of joy and the wages of sorrow' (p 86). The brooch of Thebes functions as a kind of 'forbidden fruit.' Gardner cites passages from Hugh of St Victor and John Scotus Erigene to extend the traditional identification of woman and rubies. Mars perceives his fall but can only pray that other lovers share his suffering and hope for mercy from somewhere. 'On the pagan level, the ending offers very little hope ... Mars can only ask a general complaint. But Chaucer's audience could give Mars the name of the intercessor and comforter ... here as everywhere in Chaucer, the love-scheme and the Christian are parallel' (p 88). Mars's epithets praising Venus are those commonly ascribed to the Virgin. 'This is not to ignore the fact that the adaptation of church language to the religion of love was conventional. Yet what is involved in the *Complaint of Mars* is something new, the convention viewed from its last logical extremity' (p 89).

343 Griffin, R.M. *Chaucer's Lyrics.* 1970. See **18**.

Griffin uses *Mars* at the conclusion of his discussion of Chaucer's early lyrics to mark a transition from straightforward imitation of the French complaints to a challenging of the genre as the poet becomes more concerned with moral philosophy distinguished by technical virtuosity. *Mars* is the most commented on of Chaucer's lyrics, though more for its astronomy and possible treatment of court scandal than for its technique and main themes. Griffin emphasizes the poem's comic tone. 'The comedy has a serious purpose to point up the negative effect which the courtly relationship has had on Mars' (p 74). 'After *Mars,* which discredits the entire concept of the complaint, Chaucer wrote no more "serious" complaints' (pp 83–4). 'Chaucer's early lyrics utilize several styles and conventions (primarily courtly) to deal with profound and serious questions. In this sense, all point toward the moral lyrics of the middle period' (p 84).

344 Hammond, E.P. *Bibliographical Manual.* 1908. See **37.**
Lists mss and editions. In her discussion of title and authenticity Hammond gives the various titles by which the poem has been identified and transcribes Shirley's colophons and headings (pp 384–6).

345 Hultin, Neil C. 'Anti-Courtly Elements in Chaucer's *Complaint of Mars.'*
AnM, 9 (1968), 58–75.
'The ambiguity evident in so many of Chaucer's poems springs from his use of conventions which are enriched in such a way that they carry within them the seeds of their own denial' (p 58). Hultin compares the complexity of *Mars* to that of *T&C* – 'an amalgam of courtly poetry,' an aube, a romantic narrative of 'the lady taming the knight, transforming him into a paragon of courtly virtue,' a lover's complaint, a plea for pity and sympathy, all cast in the rubric of a Valentine poem (p 59). The birds seem reassuring to courtly tradition at the outset of the poem, but they reveal a 'hevy morowe' as the ensuing narrative calls into question courtly ideals. Though the birds welcome the sun and anticipate a 'lusty morwenynge' it is 'doubly ironic since Mars will have so little joy of his' (p 62). Hultin discusses mythological antecedents of the brooch of Thebes and Chaucer's use of it. 'Mars has unwittingly revealed to us the destructive nature of the affair, through his reference to an object which gains existence only because of his determined will to remain faithful to Venus' (p 66). That determination guarantees his destruction. In discussing questions of choice and determinism in the poem Hultin links the Brooch and the planetary movements to stress the consequence of the love upon others only tangentially involved. The astrology is not of course a determining force but one which predisposes an individual to certain acts and moods. Mars remains deceived, but in view of astrological discussions by Augustine and Aquinas, biblical material on light-darkness, and traditions surrounding the Brooch of Thebes 'it is unlikely that [Chaucer's audience] did so' (p 74). 'We cannot close our eyes to the implications of the Brooch of Thebes, and it is insufficient to say that it finds its place in the poem simply because it is an object which attracts and destroys' (p 74). Hultin agrees with Stillwell **369**: the poem admonishes us to beware.

346 Kean, Patricia. *Chaucer and the Making of English Poetry.* 1972. See **114.**
In *Mars* Chaucer combines all his interests in philosophical, earthly, and courtly love in a way that is 'technically accomplished' (I, p 43). Though not great, 'it is an urbane poem and one in which, even if Chaucer's genius is manifestly not at full stretch, he is yet at ease with his audience' (I, p 44). Such poems are 'above all, social' (I, p 45).

347 Kellogg, Alfred L. *Chaucer, Langland, Arthur: Essays in Middle English Literature.* New Brunswick: Rutgers University Press, 1972.

Ch 8, 'Chaucer's St Valentine: A Conjecture,' pp 108–45, attempts to trace the development of the legend of a remote saint 'whose day of decapitation was rather curiously judged in the fourteenth century and later to be an appropriate occasion for the writing of love poems and comparable amatory observances' (p 108). Kellogg suggests it all starts with fertility rites of the Lupercalia (Feb. 14), probably the oldest of Rome's festivals. In Christian times the rites were converted to the Feast of the Presentation which was coalesced with a feast of the Purification of Mary and a Feast of Lights (a Candlemas Day). In the twelfth century St Valentine stories devolved, in which the figure took on new dimensions of a fertility saint or nature saint and fit into the 'pattern of the fertility god with considerable exactness' (eg, he inhibits rodents, drought, and plague and thereby 'frees nature to exert her powers' [p 123]). There exists no literary record of St Valentine between Baudri de Bourgueil (12th century) and Oton de Grandson (14th). 'What happened or did not happen to St Valentine is simply unknown' (pp 123–4). But he emerges as a fully developed personage whom no poet has to explain, a patron saint of mannered and erotic love, but with a 'natural fertility adjunct' (p 124) associated with both Feb. 14 and the songbirds of May. In Chaucer's three uses of the day (*CD*, *Mars*, and *PF*), St Valentine is associated with verdant nature and birds. This is not true of Grandson, where six of eight instances are one form or another of usual complaint. Kellogg discusses the relationship between Chaucer's Valentine poems and Grandson's *Songe St Valentin*, an indebtedness 'limited to what one might call the mechanical arts'; Chaucer links Valentine with nature 'and makes him again the natural saint he must have been' (p 136).

348 Kelly, Henry Ansgar. 'The Genoese Saint Valentine and Chaucer's Third of May.' *Chaucer Newsletter*, 1 (Summer, 1979), 6–10.

Kelly finds Kellogg's hypothesis (**347**) unsuccessful: 'The postulated connections range in weakness from the impossible (an early feast of the Purification celebrated in the West on February 14) to the improbable (Saint Valentine of Jumièges considered as a fertility figure) and are furthermore widely separated by missing links' (p 7). That Chaucer's Valentine poems are all set in late spring suggests that Chaucer didn't know a St Valentine of Feb. 14. Perhaps on a visit to Genoa he learned of St Valentine of Genoa, whose feast day commemorates his death on May 3. Of the three great poets first to mention Valentine's day (Chaucer, Grandson, and Gower), perhaps Chaucer was the very first. His 'fancy was touched by hearing of a holiday in Genoa at the beginning of May honoring an unfamiliar saint' (p 8). He picks up the day in his May 3 poems, which are also thus Valentine's Day poems. 'If, then, it was Chaucer who first introduced the literary world to St Valentine as a springtime matchmaker, it must be concluded that the association of the February St Valentine with the mating process is a later development' (p 9). Kelly notes how noncommittal Grandson and Gower are about the precise season. Clanvowe suggests March. 'My guess is that Clanvowe, like Grandson and Gower, did not know when Saint Valentine's Day fell' (p 9). Other devotees of St Valentine, more familiar with the Roman calendar set the feast on Feb. 14, beginning in 1400 with the court-of-love hoax of Queen Isabel in France, who was doubtless inspired by Grandson's poems. The tradition was thus speedily established.

349 Laird, Edgar S. 'Astrology and Irony in Chaucer's *Complaint of Mars.*' *ChauR*, 6 (1972), 229–31.

The narrative is conducted to indicate 'that Venus becomes Mercury's mistress' (p 229). When Venus enters Mercury's house that aspect must be sextile. 'The typically Chaucerian neatness of the arrangement is satisfying, and perhaps more important, its precision and astronomical accuracy indicate how carefully and deliberately Chaucer arranged his sextile aspect' (p 230). According to Trin. Coll. Cambridge ms R.15.18, III, ff 26–9, a discussion which is a continuation of Chaucer's *Astrolabe*, *sextile* accords with 'privy and secret love.' Thus it is 'exactly suitable for denoting a clandestine relationship between Venus and Mercury' (p 231). The planets in *Mars* enact the myth in a perpetual pattern suggesting 'an eternal and essential model of love, or at least of a certain type of love. Mars and Venus, with all their elaborate mythical and astrological associations, relate, in a richly complicated way, Knighthood to Ladyhood ... They are the general forms of such particular lovers as Troilus and Criseyde. It is therefore important to read the implications of the sextile aspect and note that the *Complaint of Mars*, like *Troilus and Criseyde*, includes betrayal among the conventional pains of love' (p 231).

350 — 'Chaucer's *Complaint of Mars*, line 145: "Venus valaunse"' *PQ* 51 (1972), 486–9.

'Valaunse' is not known to occur elsewhere in English. Skeat 1, I, pp 501–2, glossed it as *avalance* (a descent or lowering, which corresponds to *occasus*) or as OF *faillance* (a failure or defection, which corresponds to *detrimentum*). Laird explains that both Skeat's glosses are right. Venus has two houses: Taurus, where Mars is, and Aries, where Mercury is. The opposite house is called its 'determent' or 'harming.' To say that Mercury is in 'Venus valaunse,' would seem to be 'tantamount to saying he is in Venus' "determent" or "harmynge"' (p 487). The house in which the influence was greatest was called 'exaltacioun' or 'reysunge' and as long as the terms were taken literally the opposite sign was called 'fallynge.' (Cf *WBT*, III.702, 705). Alchabitius' *Isagoge in Astrolabum*, which Skeat cites for both terms, was translated into English in the fourteenth century. The translator insists that 'ther is a difference bitwixe fallinge and determent or harmynge. For determent is in the opposite of the house; fallinge, sothly, is opposite of exaltacion.' He goes on to point out that 'the mansiouns [ie, houses] beth seide the strengthe ... but not the glorie; for glorie perteyneth to honour and exaltacioun to fame, but strengthe to vigour & existence' (Trin. Coll. Cambridge ms 0.5.26, f 2v.). In this respect *valaunse* would equate with *faillance* (failure, defection, a want or lack, a non-being). 'It would be characteristic of Chaucer to use such a term with such a meaning out of sheer orderliness: *detrimentum*, *determent*, and *harmynge* are symmetrically opposed to *hous* only in the precise, specialized, perhaps even distorted sense which I suppose "valaunse" to specify' (p 489).

351 Langhans, Viktor. *Untersuchungen zu Chaucer.* 1918. See **180**. Pp 231–52. Langhans objects to attempts to allegorize *Mars*, though he thinks it has a universal application for any lover missing his Venus. The poem may even reflect Chaucer's own hopeless love for an unattainable lady, though efforts to identify her are foolish. Chaucer draws on the aubade tradition to make a detailed narrative from a single dawn song, a sort of Valentine joke decorated with astronomical and mythological lore. Langhans also discusses *Venus* and *Fortune* in this chapter, commenting on Graunson's relationship to the English court, the difficulty for Chaucer of rhyming in English, and his formal experiments in these two poems (pp 246–7). He reviews arguments on the reliability of Shirley's linking of *Mars* and *Venus* and would date composition of *Mars* ca 1375, and *Venus,* ca 1393.

352 — 'Zu Chaucers Traumgedichten.' *Anglia,* 51 (1927), 323–53. Langhans challenges Shirley's reference to a family affair of Gaunt's household to conclude: 'Die Klage des Mars ist ein lachendes Kind einer künstlerischen Laune des Dichters, ein gemütlicher und geistreicher, mythologisch und astronomisch aufgeputzter Valentinscherz' (p 341).

353 Lawlor, John. 'The Earlier Poems.' 1966. See **251**. In *Mars* the "I" of the narrator plays a negligible part – a Chaucer 'without the innumerable touches of a dramatised narrator, especially that dexterity of appearing and disappearing within and around the margin of the story' (pp 61–2). As an 'extended example of dramatic writing,' *Mars* is 'an experiment in one mode of tragic utterance' (p 63). Here for once Chaucer is 'adorning an admired species of poetry "with ful devout courage"' (p 62). 'Chaucer's is an art which springs from direct confrontation of a small audience, with whom his relationship is that of a licensed entertainer. His gifts are those proper to a training in courts – an unerring eye for pretence, for an attempt "to been estatlich of manere"' (pp 62–3).

354 Legouis, E. *Geoffrey Chaucer*. 1913. See **117**.

Legouis admires the opening line of *Mars*: 'This is a really charming dawn song. But the skylark soon comes back to earth, and the jog-trot of prose follows closely on the flight of song' (p 66).

355 Lewis, C.S. *Allegory of Love*. 1936. See **118**.

'The astronomical allusions are, I confess, too hard for me: the topical allegory is now difficult to recover and hardly worth recovering. The relation of mistress and lover in what was then conceived to be its normal or healthy condition is well described in the lines "And thus she brydeleth him in her manere / With nothing but with scourging of hir chere"' (p 170). But an opposite view is also hinted at with lines 218 ff which contrast Divine and earthly love, 'apparently to the advantage of the former. But we are now prepared for such losses of confidence at the end, or even in the midst, of an amorous poem' (p 170).

356 Lowes, John Livingston. 'Chaucer and Dante's *Convivio*.' *MP*, 13 (1915), 19–33.

Lowes traces *Mars* lines 164–6 ('Alas! that I was wroght, / And for certeyn effectes hider broght / Be him that lordeth ech intelligence') to 'the most intricate and baffling section of the *Convivio* ... Mars complains as one of the Intelligences he was created by his lord ... to fulfil the very end of his existence, which end was love. He *has* loved – has given to his lady his true service and his thought, and his love has ended in "misaventure." The cause of his complaint ... lies therefore deep enough. The fact that Dante's whole doctrine of the Intelligences is implicit in two lines is evidence again of Chaucer's power of assimilation' (pp 30–2). What Chaucer does not use of that doctrine is equally striking (p 33).

357 McCall, John P. *Chaucer Among the Gods*. 1979. See **257**.

'Much of the language and action of his *Complaint of Mars* suggest that Chaucer did in fact experiment with astronomy and myth ... and that he was aware of numerous parallels between Mars and Troilus, Venus and Criseyde. But apparently this sort of broad, mythical analogizing or "allegorizing" did not really interest him when he wrote the *Troilus*' (p 36). 'Chaucer's comic divinities live within an earthly range that extends from body humour and bourgeois bathos to mock epic and parody. They are reduced to everyday ordinariness or they are inflated into grand grotesques' (p 131). 'In truth, when Geoffrey Chaucer strolled among the gods he walked with both feet on the ground' (p 158).

358 Manly, J.M. 'On the Date and Interpretation of Chaucer's *Complaint of Mars*.' *Harvard Studies and Notes in Philology and Literature*, 5 (1896), 107–26.

'The poem is so packed with astrological allusions and conforms so closely to astronomical relations and movements, that it can hardly be regarded as anything else than a mere exercise in ingenuity in describing a

supposed astronomical event in terms of human action and emotion ...
Whether there may lie behind the poem some hidden ligature connect-
ing it with an amour of John Holand and Isabel Langley, can perhaps
never be definitely decided. But we know how easily the existence of
this poem and the reputation of Isabel for lightness would suggest the
connection of the two; gossip was probably governed by the same laws
that govern it to-day' (p 124–5). Manly thinks it would be, 'to say the
least, hazardous' to try to date the poem on the basis of its astronomical
data (p 113).

359 Merrill, Rodney. 'Chaucer's *Broche of Thebes:* The Unity of *The Complaint
of Mars* and *The Complaint of Venus.' Literary Monographs*, 5 (1973), 3–61.
Merrill attempts to show that *Mars* and *Venus*, though not initially
planned together, were designed as a sequence which 'yields to no other
of Chaucer's in subtlety, and which exceeds many in concentration' (p 3).
The completed poem includes the bird's proem, the narrative of Mars,
the complaint of Mars, the complaint of Venus, and the Lenvoys (p 15).
The title of the completed work should be 'The Brooch of Thebes.' Ms
evidence supports this interpretation; mss which separate them or include them alone are late and not good. Shirley's rubrics link them with
paired titles. 'To suppose them originally separate is to postulate at least
two copies of the originally distinct complaints which, however differing
in other respects, agree in viewing them as a sequence' (p 6). In short,
'There is not one iota of evidence in the manuscript tradition which
would justify separating the poems' (p 7). When read together they reveal a characteristically medieval kind of unity: 'Medieval writers could
entertain a liberal notion of a "unified" structure, just as medieval ma-
sons were quite ready to adapt the design of a single cathedral to changing needs and stylistic expectations' (p 7). Merrill considers but rejects
readings of the poems as historical allegory. Cowling's notion (**336**) that
the poem 'dignifies' scandal in Gaunt's household is unsound. 'Even a
superficial glance at the poem would show how far from dignified the
fiction is' (p 8). Gaunt could hardly be happy to see his daughter in the
title role; and if the poem is an exposé, 'the ferocious Holande would
certainly have inspired as much fear as York' (p 8). 'What seems more
likely is that Chaucer could expect his audience to enjoy a well-contrived
joke ... The poet's urbane sense of the ludicrous never allows him to forget the universal implications of his fictions; even particular objects of
wit can feel the sympathy in his portrayals of them' (pp 8–9). Merrill
thinks *Mars* was composed first. Then *Venus* was added later as a
response to Graunson's writing on behalf of Isabel of York. Chaucer a-
dapts the first, fourth, and fifth of Grandson's balades as a complaint to
be put in the mouth of the lady herself. For initiates, he adds the allusion to Grandson in L'envoy, pretending to be following the French poet

'word by word,' though he is not, having even changed the sex of the persona. The title *Broche of Thebes* (cf, rubrics and Lydgate's reference by that title) is justified precisely because it at first seems inappropriate. The poem is morally complex: 'Chaucer wants not merely to condemn foolish love but to show how it drives the lover himself – even the pagan Mars or Venus – to discover the central problems of worldly existence ... The astronomical conjunction ... is an economical and vivid way of representing the irresistible force of sexual feeling which is a central theme of medieval love poetry; against it may be seen the complexity of psychological response and moral evaluation' (p 20). There is also the complexity of the court situation. 'Chaucer has created an image of Boethian Fate' (p 21). The poem begins in a high style: 'The narrator of this mock epic believes in himself and his task; yet by his attempt to raise and dignify the episode, he unwittingly points out to us its essential comedy' (p 22). The 'arming of the hero' at the moment of crisis is 'not only fruitless, it's a hindrance'; Merrill argues that Venus does not take up with Mercury, however; rather Mercury provides needed friendship and consolation, but 'not of passion' (pp 191–2, n 28). In Venus' complaint, though she attempts to justify herself according to the standard she imputes to the world at large, as she meditates on her conduct and desires, the poem is not in fact a great 'penaunce,' but the reverse, 'a superabundant joy in literary creation' (p 24). Groaning about 'skarsete of rym,' Chaucer is 'clearly having a little joke at the expense of this standard complaint' (p 24); his extreme self-consciousness is like that of the birds and the lovers, and it reminds us of the dazzling artifice of the poem's multiple structures, varying stanza forms, tonal range, and intricate movements between rapid action and private meditation. Merrill suggests numerical relationships between parts, comments on the lack of transition between poems (which amounts to a confrontational device), and compares the overall poem to a jewel with many faces expressing unity in diversity. Three is a key number and, deep beneath the surface, Merrill sees hints of divine love beyond the comprehension of the participants (p 29). Ch 4, 'The Sentence: "The Complaint of Mars",' pp 30–42, explores religious analogues behind allusions in the poem which reveal a Christian humanism that transcends the bleak choices between asceticism and damnation. Mars, even in his attempt to alleviate the love pain with his rhetoric, raises the question of God's responsibility (p 38), though questions of determinism and free choice are not resolved until *Venus*. The Broche is a symbol of 'any object of human desire,' 'the world itself as it is present to man's cupidity' (p 40). Mars echoes supplications to the Virgin, though he does not perceive what he is doing. 'It is important to see how Mars' own ignorance of this high application is functional. His emotional need, combined with his rhetorical appeal for justification ... has caused him to project a lady whose perfections are contradicted even by his own deepest sense of her, to say nothing of the "objective" truths of her mythical capriciousness and cruelty. We see arising from within the depths of a foolish lover's ignorance those very needs which can only be satisfied by the recognition, based on faith, that there is indeed a Lady who is so gentle, so humble, so honorable, and at the same time so powerful in doing "socour" to the distressed mortals' (p 42). In the last chapter Merrill reads Venus' praises of love also in a higher way, as a parody of Christian love. 'In the very pretense that her decision to love is a matter of free choice, Venus shows that profound desire for freedom which is only realized by the Christian's decision to love God. Thus the two ways of reading the poem are dynamically related, not mutually exclusive' (pp 59–60). Venus' very insecurity in love demonstrates the operations of the Broche of Thebes which 'raises expectations of comfort and happiness only to render them impossible by the very fact of being possessed ... The final function of the Broche is to raise our attention to its "worcher"' (p 60).

360 North, John D. 'Kalenderes Enlumyned Ben They.' *RES*, 20 (1969), 137–42. According to astronomical references there are two dates in the poem: Feb. 14 (St Valentine's Day) and April 12. Chaucer's astrological language and determinations are so precise as to restrict the year to April 12, 1385–Feb. 14, 1386. 'We are probably ... not far off the truth if we take 1386 as the year of composition ... taking the song as analogous to the act of authorship' (p 142).

361 Norton-Smith, John. *Geoffrey Chaucer*. London: Routledge and Kegan Paul, 1974.
'There is nothing quite like the *Complaint of Mars* in the Middle Ages in either Latin or the vernacular. Yet, in its own nature it displays typical Chaucerian literary characteristics: complexity of construction, amalgamization of hitherto unrelated material, humanist wit, Ovidian aetiological fabulizing, and a penetrating philosophical interest in the perplexities (and eventual heartache) of human love' (p 23). Smith admonishes critics to view Shirley's rubric and colophon as separate statements, the one a straightforward assertion, which 'may be perfectly correct,' namely that *Mars* was composed at the authoritative request of John of Gaunt; but the other, the colophon, 'amounts to mere additional gossip – "some men sayne" ... There is no need to go further in the constructing of fantasies out of the colophon' (p 24). *Mars* is closely tied to *T&C* – 'a miniature *Troilus*' (p 28) – embodying 'a poetical application of astronomy to an aetiological myth in an attempt to establish an archetypal plot or pattern of tragic love, a complex yet compressed *exemplum* of doomed, unfortunate *fine amour*' (p 28). Smith contrasts the tone and effect of *Mars* with Shakespeare's *Venus and Adonis* (p 29). 'The idea of adopting Statius'

description of the *monile Harmoniae* (*Thebaid*, II, 266ff) for the purpose of providing an interpretative, philosophically-oriented conceit, is as poetically original as Chaucer's initial decision to incorporate and elaborate the astrological plot sequence' (p 32). What had been a simple passage of *amplificatio* in Statius, Chaucer turns into a *significatio* (pp 32–3). The whole poem exhibits a 'typically undogmatic Chaucerian interest in stellar determinism and free will.' Mars and Venus are presented as having free will and predestined actions (p 34).

361a Oruch, Jack B. 'St Valentine, Chaucer, and Spring in February.' *Speculum*, 56 (1981), 534–65.

Oruch identifies 'pertinent notices of Valentine in literature and church documents from the fourth to the sixteenth centuries' to suggest 'a rationale for the inclusion of Valentine in the poetry of love and spring' (p 535). Oruch argues that Kellogg's linking of the Lupercalia, Valentine, and Chaucer 'is based upon faulty assumptions and misunderstood data' (p 540), particularly in the interpretation of Baudri de Bourgueil. Oruch notes that Hyde Abbey (New Minster) claimed the head of St Valentine among its relics; that monastery in Chaucer's day owned the Tabard Inn in Southwark (p 544). However, the association of St Valentine with spring, birds, and lovers lies outside saints legends and pious literature. The key lies in early calenders, natural history, and popular romance (p 549), wherein February is 'firmly established as a spring month' and the time of mating birds and natural fertility, the sowing of hardy vegetables, and of lenten love longing. Links between Valentine and fertility and fertility celebrations probably existed in folklore prior to its appearance in Chaucer, Granson, Clanvowe, and Gower (p 557). Oruch agrees with Brewer (Ed., *Parlement*, pp 6, 131) that Granson is likely to have imitated Chaucer (pp 557–8). 'At the time of Chaucer's death in 1400 the transformation of Valentine into an auxiliary or parallel to Cupid as sponsor of lovers was well under way. In that year the *Cour amoreuse* was formed in Paris on February 14 with a membership of six hundred men, including King Charles VI and most of the Burgundian faction at court; it met monthly to foster music and poetry and to hear "cases" relating to love' (p 558). Other societies followed. The English Valentine poems derive from Chaucer (pp 559–61). 'Chaucer's innovation in setting the occasion of the *Parlement* and *Mars* ... was to shift the time of the typical spring poem back from the familiar, even commonplace April and May to mid-February, a choice which throws into sharper relief the contrasts between the two seasons and hence also between the lover's emotion of warm love and his cold comfort' (p 564). Chaucer is 'the original mythmaker in this instance' (p 565).

362 Owen, Charles A., Jr. 'The Problem of Free Will in Chaucer's Narratives.' *PQ*, 46 (1967), 433–56.

Owen sees a development from concern with philosophical problems in Chaucer's earlier works to a love of character in the later ones, though throughout his career Chaucer uses similar Boethian matter to create an illusion of reality. Owen traces the development from *Mars, KnT,* and *T&C,* to *CT.* In *Mars* love is a compulsion visited on creatures by the Creator, but yielding fitful satisfaction because of overwhelming forces both external and internal arrayed against it. 'Venus, through no will of her own, must flee twice as fast as her lover, and Mars can don his mighty armor and threateningly shake his spear, all to no avail in Taurus. The two, inexorably separated by their own predetermined movements, can only lament their plight and await a more fortunate disposition of the spheres' (p 434). 'In outline the story of Mars and Venus resembles *Troilus and Criseyde*. The transformation of the lovers through love, their brief enjoyment of one another, and their separation and grief occur in both works. The *Mars* lacks the betrayal and any mention of a Creator "who will falsen no wight"; it lacks the detail of event and speech and motive that make the characters vividly alive for the reader; it lacks the proportions that make both love and its loss so poignant. What the *Mars* does is to throw into abstract relief the haplessness and helplessness of its characters. They have no choice but to fall in love and, as the bird puts it in his imperative, "paciently taketh your aventure." Their will plays no part in their separation. They become exemplary figures in a mechanical universe, moved hither and yon by alien forces, the more unhappy for the awareness of their plight. The combination of astrology and myth results in Chaucer's most deterministic poem' (p 435).

363 Piaget, Arthur. 'La Cour Amoureuse dit de Charles VI.' *Romania,* 20 (1891), 418–54.

Piaget argues that by 1400 there was a social organization publicly celebrating St Valentine's Day in France.

364 Robbins, R.H. *Companion to Chaucer Studies.* 1968/1979. See **136**.

Robbins praises and draws upon Clemen **334** and Stillwell **369**, to conclude: '*The Complaint of Mars* treats realistically a serious problem: what happens to illicit lovers who are caught in the act? When characterization becomes more complex, frame more elaborate, problems more immediate, then the complaint breaks down. The way out leads to *Troilus and Criseyde*' (p 324/391).

365 Root, R.K. *The Poetry of Chaucer.* 1900/1922. See **140**.

Mars is 'a conventional poem, supposed to be sung by a bird on St Valentine's Day, in which mythology and astronomy are curiously blent together to the greater glory of illicit love ... The *Complaint* has little claim to attention save for the fact that a somewhat difficult 9-line stanza is handled with a good deal of skill' (p 63).

366 Saintsbury, G. *History of English Prosody*. 1906. See **72**.

Saintsbury notes metrical experimentation in *Mars*, especially the prominent use of the stopped final stanzaic couplets and 'ample exercise in enjambment' (I, p 152).

367 Saville, Jonathan. *The Medieval Erotic Alba: Structure as Meaning*. 1972. See **141a**.

Saville gives some consideration to the influence of the alba on Chaucer, especially in *T&C* and *ReeveT*, but also in the story of the Brooch of Thebes and *Mars*, 'a rumination on time and love closely connected to the themes of the *alba*' (p 238).

368 Skeat, W.W. *Oxford Chaucer*. 1894/1899. See **1**.

Skeat would date *Mars* ca 1374 on the basis of its alleged connection with Isabel of York. 'It is somewhat curious that the Princess Isabel, in a will made twelve years before her death, and dated Dec. 6, 1382, left, amongst other legacies, "to the Duke of Lancaster, a *Tablet of Jasper which the King of Armonie gave her*" [cf Furnivall **340**, p 82)]. Here *Armonie* means, of course, Armenia; but it is also suggestive of *Harmonia*, the name of the first owner of the brooch of Thebes. It seems just possible that the brooch of Thebes was intended to refer to this tablet of jasper, which was doubtless of considerable value and may have been talked about as being a curiosity' (I, p 66). Skeat's edition gives titles to each of the balades in the compleynt itself: after the Proem, 1) Devotion; 2) A Lady in fear and woe; 3) Instability of Happiness; 4) The Brooch of Thebes; 5) An appeal for sympathy (I, pp 323–34).

369 Stillwell, Gardiner. 'Convention and Individuality in Chaucer's *Complaint of Mars*.' *PQ*, 35 (1956), 69–89.

Stillwell considers the poem in relation to the literary types and conventions with which it has affinities – 'Ovid moralized and astrologized, the aubade, the Valentine-poem, the lover's complaint, and themes of courtly love' (p 69). From this background emerges a highly original poem, 'a work deliberately and amusingly atypical in its treatment of conventions' (p 69). Much of the reader's pleasure lies in the contrast between 'the conventional gaiety and grace of the first three stanzas or so and the lively realities that follow' (p 71). It would seem that if the lovers follow the advice given in the Proem they are headed for woe. 'Chaucer's fun is that of telling lovers exactly the opposite of what they ought to be told or hope to be told on St Valentine's Day' (p 72). In this poem everything is topsy-turvy. 'The regrets expressed in an aube or aubade should be sung or spoken at the first signs of approaching dawn, shortly before the lover makes his getaway, not after he has been caught' (p 73). The aubade is supposed to scold; but here the sun really is the enemy. 'Mars is almost roasted to death, and has reason to bewail the influence of Phoebus' (p 74). Stillwell contrasts Chaucer's treatment of the story with the *Ovide Moralisé*: 'All in all, the *Ovide* gave Chaucer relatively little for *Mars* – not much more, if anything, than the idea for the combination mythology-astrology-generalization' (pp 76–7). The Valentine matter in *Mars* is markedly different from the Valentine matter in Gower and Graunson. 'Chaucer seems to say, "Ye lovers, take note." Even your revered goddess is governed by a force over which she has no control. Knights, observe how helpless in this situation is Mars, the pattern of your hardihood' (p 82). When the god and goddess meet, "Ther is no more, but unto bed thei go": 'Chaucer knew that this line was prosaically and inappropriately factual ... We have come down from high romance'; Mars, upon the arrival of Phoebus, is 'no more effective than Sir Thopas before Sir Elephant' (p 83). 'In the Complaint itself, Chaucer achieves a climax of increasing originality and wit, of increasing breadth of generalization, of increasing directness in addressing his audience' (p 85). 'To his Valentine's Day audience, then, the unpredictable Chaucer expresses an attitude toward young lovers very much like that of the *Knight's Tale* or the *Troilus* ... This attitude Chaucer expresses with remarkable felicity' (pp 88–9).

370 Storm, Melvin G., Jr. 'Chaucer's Poetic Treatment of the Figure of Mars.' *DAI*, 34 (1973), University of Illinois dissertation, 1972. 742A.
Storm discusses the two interpretative traditions of the Mars-Venus adultery – the one demonstrating the power of love to overcome violence, cruelty and war, and the other representing the debilitating effect of lust upon manly strength and virtue. Chaucer draws chiefly upon the latter when he deals with martial figures in his poetry.

371 — 'The Mythological Tradition in Chaucer's *Complaint of Mars*.' *PQ*, 57 (1978), 323–35.
'The Complaint of Mars is typical of a larger pattern in Chaucer's works, where we discover that the skills and strengths of warfare do not translate well to the Ovidian field of amorous combat' (p 327). The war god making love songs is like one 'using a handbook, checking the definition of his form and laboring to remain true to it' (p 328); Mars tries to show a lover's skill by following a conventional poetic form, but is not fully successful in doing even that (p 329). Ignorant of Venus' new situation he bears the marks of the fatal pattern of other warrior lovers like Hercules and Samson who, weakened by love, fall into bondage and become powerless. The oblique reminder of Harmonia suggests ultimate misfortune in the outcome. *Mars* is more fatalistic than *T&C*.

372 Williams, George. 'What is the Meaning of Chaucer's *Complaint of Mars?*' *JEGP*, 57 (1958), 167–76.

Williams works from the premise that many clues to the poet's private life may be found in his poetry, especially in a poem like *Mars*.

Chaucer's Mars, who is in 'the thridde hevenes lord' (line 29), suggests to Williams John of Gaunt who was Edward III's third son, third in succession to the throne, the third most powerful man in England, and the third most celebrated military figure in the realm. This 'thirdness' existed for John up until the death of the Black Prince on June 8, 1376. He was truly 'by desert' and 'by hevenysh revolucion' the 'thridde hevenes lord' (p 168). If Gaunt is Mars, then Katharine Swynford must be Venus; the actual complaint is 'a plea for tolerance of Mars' illicit love that has been harshly rebuked' (p 169). John, who lived with Katharine nearly thirty years and eventually married her, must really have loved her and must have been hurt by the vilification to which he and she were subjected by the court. Perhaps Shirley's statement that the poem was written at Gaunt's request is 'correct, after all' (p 170). Cilenio's Tower, where Venus hides, is Chaucer's house. Cilenio (Mercury) equates with eloquence and commerce, which is apt for the poet and controller of customs. She hides in a dark smoky cave 'two pas within the yate.' Such a cellar was to be found at Aldgate and is mentioned in Chaucer's lease (p 171). There is no direct evidence of such a visit by Katharine, of course, but she may well have had to hide out. 12 April 1377, is a likely date. Chaucer had just returned from a mission to Flanders (cf Mercury 'rydinge in his chevache'). 12 April 1376, is also a possibility, just prior to the assembling of the Good Parliament which attacked Gaunt. It is possible that, with Gaunt 'the most unpopular man in England at that time,' John and Katharine had to separate. William Courtenay, Bishop of London, was the principal enemy (the Phoebus); his arms were three balls – 'firy torches red' (lines 83, 91), with a pun on *torche* and *torteau* (disk). Venus 'rysen among yon rowes rede' might be a pun on Roet's red (nb, the three wheels on the Roet arms). She is aptly labeled 'queen' since she had born John two children. 'All this ... is highly speculative and conjectural. But, after nearly six hundred years, speculation and conjecture must play a major role in all Chaucerian scholarship' (p 176).

373 — *A New View of Chaucer*. 1965. See **275**.

Ch 3, 'What is the *Complaint of Mars?*,' pp 56–65, is an adaptation of **372**. Williams thinks that the most significant thing about his speculation is that it holds so consistently together many details that form the pattern and also illuminates the poem as a whole. It makes possible an account of some of Chaucer's personal relationships and offers a picture of an intensely interesting moment in the lives of three great personages (p 65).

See John Gardner **171** on Williams' equations of Mars (Gaunt), Venus (Katharine), Mercury (Geoffrey): 'Williams' theory is pretty crazy. What poet in his right mind would compliment his friend by reminding him of the time "you'd've had it old boy, if it wasn't for you-know-who!"' (p 353, n 10).

374 Wise, Boyd Ashby. *The Influence of Statius upon Chaucer.* 1911. See **278**. Wise notes that 'the monile Harmoniae' (Brooche of Thebes) comes from Statius (pp 42–4).

375 Wood, Chauncey. *Chaucer and the Country of the Stars: Poetic Uses of Astrological Imagery.* Princeton: Princeton University Press, 1970. Pp 103–60. After raising logical objections to readings of historical allegory into *Mars*, Wood argues that the poem takes 'a conventional attitude toward a standard theme with astrological details that ... echo the customary attitudes toward the events' (p 108). He reviews versions of the Mars-Venus story in Western literature (pp 108–15), from Homer and Ovid to Plutarch, Statius, and the Vatican mythographers, to conclude that *Mars* is 'modelled after a humorous Ovidian story, and the sub-theme of Mars' change from warrior to lover, effected by Venus, is put to comic, not philosophical use' (p 114). Although Chaucer took the basic elements of the story from Ovid, 'he cast them in a significant astrological form that is not classical' (p 115). Astrological commentaries on the conjunction of the two planets suggest adultery and lechery, and support the view that Chaucer is satirizing 'those love relationships in which men subject themselves to women' (p 115). 'From its classical background Chaucer's audience would expect the story to be funny; from its astological nature, to be unfortunate' (p 120). Aided by various Ovidian mythographers Wood discusses in detail the iconography of the Fairfax illumination of the lovers (pp 133–41). Mars is 'a poem showing the penalties of the wrong kind of loving' (p 141). Comparisons with Boethius point up the ironies of Mars' 'determined' lot (pp 155–8). At the end of the poem 'compassion and pity are very much in order' for the complaining Mars, but 'not as Mars thinks, for his woe, but rather for his unreasonableness ... Chaucer has been concerned with proper and improper love throughout ... What is remarkable is not the subject, but the dazzling execution of it' (p 160).

The Complaint of Venus

See also **332, 336, 340, 351.**

376 Braddy, Haldeen. 'Sir Oton de Graunson – "Flour of Hem that Make in Fraunce".' *SP*, 35 (1938), 10–24.

The influence of Graunson's poetry was widespread in his own time in Spain, Portugal, Prussia, Italy, and England, as well as France and his native Savoy. He served under Gaunt in England, Spain and Portugal and was well known personally in the English court. 'No other French poet was nearly so well known in England ... To justify Chaucer's estimate, one need only consider Oton's contemporary reputation. Unique as the appraisal of the works of a personal friend, Chaucer's description accords closely with popular opinion; for in the fourteenth century there was ample justification for calling Sir Oton de Graunson the "flour of hem that make in Fraunce"' (p 24). That he is now not highly regarded is due to the changing of poetic vogues. 'He studied assiduously the practices of the authors of the *Roman de la Rose* and could not free himself from the traditions which almost suffocated even Machaut ... The blemishes of his verse are the mistakes of the age' (p 22).

377 — 'Chaucer and Graunson: The Valentine Tradition.' *PMLA*, 54 (1939), 359–68.

The Valentine tradition mentioned in *PF* and *Mars* is akin to the sequence of Valentine poems by Graunson 'who seems to have been the first to popularize this type of verse in fourteenth-century England' (p 359). Apparently the Valentine poems served personal goals. Braddy discusses Graunson's attachments to Gaunt's household and Isabel of York; also he stresses the importance of Shirley's testimony on Graunson's links with Chaucer and comments on the literary circle of a later generation in which Shirley moved (Suffolk and Orkens). 'We seem to have both striking external and internal evidence that *The Complaint of Venus* was undertaken at the request of Isabel, Duchess of York' (p 367).

378 — *Chaucer and the French Poet Graunson*. 1947. See **84.**

Ch I, ' ... flour of hem that make in Fraunce' draws upon **376**, though it is more full in detail in its discussion of Graunson's involvements with the courts in England, Spain, and Portugal, including an account of his death in a duel of honor in 1397. Braddy argues, as before, that *Venus* was written at the request of the daughter of the King of Spain (Isabel of York), 'whose knowledge of Oton's unsurpassed reputation among French poets' would have justified Chaucer's praise (p 21).

379 Dodd, W.G. *Courtly Love.* 1913. See **96.**

Dodd comments on Chaucer's changing the speaker to a lady and offers a detailed comparison of the poem with Granson, whom he translates (pp 97–8).

380 Donahue, J.J. *Chaucer's Lesser Poems.* 1974. See **21.**

There is no point in reading *Venus* as sequel to *Mars*; it is 'an entirely independent love lyric.' Scholars, in their absorption with the poem's form, underestimate the poem. Its envoy is entirely original and 'is rather touching' (p 240).

381 Gardner, John. *The Poetry of Chaucer.* 1977. See **103.**

Gardner thinks *Venus* and *Mars* are related poems. 'The argument that the title of the *Complaint of Venus* is wholly inappropriate is nonsense' (p 89). The envoy is a separate piece of work, 'a tag probably added later when the poet decided to send in the poem as a plea for favor. It has nothing in common with the subject matter of the complaint' (p 89). That the envoy speaks of 'this compleynt' in the singular does not mean that Chaucer himself never thought of Mars and Venus as 'companion pieces ... At all events, the poems are built on the same principles and work well side by side' (p 90). In *Venus* Chaucer adapts church language for love as he did in *Mars* (see **342**); Venus' complaint 'parallels the Christian vision without ever becoming subject to it' (p 91). The lines do not refer to Christ, in Venus' mind, nor do they suggest that Venus ought to look to Christ rather than Mars, but a 'legitimate parallel' is implied, nonetheless, in all three ballades (pp 91–3). 'Taken by itself, the *Complaint of Venus* has perhaps nothing in it that urgently signals us beyond the most literal reading. (I don't really believe that. The more one reads of medieval literature, the more blatant these seemingly faint hints become, whether the purpose, in a given case, be religious, blasphemous, or something else.) But read in the light of techniques and ideas set up in the *Complaint of Mars*, techniques and ideas seen again and again in the poetry of Chaucer and in the courtly-love tradition in general, the *Complaint of Venus* becomes a richer poem. Chiefly, it gains dramatic force as a result of our sense, partly developed in the earlier complaint, of Venus as, in psychology at least, a lifelike woman' (p 93).

381a — *Life and Times of Chaucer.* 1977. See **171.** Pp 286–7.

On *Venus*, lines 76–8, beginning: 'For eld that in my spirit dulleth me': though these lines may be a later addition, they sound 'like the serious lament of an old man annoyed at his inability, of late, to write poetry as he once did' (p 286). Cf Chaucer's remarks on his aging in *Scogan*. 'Yet the envoy to Scogan shows anything but a decline in poetic power ... We have fairly good evidence that what actually happened is that in his last years Chaucer did *not* write less brilliantly than he'd written before (though he was now writing less), but, rather, wrote in a quirky new

way. He became less interested in poetry as mimesis, or the imitation of
character and action, and increasingly interested in poetry as an exalted
and significant form of – in the most literal sense – clowning. Though
he may have had doubts about the odd new direction in which his art
had moved, he was in fact discovering an approach to art that would
come into general favor among artists only in the twentieth century'
(p 287).

382 Mason, Harold Andrew. *Humanism and Poetry in the Early Tudor Period.*
London: Routledge and Kegan Paul, 1959. Pp 161–7.
'Chaucer was quite easy with the French modes and by no means their
slave. A good example is *The Complaint of Venus,* where we can see
Chaucer inserting traditional English phrases into his translation'
(p 162). He 'did not feel that the assimilated French manner required
very strict decorum' (p 163). Mason borrows Deschamps' epithet for
Chaucer to label Wyatt 'great translateur' for the humanists (pp 171–235).

383 Merrill, Rodney. 'Chaucer's *Broche of Thebes:* The Unity of *The Complaint
of Mars* and *The Complaint of Venus.'* 1973. See **359.**
Merrill argues that *Venus* was deliberately added to *Mars* and that the
two should be looked upon as a single poem to be entitled *Broche of
Thebes.* See **359** for complete annotation.

384 Piaget, Arthur. 'Oton de Granson et ses poésies.' *Romania,* 19 (1890),
237–59; 403–48.
Discusses the discovery of the French originals of *Venus,* pointing out the
accuracy of Shirley's statement of the ballades' source. Piaget feels that
Complaint of Venus is not an apt title for Chaucer's poem, however, since
the poems in the source have nothing to do with Venus (pp 411–6).

385 — 'Oton de Grandson, Amoureux de la Reine.' *Romania,* 61 (1932), 72–85.
Piaget argues that Grandson's Valentine poems are autobiographical and
that the woman is Queen Isabel of Bavaria. 'Il lui a rendu un éclatant
hommage. Il a loué non seulement la beauté et la grâce d'Isabel, mais
aussi sa piété et sa dévotion, sa bonté et sa vertu qui triomphait de toutes
les embûches' (p 82).

386 Robbins, R.H. *Companion to Chaucer Studies.* 1968/1979. See **136.**
Venus is not about Venus. 'In Graunson, a man addresses his "douce et
plaisant dame." In Chaucer, a woman speaks. Yet court-courtly expressions of love are so interchangeable that no reorientation was necessary.
The second ballade could serve either sex; all the first and third need is
a change of pronoun ... *The Complaint of Venus* underscores better than
most love lyrics the complete artificiality and unreality of the game of
love, by its disregard of the distinctive psychology of the sexes'
(p 322/389).

387 Skeat, W.W. *Oxford Chaucer*. 1894/1899. See **1**.

Skeat gives separate titles to each of the balades: I. The Lover's worthiness; II. Disquietude caused by Jealousy; III. Satisfaction in Constancy. His edition prints the French originals at the bottom of the page (I, pp 398–404). 'This poem is usually printed as if it formed part of the Complaint of Mars; but it is really distinct' (I, p 86). Skeat thinks the word *Princess* at the beginning refers to the Princess Isabel of Spain (Duchess of York), which would date the poem ca 1393, about the time Graunson received his annuity. The title is from Shirley and 'by no means a fitting one. It is not suitable for Venus, unless the "Venus" be a mortal; neither is it a continuous 'Compleynt,' being simply a linking together of three separate and distinct Balades' (I, 87). The three balades thrown together would seem to be a command performance for Isabel of York.

388 Williams, George. *A New View of Chaucer*. 1965. See **373**.

Venus 'does not quite belong among those poems whose center of gravity is Gaunt and his circle' (p 165). The poem is 'sadly misnamed,' addressed to a 'Princess' who must be Joan, wife of the Black Prince. Chaucer must have translated the three poems of Oton at her request or for her benefit as 'an expression of her love for the Black Prince.' Chaucer's apology in the envoy 'for not having made a better translation would sustain this interpretation' (p 165). Williams would date the poem ca 1385.

**A Complaint to his Lady
also called A Balade of Pity**

See also **92, 150**.

389 Birney, Earle. 'The Beginnings of Chaucer's Irony.' 1939. See **83**.

In *Lady*, like *Pity*, the 'same irony of unrequited love becomes the central topic.' Birney stresses the poem's 'unusual grace, a playful savoring of the situation,' and its 'singleness of ironic effect which is scarcely surpassed in the very latest of Chaucer's shorter poems.' Chaucer works with conventional conceits, the 'bromides of the courtly *erotica*' (p 640).

390 Clemen, W. *Chaucer's Early Poetry*. 1963. See **92**.

Lady is even closer to the French school than *Pity*; it is almost like three separate exercises. 'In this poem Chaucer is experimenting and practicing; we must not regard it as a finished and final expression of his art' (p 186).

391 Clogan, Paul M. 'The Textual Reliability of Chaucer's Lyrics: *A Complaint to His Lady.' M&H*, ns, 5 (1974), 183–9.

'A reliable text does not have to represent the author's final intention ... but it does bring the reader as close as possible to the true text of the author's work. Yet a reliable text can survive only as long as the market will support it; when it disappears, it has to wait the arrival of a young Turk to rediscover it and dress it up for a new audience' (p 183). After commenting on the lack of popularity of Chaucer's lyrics, Clogan considers the problem of dealing with a poem like *Lady* – 'a series of experiments in rhyme which Chaucer apparently left unfinished, but from which he later borrowed individual lines for the composition of *Anelida and Arcite*' (pp 185–6). 'Since there are a number of parallels in *Lady, Pity,* and *Anelida and Arcite, Lady* may well be the earliest in composition and represent the poet's draft of experiments in three distinct rhymes from which he later borrowed individual lines and phrases' (p 186). Clogan questions whether, in view of the experimental and unfinished quality of *Lady,* emendations to perfect rhyme or meter are justified. He discusses emendations by Skeat, Koch, Pollard, and Robinson, especially the repetition of line 14 at the beginning of the first terza rima stanza. 'This search for metrical regularity has deprived the lyric of its distinctive style and versification' (pp 186–7). 'Like French poetry of the fourteenth century the lyric represented a series of variations on a theme, with no attempt at continuous development or logical connections. *Lady* is an exercise in different keys on the conventional theme of unrequited love, and this is clearly indicated by the contrast achieved through the use of a different meter for each section' (p 187). Though *Lady's* subject is that of the French complaints, it differs from them in its 'noted absence of the rhetorical figures' which marked the French style. Instead, Chaucer's diction is appropriate to natural speech, without pause at the end of the lines as in Machaut. Chaucer's style has a greater fluency and is less limited to the verse line as a unit of thought; it utilizes a dialogue effect where one 'begins to hear for the first time the poet's so-called "speaking voice" which later becomes the voice of the narrator in his major works' (p 187). The value and significance of Chaucer's metrical experiments and innovations are 'severely undercut by editorial emendations to perfect rhyme or meter' (p 187).

392 Donahue, J.J. *Chaucer's Lesser Poems.* 1974. See **21**.

'That the work is disjointed and fragmentary is ... unimportant since the lines aim at little more than they already achieve – merely a striking repetition of the same lament' (p 49).

393 Hammond, E.P. *Bibliographical Manual*. 1908. See **37**.

Hammond places 'Ballad of Pity, or, Complaint to His Lady' in the doubtful category. The poem follows immediately upon Chaucer's *Pity* in Harley 78 where a horizontal line drawn by Shirley divides it from the earlier poem. A marginal asterisk marks the running title to both poems, 'The balade of Pytee by Chauciers.' 'The most weighty external evidence for Chaucerian authorship is the continuing of Shirley's running title to include this poem as well as the Pity; weighty internal evidence is the use in the poem of terza rima, an Italian verse-form presumably unknown to any fourteenth-century English poet but Chaucer' (p 411).

394 Hussey, S.S. 'The Minor Poems and the Prose.' 1970. See **112**.

Hussey finds the least attractive of Chaucer's short poems those like *Lady* which 'are allegorical in manner and heavily dependent on courtly love' (p 258).

395 Lewis, C.S. *Allegory of Love*. 1936. See **118**.

'The *Compleynt unto Pite* and the *Compleynt to His Lady* illustrate the use of personification at its lowest level – the most faint and frigid result of the popularity of allegory' (p 167). The figures fail to interact or even be pictorial as in a true allegory.

396 Timmer, B.J. 'La Belle Dame Sans Merci.' *ES*, 11 (1929), 20–2.

Timmer questions Skeat's assertion (**1**, I, p 526) that 'Faire Rewthelees' in *Lady* (line 27) is a translation of the French phrase 'la belle dame sans merci.' Timmer cannot find the phrase in Machaut, Deschamps, or Granson. The stock figure of the pitiless woman is there, but 'no such definite title as *Belle Dame sans Merci* can be found in them' (p 21). The figure of the ruthless woman came from Provençe to Northern France, then to Italy and England. Possibly the phrase comes from Italy, though Timmer does not find it in Petrarch. Perhaps Alain Chartier translated the phrase *La Belle Dame sans Merci* from Chaucer's 'Faire Rewthelees,' though this is not likely. Probably the two phrases were formed independently of each other (p 22). Or perhaps 'Faire Rewthelees, the Wise, yknit unto Good Aventure' is a pseudonym, as Cowling suggested (*Chaucer* [Methuen, 1927], p 106).

The Complaint unto Pity

See also **89, 92, 340**.

397 Baum, Paull Frank. *Chaucer's Verse*. 1961. See **58**.

In discussing meter Baum chooses *Pity* as an early example of Chaucer's experimenting with a 5-stress line; using *GP* as a later work for comparison, he comments on metrical feet, inversions, and kinds of stress (pp 13–26).

398 Birney, Earle. 'The Beginnings of Chaucer's Irony.' 1939. See **83**.
Pity, 'although one of the most conventional of his love lyrics, contains definite anticipations of the manner of the "mature" Chaucer. The central allegory of the poem is a dramatic irony. The lover comes with an elaborate bill of complaint against Pity, only to find her dead. The *contretemps* is toyed with in a manner that is almost lugubrious' (pp 639–40).

399 Bright, James W. 'Minor Notes on Chaucer.' *MLN,* 17 (1902), 278–80.
Bright would punctuate line 31 – "So many men as in her tyme hir knew" – so that it is set off as a parenthetical aside. He finds a similar construction in *Lady,* lines 110–1. Robinson **12** follows Bright's suggestion, but Fisher **23** does not.

400 Brusendorff, A. *Chaucer Tradition.* 1925. See **28**.
Brusendorff notes that 'the text is in a very unsatisfactory state' (p 270). He discusses metrical experimentation in the poem (pp 272–3).

401 Clemen, W. *Chaucer's Early Poetry.* 1963. See **92**.
Pity, a poem of 'little originality,' is 'perhaps the only truly allegorical of Chaucer's poems. An inner experience has been completely rendered by means of personification' (p 179). In this respect it is Chaucer's only poem which is 'based on the design of the *Roman de la Rose*' (p 181). Though evidences of its material may be found in Machaut, Deschamps, and Petrarch, no main source has been traced. 'An elaborate screen of rules and forms seems to shut off any immediate expression of feeling; a scaffolding of abstraction is erected' (p 182). Clemen comments on the early use of rhyme royal (a French stanza), but notes Chaucer's frequent use of enjambement, even in this early work, to create 'something approaching colloquial language' (p 183).

402 Clogan, Paul M. 'Chaucer's Use of the *Thebaid.*' *EM,* 18 (1967), 9–31.
The calling of Pity 'Herenus quene' reveals the influence of Statius' personification of *Pietas,* who has the power to overrule the Furies but who, as the Theban war progresses, is put to shame by Tisiphone.

403 Dodd, W.G. *Courtly Love.* 1913. See **96**.
Dodd finds the allegory to be well sustained. 'The poem is thoroughly in the style of the love lyrics of Deschamps and Machaut. There is some ingenuity displayed in the allegory; but it is no greater than we have seen in the French poems' (p 93).

404 Donahue, J.J. *Chaucer's Lesser Poems.* 1974. See **21**.
Although the poet personifies all his lady's attributes 'in a trite fashion, at least his use of the convention is novel enough.' Today the poem's 'little set of delights have lost their power to please the greatest number.' Some charm remains, but its greatest contribution is that 'it launched rime royal for better tasks' (p 44).

405 Flügel, Ewald. 'Chaucers Kleinere Gedichte.' *Anglia,* 23 (1901), 195–224.
Flügel discusses ms variants and the relationship of *Pity* to Deschamps
and Machaut. He draws parallels with Gower's *CA* and Hoccleve's *De
Reg. Princ.* Moreover, he gives some attention to the poem's terminology
(nb, *herse;* the virtues such as *Plaisence, Beaute,* and *Honestee; Herenus;* and
Regalyle).

406 Gardner, John. *The Poetry of Chaucer.* 1977. See **103.**
In *Pity* 'the controlling device is Chaucer's old gimmick, the myopic,
dim-witted narrator, caricature of himself, whose literal-mindedness
makes the complaint a comically "realistic" treatment of allegorical devices and conventions – roughly the medieval equivalent of the man who
shoots back at the movie screen.' When the narrator, finding Pity dead,
presents his complaint to the reader instead, 'the comic revelation of
what cannot be revealed is like Donne's revelation of what cannot be revealed in "The Undertaking"' (p 81). 'From the conventional viewpoint
a lover's unwillingness to take a chance for the sake of love would be ludicrous (even today, cartoon books tell us, the lover is supposed to go
down on his knees to propose marriage); from a realistic viewpoint, the
folderol of love is ridiculous. In the *Complaint unto Pity,* each viewpoint
throws the other into comic perspective; lighting up the age-old paradox:
what the lover does to show his love is ridiculous, no man of sense
would do it; but lovers are nobler (more daring, more selfless) than people with dignity and good sense' (pp 81–2).

407 Gray, Douglas. 'Chaucer and "Pite",' in *J.R.R. Tolkien, Scholar and Story
Teller: Essays in Memoriam.* Ed. Mary Salu and Robert T. Farrell. Ithaca:
Cornell University Press, 1979, pp 173–203.
Pite, a near synonym for *routhe,* was among Chaucer's favourite words.
'An obvious, though humble, starting-place' for studying the term is *Pity,*
a poem not much admired by the critics. Nonetheless, the poem is 'a
polished example of its kind, written with ease and eloquence, and the
simple allegorical situation is handled with a happy blend of elegy and
argument' (p 173). In *Pity,* 'pite' is a virtue seen exclusively in the context of a specific love situation; the background here is *RR,* especially
Jean de Meun's 'splendid allegorical battle' between *Pitie* and *Daunger*
(pp 174–5). Pite, as a desirable and benevolent aspect of the landscape of
the beloved lady's heart, is rather 'done to death by court poets.' Gray
comments on her appearance in *La Belle Dame sans merci* (p 175). But pite
also appears in subtler forms in *T&C, LGW, KnT, Mel, PhysT, PriorT,* and
MLT. Pite relates to Latin *pietas* with its suggestion of duty and moral
obligation, but also natural affection. In Chaucer there is invariably a
close connection between pite and gentilesse, a virtue expected of a good
knight as well as a lady. The Parson associates it with *misericorde* (so too
in *ABC*). After an extended discussion of the virtue in *MLT,* lines 191–7,

and *ClerkT*, lines 197–203, Gray concludes: 'The modern reader is often rightly disturbed by what he considers the extreme passivity of the virtue, the abandonment of action, which he suspects may easily lead to a-dulation of suffering in itself' (p 201). But we must keep in mind that pite is a duty and an active principle, an effect, with something of the quality of wisdom and fortitude, that is, the 'stableness of corage' (p 202). We should add to laudatory phrases applied to 'our greatest medieval poet that old gloss – '*humanus, fulle of pytie*' (p 203).

408 Griffin, R.M. *Chaucer's Lyrics*. 1970. See **18**. Pp 32–43.
Chaucer's first poem in rhyme royal is not an unqualified success. The contrast between coarse sexual implications and higher philosophical and religious questioning of the Bill of Complaint are not so much resolved as ignored.

409 Hammond, E.P. *Bibliographical Manual*. 1908. See **37**.
Hammond lists mss, printed editions, discussions of text, and considers the poem's date and authenticity. Since the lyrics are so short and occur in a variety of ms contexts they are given a great variety of titles. She lists about a dozen variant titles for *Pity*, ranging from *The Complaynt unto Pyte* in Bodley 638 and Bale's *De misericordia sepultura* and Leland's *De pietate mortua* to Thynne's special title page 'Howe pite is ded and beried in a gentyll hert.' Cambridge Ff 1,6 heads the poem with the name of *Jesus* (pp 390–1).

410 Heath, H. Frank, ed. ['Pity'] in *The Works of Chaucer*. London: Macmillan, 1898, p xxxv.
Pity is 'a better poem' than *ABC*; 'the mark of sincerity and deep feeling is upon it, though the metaphor is carried too far here and there for clearness.'

411 Lowes, John Livingston. 'Chaucer and Dante,' *MP*, 14 (1917), 705–35.
In *Pity*, lines 92–3, 'thou Herenus quene' is identified with Pity, but also suggests Proserpine. 'It is clear that Chaucer must have known Proserpine as the queen, not only of the rest of the underworld, but also of *Elysium*, and so of the realm of *mercy*. At all events, "Herenus quene" *is* also queen of the "feld of pitee"' (p 723). Perhaps she is also, as in Dante, to be understood as Proserpine in her well-known guise of Luna or Lucina, as in line 94, 'Let som streem of your light on me be sene.' The form 'Her*enus*' suggests the word was new to Chaucer, and 'I suspect that the phrase may be about the very first of his responses to the influence of Dante' (p 724).

412 Nolan, Charles J. Jr., 'Structural Sophistication in "The Complaint Unto Pity".' *ChauR*, 13 (1979), 363–72.
'It is clear ... that Chaucer is making use ... of the amorous complaint form. What has not been generally recognized, however, is that he also employs the structure of the legal bill in the second half of his work.

Usually prepared in advance, as Chaucer's is here, such documents had a tripartite division consisting of an address, a statement of grievance, and a prayer for remedy' (p 364). 'Chaucer ... conforms to custom in elaborating his statement of injustice. The only embellishment allowed in legal bills involved indicating the frightfulness of the crime and the resultant hardship, possibly with some exaggeration' (p 367). 'The blending of the amorous and the legal complaint adds a new dimension to the second use, the contest. Pity and Cruelty are no longer just courtly virtues personified but become in addition antagonists at law. Of course, the result of raising their struggle to the level of legal combat is to imply that the outcome has not only personal but social consequences as well. Thus the mixture of forms enriches the personification as it does the language' (p 371).

413 Norton-Smith, John. *Geoffrey Chaucer*. 1974. See **361.**

'Complaint' is a loose genre: 'The longer the complaint, the more obvious becomes the basic weakness of the form' (p 21). Chaucer compensates by adding narrative complexity in *Pity*, 'an "allegorical episode" where any pattern which would give the simple impression of a consistent sequence of events was avoided. Instead, the episode contains a series of compressed or oblique conceits which ... correspond to an actual psychological occurrence in the lady's mind' (p 21).

414 Pittock, Malcolm. 'Chaucer: The Complaint Unto Pity.' *Crit*, 1 (1959), 160–8.

'The interplay between the real and apparent plots makes the poem complex and sophisticated. The apparent plot, cut to a conventional pattern with which the contemporary reader was familiar, served as a link between the author and his public, and through its deliberate narrative quality enabled him to refer obliquely to the structure and values of the society for which he was writing' (p 161). Pittock charts the 'emotional course' of the poem: 'By envisaging Pity as a person whom he is seeking for protection against the great Lord Love (later Cruelty), the poet absolves himself from any responsibility for the emotion he feels and makes the Lady appear churlish for not responding to him' (p 163). At first we read completely seriously the poet's prayer for salvation. Later we see he is deliberately hyperbolic. Nonetheless, Pity becomes more than sexual responsiveness; rather it is a need for compassion, 'a fundamentally important quality the lack of which betokens a serious moral condition: the Lady's soul really needs praying for; she is no better than an inanimate body if she is incapable of pity' (p 164). The complaint is a serious exhortation to true compassion and real spiritual beauty. 'The courtly love element is allowed to predominate' (p 165).

415 Robbins, R.H. *Companion to Chaucer Studies*. 1968/1979. See **136**.
'For love lyrics like Chaucer's in *formes fixes*, literary and social conventions form the underpinning and must be accepted without deviation. Making and reading such lyrics was one of the games people played, and provided sophisticated fun for poet and a knowledgeable audience. Court verse explored the rules of social ritual: how should a lady and gentleman behave toward each other? ... This other-world of courtly dalliance existed primarily in the mind. Its justification lay in its unreality; it was an escape from the pressures and tensions of the work-a-day life that stifled the niceties of love-making. Any discussion of real social problems, like those of adulterous relationships, was taboo' (pp 317–8/384–5). *Pity* is 'simple polite verse: narrative does not overwhelm complaint, and biographical allusions are absent' (p 321/388). Robbins disagrees with Pittock **414** that the poem explores compassion: 'Rather is Chaucer exploring the genre to see how far he can stretch it without breaking. That he succeeded can be gauged from its fifteenth-century imitations' (p 321/388). The poem is not ambiguous.

416 Root, R.K. *The Poetry of Chaucer*. 1900/1922. See **140**.
Perhaps Chaucer, like Aurelius in *FrankT*, wrote complaints to ease his love-lorne youthful heart (cf the eight year sickness in *BD*). 'It is quite possible that when Chaucer would launch himself as a courtly poet' he tried to serve his lady love as Don Quixote did. But 'personally, I find the idea of a hopeless love, protracted through eight long years, out of harmony with the eminent sanity of Chaucer's nature. But who shall say?' (p 58). *Pity* is 'a conventional love poem on the French model ... in all probability one of Chaucer's earliest extant works' (p 58).

417 Saintsbury, George. *A History of English Prosody*. 1906. See **72**.
Pity is Chaucer's first experiment in rhyme-royal, the stanza he later brings to perfection and 'which long held the premier place among our stanza forms.' In this early work 'the poet's instinct is true, but his craftsmanship is as yet incomplete' (I, p 150).

418 Snell, F.J. *The Age of Chaucer*. 1901. See **143**.
Snell warns against reading autobiography into such poems as *Pity* (pp 132–5). 'There is reason to suspect that the *Complaint to Pity* is not typical of Chaucer's youthful lyric, that something of the roguish humour so characteristic of his later muse was expressed in his early verse as well' (p 135).

419 Wise, B.A. *The Influence of Statius upon Chaucer*. 1911. See **278**.
Wise expands 'Professor Skeat's brilliant explanation of Herenus' (p 39; cf **1**, I, p 62, lines 57, 64, 92, and *Academy*, Jan. 7, 1888, p 9). 'If Dr Furnivall [*Trial Forwards*, p 12] is right in regarding this poem as Chaucer's earliest work that is not a translation, then it represents his first borrowing from Statius' (p 41). Furnivall dates the poem ca 1367.

The Former Age

See also **47, 89, 194.**

420 Brusendorff, A. *Chaucer Tradition*. 1925. See **28.**
Brusendorff discusses the mss and argues that what we have is not a finished poem; it is rather 'clearly a fragment copied from one of the poet's drafts' (p 293).

421 Cipriani, Lisi. 'Studies in the Influence of *RR* on Chaucer.' 1907. See **162.**
Suggests influence of Jean de Meun as well as Boethius on *FA, Fortune,* and *Gent.*

422 Donahue, J.J. *Chaucer's Lesser Poems*. 1974. See **21.**
FA has the greatest title to membership in a Boethian group; it is one of a handful of sober lyrics in which Chaucer stirs a larger audience to philosophical meditation and 'a moral cry' (p 247).

423 Gardner, John. *The Poetry of Chaucer*. 1977. See **103.**
'Unlike Boethius' poem, Chaucer's is rich in concrete imagery; the contrast between the Golden Age and the troubled modern world is sharp. But Chaucer's imagery is not designed merely to lend vividness. It's also symbolic' (p 94). Chaucer introduces several words from the Christian idea of Eden which have no parallels in Boethius, like *blisful, fruits, colde welle* (instead of streams), *grain, vine, lambish,* and *Nimrod,* all of which fuse the pagan First Age and the Christian. Chaucer also adds the Neoplatonic notion of unity giving way to chaos. 'With the breaking of divine unity, the corruption of the relationship between god and man, the rise of tyranny, and the dispersion of mankind, all order collapses and all mankind are at one another's throats. As in Boethius or Plotinus, or as in musical theory on mismatched proportions, with the collapse of love Oneness explodes into Manyness [ie, "doubleness" "mordre in sondry wyse"] ... This same idea of the tragic conflict within the realm of the many will be a focal idea in ... *Troilus and Criseyde*' (p 95).

424 Griffin. R.M. *Chaucer's Lyrics*. 1970. See **18.**
Griffin comments on the 'musical ordering of interwoven images' (p 106). 'The ending is powerful, but not altogether satisfactory ... an attempt at climax, but in its abstract brevity it is only a rough draft for a conclusion never written' (p 111).

424a Levin, Harry. *The Myth of the Golden Age in the Renaissance*. Bloomington: Indiana University Press, 1969.
See pp 6, 23, 133. 'The emblem of Jesus, the lamb, tinges Chaucer's picture of "The Former Age"' (p 6), and provides an early instance of pastoral motifs in the representation of the Golden Age. Ovid demonstrates why the iron age is aptly named, as men disembowel the earth for treasure. Boethius wonders why men need to dig; Chaucer twists the idea into a curse in *FA* (p 23).

425 Norton-Smith, John. 'Chaucer's *Etas Prima.' MAE*, 32 (1963), 117–24.

The fact of its presence in Cambridge University Lib. ms Ii.3.21, side by side with Boethius' *De Consolatione*, would seem to indicate that by the mid fifteenth century "The Former Age" had become more or less associated with Boethius' (p 117). Nonetheless, 1) Boethius, II.m.5 is not really a separate poetical entity, nor is Chaucer that close to it. 2) Chaucer's organization in *FA* derives more directly from Jean de Meun's adaptation of Boethius (*RR*.8355 ff.) where the style consists of a rigid catalogue laced with anaphora and clauses of similar grammatical construction. 3) Neither Boethius nor Jean may be considered 'the total creative poetic impulse (Geoffrey''s "archetypus') of Chaucer's poem' (p 117), for he adds much new material after stanza four. 4) The moral intention of *FA* is not identical with that of Boethius II.m.5. Ms Camb. Lib.Hh.4.12 entitles the poem *Etas Prima*; that title is perhaps a better guide for reading the poem as 'a separate, unattached entity' (p 118). 'Boethian' poems like those of Deschamps specify Boethius as their source and are more moralistic than Chaucer's poem, which 'nowhere ... offers any ethical advice or implies any positive moral attitude' (p 119). Chaucer's style is 'empirical' in its 'enumeration of detail ... not a symptom of nostalgia as has sometimes been suggested'; rather it is more a catalogue 'as accurate, inclusive, and up-to-date as possible' (p 119). Neither the tone nor language is Boethian. 'The last stanza shows Chaucer moving further away from Boethius in the introduction of his finest imagery: the double *exemplum*, one mythological, the other historical' (pp 120–1). The tradition behind Chaucer's Nimrod is not simply that of builder of Babel but rather that which regarded him as the first tyrant. Chaucer criticizes both people and ruler: 'The sobre enumeration of the insane principles of modern life allows no positive moral position. The Chaucerian outlook is bleak and depressed' (p 122). Norton-Smith relates the central poetic impulse of *FA* to Seneca's Epistle 90, which lies behind Boethius, II.m.5, and also Ovid's account of the first age in Ovid's *Metamorphoses* and Tibullus, I.3.lines 35 ff. Perhaps the poem is not of the early 1380's but rather, like *Lak of Stedfastnesse*, of the 1390s, perhaps even as late as 1398–9 when Richard pillaged the people with blank charters and when seventeen counties had to pay a tax of a thousand marks apiece 'for the recovery of the King's pleasure' (p 124).

426 Preston, Raymond. 'Poyson, Man-Slaughtre, and Mordre in Sondry Wise.' *NQ*, 195 (1950), 95.

There is no reference to poison in Boethius, II m.5; Chaucer seems to be drawing on Ovid, *Metamorphoses*, I.144–8 (the account of the first ages).

427 Robinson, F.N. *The Works of Chaucer*. 1957. See **12**.

'The *Former Age* cannot be attached to any definite occasion, though the reflections on the happiness of man's primeval state might well have been prompted by the troubled conditions of the reign of Richard II' (pp 521–2). Cf Pace **47**.

428 Root, R.K. *The Poetry of Chaucer*. 1900/1922. See **140**.

'Poets have always been ready to sing the praises of long ago ... Doubtless Chaucer was wise and practical enough to see the fallacies of a general "return to nature," and to recognize that civilization has brought its blessings as well as its curses; but he was also philosopher enough to see that "covetyse" was really at the bottom of all the most serious evils of his day, as it is of our own' (p 70).

429 Schmidt, A.V.C. 'Chaucer and the Golden Age.' *EIC*, 26 (1976), 99–115.

'One envies rather than begrudges Chaucer the flexibility of dialect word-choice which helped him cope with the "skarsetee of rym in English"' (p 102). In *FA* the sonority of the decasyllabic line, the architecture of the *ababbcbc* stanza, and the learned vocabulary create a sort of 'creative mythology' (a phrase borrowed from Joseph Campbell), which is unusual for Chaucer and which contributes to the poem's 'air of *gravitas*.' The 'unusually learned and solemn tone' of the poem suggests that Chaucer possibly had in view 'a restricted readership consisting of likeminded people (such as the poet Gower) rather than the court-audience of the long poems' (p 103). The poem begins closely to the Boethius, though Ovid is the principal source. Still, the quality is Boethian. 'Some of his additions serve to spell out the sense with a pedantic insistence that is more Elizabethan than medieval' (p 107). The myth of the First Age serves not to *justify* the ways of men but to condemn them, to show how irretrievably complete the falling off has been. 'Hence the sombre, plangent tone and the mood of deep pessimism that find no parallel elsewhere in Chaucer's work' (p 113). 'Unlike primitive myths, *The Former Age* is not a story, only an image: of regret, not nostalgia; and, if we employ the word with due care, of aspiration' (p 114). Like Eliot's *Burnt Norton*, the poem offers the 'perpetual possibility' (p 115).

429a — 'Chaucer's *Nembrot*: A Note on *The Former Age*.' *MAE*, 47 (1978), 304–7.

Nimrod is the only figure from the Bible among Chaucer's classical sources for the ideas and imagery of *FA*. Schmidt notes Nimrod glosses on the giants' catastrophic attempt to scale the height of heaven in Ovid mss, which link classical and biblical matter. In an oft-repeated comment Jerome pointed to Nimrod as 'the first to seize absolute power over people, something not known before' (p 305). Josephus, in a passage widely circulated in monastic libraries after the sixth century, likewise presented him as a tyrant. Chaucer may have got the tyrant idea from Bede, but more probably from Walafrid Strabo's *Glossa Ordinaria*. In *FA* Nimrod's towers represent more than just pride; rather, they 'represent fortified structures of any and all periods, emblematic of man's domination of his fellows' (p 307). Chaucer 'debiblicises' Nimrod 'who now becomes an almost purely symbolic figure operating on the same imaginative plane as Jupiter' (p 307).

430 Skeat, W.W. *Oxford Chaucer*. 1894/ 1899. See **1**.

Both mss copies of *FA* are from the same source, 'as both of them omit the same line, viz line 56; which I have had to supply by conjecture' (I, p 78). Skeat also notes misspellings and mistakes in riming which he has corrected. 'But the poem is a beautiful one, and admirably expressed; and its inclusion among the Minor Poems is a considerable gain' (I, p 79). Skeat prints Chaucer's *Boece* II.m.5, marking the appropriate passages according to the stanzas of *FA*, noting that 'the likeness hardly extends beyond the first four stanzas' (p 79). In Cambr. Univ. Lib. ms Ii.3.21 *FA* and *Fortune* are 'actually introduced into Chaucer's translation of Boethius, between the fifth metre and the sixth prose of the second book' (I, p 80).

431 Tatlock, J.S.P. *The Mind and Art of Chaucer*. 1950. See **147**.

Tatlock contrasts the picture of the first age in Boethius with that in Hebrew tradition, both of which Chaucer draws upon. In the classical tradition, 'the picture is more attractive, especially to the imaginatively indolent, than the Garden of Eden, where man must till the soil. Hebrew literature throughout had the ethical spirit of the prophets. The classical ancients, while they also had a more strenuous picture of the golden age, could surrender their ethics and their good sense for a while to an existence of lolling; even so strenuous an idealist as Boethius could surrender to its combination with peaceableness; it would appeal as much at moments to Christians who accepted the orthodox unstrenuous idea of heaven' (p 84).

431a Witlieb, Bernard. 'Jupiter and Nimrod in *The Former Age*.' *Chaucer Newsletter* 2 (Summer, 1980), 12–3.

Chaucer's depiction of a sensual Jupiter and ambitious Nimrod (*FA* vv 56–9) derives from the *Ovide Moralisé*. 'The link between Jupiter and Nimrod becomes clear when one considers that the *Ovide Moralisé* reconciles Ovid's story of the giants' rebellion against Jupiter with the construction of the tower of Babel and God's anger ... Jupiter's power excesses have their counterpart in Nimrod's seizure of Babylon, which Chaucer exploits as his culminating allusion to the warlike state of contemporary mankind' (p 13).

Fortune: Balades de Visage sanz Peinture

See also **42, 351.**

432 Bilderbeck, J.B. 'Chaucer's "Fortune".' *Athenaeum*, Jan. 18 (1902), pp 82–3.
The 'beste frend' in the envoy to *Fortune* is Richard II; the 'three' or 'two'
(line 76) would be Lancaster, York and Gloucester, who, according to the
minutes of the Privy Council 8 May 1390, would be required to approve
any gift the king might wish to bestow. Bilderbeck would date the poem
between the middle of 1391 and the autumn of 1394, or possibly in 1396,
when Chaucer again 'seems to have been in anything but flourishing
circumstances' (p 83).

433 Brusendorff, A. *The Chaucer Tradition.* 1925. See **28.**
Fortune is marked as Chaucer's by Shirley and Fairfax 16, 'so ... its
genuineness is beyond doubt' (pp 241–2). Shirley notes that the poem
was 'translated oute of ffrenshe'; however, no direct source is known and
thus the note is not usually given much credence. Brusendorff examines
Deschamps as a possible influence.

434 Galway, Margaret. 'Chaucer among Thieves.' *TLS*, April 20, 1946, p 187.
Fortune may be an occasional poem linked to the double robbery of
Chaucer in Sept. 1390. Perhaps Chaucer was mocked at court for having
'translated Boethius' "Consolations of Philosophy" for the edification of
Richard and his court, to whom he must now present himself as a bat-
tered suppliant. He was not likely to escape quizzical inquiries as to
whether, under these blows of Fortune, he could practice the noble stoicism he had preached and, like the pauper in the "Consolations," sing as
he walked the roads. In his poem on Fortune, written about the time of
this outstanding test of his Boethian philosophy, Chaucer alludes to a
dire misfortune inflicted on him by crafty enemies. He maintains his
discipleship to Boethius in the tone of the refrain: "For fynally, Fortune,
I thee defye!"' (p 187). The phrase *visage sanz Peinture* may allude to the
'rainbow coloured bruises' he got while trying to retain possession of his
money bags.

435 Griffin, R.M. *Chaucer's Lyrics.* 1970. See **18.**
Notes the prominence of sexual puns in *Fortune* (pp 138–54).

436 Hammerle, Karl. 'Das Fortunamotiv von Chaucer bis Bacon.' *Anglia*, 65
(1941), 87–100.
Chaucer's ideas of Fortuna in *Fortune* and *T&C* derive largely from
Boethius and Jean de Meun. His first important follower in the literary
treatment of Fortuna is Lydgate in *Fall of Princes*. The motif recurs in
Machiavelli, Spenser, Marlowe, Shakespeare (*Titus Adronicus*), and
Raleigh's *History of the World*.

437 Patch, Howard Rollin. 'The Tradition of the Goddess Fortuna: In Roman Literature and the Transitional Period.' *Smith College Studies in Modern Language*, 3,iii (1922), 131–77.

Patch describes the nature and functions of Fortuna in Roman literature. 'As a deity, she was mother, nurse, provider, guardian, friend, and enemy, to the Roman, and the child of Jupiter himself' (p 133). The late Roman Fortuna was a deity who absorbed many others who were more ancient. Patch considers treatments of the goddess in Sallust, Cicero, Horace, Ovid, Seneca, Virgil, and Juvenal. She was most popular under the empire. Her cults were involved in divination, which was repulsive to early Christians. Patch discusses Martianus Capella as a transitional figure between Roman and Christian attitudes toward Fortune.

438 — 'The Tradition of the Goddess Fortuna: In Medieval Philosophy and Literature.' *Smith College Studies in Modern Language*, 3, iv (1922), 179–235.

Patch traces the alteration of the pagan idea of Fortune as it was made to conform with Christian philosophy. He first considers Lanctantius, St Augustine, St Jerome, and St Thomas Aquinas, all of whom in effect annihilate the goddess. Boethius offers a compromise between pagan acceptance and Christian annihilation. Though he is philosophically consistent, he is inconsistent in his portrayal of Fortune (p 192), presenting three distinct pictures which depend on points of view: to the person who is bound to Fortune, she is a powerful taskmaster; to the one who is philosophically free of her influence, she is nothing; from God's perspective she is a positive influence (evil fortune becoming good fortune as she instructs men in the true nature of false goods). The idea, as Boethius leaves it, is as orthodox as that of St Thomas, but with poetic insight as well (p 195). Patch also discusses the views of Alanus de Insulis, Henricus Septimellensis, Albertus Magnus, Dante, Petrarch, Boccaccio, Federigo Frezzi, Aeneas Sylvius, Boiardo, Leon Battista Alberti, Pico della Mirandola, Ariosto, Cardinal Bembo, Tressino, Machiavelli, and others. The essay includes a bibliography of primary sources.

439 — 'Fortuna in Old French Literature.' *Smith College Studies in Modern Languages*, 4, iv (1923), 1–45.

Patch considers treatments of the goddess by Simund de Freine, *Le Roman de Philosophie* (ca 1180); *Le Roman de la Rose*; Phillipe de Beaumanoir, *La Manekine* (ca 1250–96); Pierre de la Broche; Watriquet de Couvin, *Li Mireoirs as Dames* and *Uns Dis de Fortune*; Baudouin de Condé, *Prisons d'Amours*; Nicole de Margival, *La Panthère d'Amours* (ca 1295); *Le Roman de Fauvel* (1310–4); Jean de Condé, *Li Dis de Fortune* (1310–40); *Les Echecs Amoureux* (late 14th cent.); Guillaume de Guilleville, *Pèlerinage de l'Homme*; Guillaume de Machaut, *Remede de Fortune*; Jean Froissart; Eustache Deschamps. The fifteenth-century writers Patch discusses are Christine de Pisan, *Le Livre de la Mutacion de Fortune*; Charles of Orléans;

Martin Le Franc; Pierre Michault, *Dance aux Aveugles*; Alain Chartier, *L'Esperance ou Consolation des Trois Vertus*. Patch offers a synopsis of each of the named poems and cites scattered references or attitudes in unnamed lyrics. He adds a note on the influence of Boethius (p 34) and a note on French translations of Boccaccio's *De Casibus* (pp 35–9).

440 — 'Chaucer and Lady Fortune.' *MLR*, 22 (1927), 377–88.
After a brief survey of medieval attitudes toward Fortune Patch comments on the role of Fortune in *BD, HF, Fortune, KnT, T&C, MonkT, MLT*, and *NPT*. In Boethius Chaucer 'found a wealth of detail regarding the pagan Fortune ... much of which he uses later, and he also found certain implications which lead naturally to the Christian figure' (p 380). The dialogue in *Fortune* is strikingly Boethian; Patch would date the poem shortly after completion of *Boece*. Though the gods are capricious, behind all is a righteous God. The poem is 'at once a pat on the shoulder and a tap on the back, and both without a coward's whine' (p 381).

441 — *The Goddess Fortune in Medieval Literature*. Cambridge: Harvard University Press, 1927.
Patch explores attitudes toward Dame Fortune from ancient sources through the Middle Ages, devoting special attention to the philosophy of Fortune, traditional themes of Fortune in medieval literature, the functions of Fortune, her activities and her cults, her dwelling-place, and her famous wheel. The essay includes a bibliography and twelve plates in addition to a frontispiece (mainly from 15th-century mss). Patch cites Chaucer's balade on the subject to illustrate the notion that poverty is proof against the turns of Fortune. The theme of the poem he feels is that of 'friend in need' (p 74).

442 Rideout, Edna. 'Chaucer's "Beste Friend".' *TLS*, Feb. 8, 1947, p 79.
Rideout would link the outcry in *Fortune*, line 78, to Chaucer's loss in 1386 of his two offices as Comptroller of Customs in the port of London. The political events surrounding Thomas of Gloucester may have been the cause of the poet's demotion and the 'beste frend alyve' must refer to Richard II who does later help to restore Chaucer. Perhaps Chaucer's own death in 1400 was hastened by grief over that of Richard, his 'beste frend,' in 1399.

443 Root, R.K. *The Poetry of Chaucer*. 1900/1922. See **140**.
Though little more than a restatement of Boethian teachings, *Fortune* is not 'a mere literary *tour de force* ... Chaucer assimilated the philosophy of Boethius into his own soul, and made it the guiding principle of his life' (p 71). The thoughts of the poem are 'noble thoughts ... nobly spoken forth, not only with art, but with conviction ... Before the poem closes, its stoicism becomes a Christian stoicism' (p 71). The rhyme scheme is difficult, requiring twelve b-rhymes; 'yet there is scarcely a line in which one is conscious of any conflict between versification and thought' (p 72).

444 Wimsatt, James I. 'Chaucer, Fortune, and Machaut's "Il m'est avis".' In *Chaucerian Problems and Perspectives: Essays Presented to Paul E. Beichner.* Ed. Edward Vasta and Zacharias P. Thundy. Notre Dame University Press, 1979, pp 119–31.

Though *amour* is the dominant topic in Machaut, 'a substantial number of his works center on politics and morals, reflecting his public careers as courtier and clergyman' (p 119). 'Il m'est avis, qu'il n'est dons de Nature' is a vigorous and attractive ballade decrying the power of fortune and her friends in high places. Chaucer draws on the poem in *BD, Boece, MerchT, Fortune* (ll 125–8), and *Sted*. It is a relatively prominent Machaut poem, appearing thirteen times in eight of the best mss. Wimsatt reprints the French text and a modern English translation, then discusses its relationship to each of the five Chaucerian works. Though Boethius is the main source for *Fortune*, there are others too, as Shirley knew when he suggested a French source. That Chaucer wished to tie the poem to French poetry is evident by its French title, French rubrics, and French refrain line. Other lines seem to have French originals or bear the French influence of *RR* and poems of Deschamps. But 'taking all factors into account, *Fortune* has stronger connections with "Il m'est avis" than any other work of Chaucer,' though *Sted* is 'more like the Machaut lyric in its limited aim of commenting on the times' (p 128).

Moral Balade of Gentilesse

See also **29, 42, 106.**

445 Brittain, Robert E. 'A Textual Note on Chaucer: *Gentilesse*, 20.' *MLN*, 51 (1936), 433–5.

On the basis of Cotton Cleopatra D.vii (C) and Harley 2251 (H$_2$), which reads 'that maketh his heires hem that him queme,' Brittain would emend Skeat's line 'That maketh him his heir, that can him queme' to 'That maketh him his heires that him queme,' thus maintaining meter and not altering any word in the C–H$_2$ reading. Robinson **12** and Fisher **23** follow Brittain's reading.

446 Brusendorff, A. *The Chaucer Tradition.* 1925. See **28.**

The authenticity of *Gent* is attested by Shirley and Scogan, and is beyond doubt. Scogan introduces the poem into his own 'Moral Balade' and interprets Chaucer's 'firste stok' as God or Christ in his introductory stanza. Chaucer's poem is 'in the spirit of Dante' *(Convivio)*, though it also reflects Boccaccio's *Filostrato*, VII.87 ff.

447 Donahue, J.J. *Chaucer's Lesser Poems*. 1974. See **21**.

The verses of *Gent* are 'among Chaucer's noblest,' to be placed beside *Truth* as 'a foremost philosophic poem' (p 256).

448 Donaldson, E.T. *Chaucer's Poetry*. 1958/1975. See **14**.

The doctrine of gentilesse, which 'has its origins in Christ's teaching, implies only the moral democracy of mankind and was never transferred by the Middle Ages into the political or even sociological realm. The same man who, like Chaucer, would argue for the moral equality of men, would support political and social autocracy to his dying day' (p 963/1127).

449 French, Robert Dudley. *Chaucer Handbook*. 1927. See **99**.

French dates the poem 1390–5 and cites *Consolatio*, Bk. III.pr.6, and m.6, along with *RR*, ll 18, 607 ff, as the main sources. The whole poem is restricted to three rimes. 'In one of the manuscripts, Chaucer's poem is inserted in a "Moral Balade," which, according to Shirley, was addressed "to my lorde the Prince, to my lord of Clarence, to my lord of Bedford and to my lorde of Gloucestre, by Henry Scogan, at a souper of feorthe merchande in the vyntre in london at the hous of Lowys Iohan." Henry Scogan was undoubtedly the person addressed by Chaucer in the famous Envoy, and the princes named by Shirley were the four sons of Henry IV. In introducing the *Gentilesse* into his "Moral balade," Scogan refers to "My maistre Chaucier, God his soule have, / That in his language was so curyous"' (p 108).

450 Green, A. Wigfall. 'Structure of Three Minor Poems by Chaucer.' *UMSE*, 4 (1963), 79–82.

Green finds the link between the title of *Gent* and its refrain to be remote. Largely because of its envoy *Truth* 'has more charm than "Gentilesse," but the structure of the latter is more skillfully wrought' (p 82).

451 Griffin, R.M. *Chaucer's Lyrics*. 1970. See **18**.

'Although *Gentilesse* appears at first to be a simple and straightforward handling of a commonplace sentiment, it is ... an extremely complex and sophisticated poem. The simplicity of the *sentence* ... is precisely what frees Chaucer to attempt such stylistic refinements, and allows him to create in *Gentilesse* what is perhaps the most delicate and precise of the moral lyrics' (p 124).

452 Hammond, E.P. *Bibliographical Manual*. 1908. See **37**.

Under *source* Hammond cites Boethius, III.pr.6 and *RR* 18807 ff, with cross-references to *WBT* 253 ff, Dante, *Purg*. 7, 121; *Convito* IV canzone 3; *CA* IV, 2200 ff; and *Dis de Gentilesse*, in the works of Jean de Condé, III, 97 (p 372).

453 Jefferson, B.L. *Chaucer and the Consolation of Philosophy of Boethius.*
Princeton: Princeton University Press, 1917.
Jefferson considers *Gent* in his discussion of True Felicity (pp 94–104).
After commenting on the pervasiveness of the theme of gentilesse in
Chaucer he examines Lowes' argument on Dante and Chaucer (**454**) to
show that many influences that Lowes claimed for the *Convivio* could
also come directly from Boethius. 'The influence of the two authors
seems to be fused almost beyond separation' (p 101). Jefferson traces the
theme in several of the *CT*, especially *WBT, SqT, FrankT, MancT,* and
ParsT.

454 Lowes, John Livingston. 'Chaucer and Dante's *Convivio.' MP,* 13 (1915),
19–33.
Chaucer draws on Jean de Meun as well as Boethius and the *Purgatorio*
in his treatment of *gentilesse.* But 'it is the spirit of the *Convivio* with
which the whole treatment is pervaded' (p 20). Eg, 'old richess,' which
Chaucer uses twice in *WBT* and once in *Gent* occurs six times in *Convivio*
(*antica ricchezza*). Cf Koeppel, *Anglia,* 13 (1891), 184–5. In *Gent* we find 'a
characteristic mingling of all the springs of his inspiration. As in the
Fortune *balade,* Jean de Meun, Boethius, and Dante are all present – the
heart of their teaching grasped and assimilated in Chaucer's own
thought, and fused in a new and individual expression by his ripened
art. There is here no question of originality. Few passages in Chaucer –
unless it be the Fortune *balade* itself – show with greater clearness his
consummate gift of gathering together and embodying in a new unity
the *disjecta membra* of the dominant beliefs and opinions of his day. To
overlook that in any study of external influences on Chaucer is to take
the chaff and leave the corn' (p 27).

455 Maynard, Theodore. *Connection Between the Ballade.* 1934. See **67.**
Gent could have been written at almost any time in Chaucer's career.
'The fact that it is colored with Boethian philosophy would not necessarily prove that it was written after the *Boece.* For Chaucer may well
have been saturated in Boethius from his youth, as were so many men of
the middle ages' (p 60).

456 Toynbee, Paget. *Dante in English Literature.* 2 vols. London: Methuen, 1909.
Toynbee notes the large influence of Dante on Chaucer, ranging from
T&C, HF, SNT to *AA, WBT* and *Gent* (I, 1–16). He quotes the passage on
gentilesse from *WBT* and notes that the discussions on true nobility
there and in *Gent* owe much to *Convivio* (I, 14).

457 Robbins, R.H. *Companion to Chaucer Studies.* 1968/1979. See **136.**
Robbins relates the theme of *Gent* to *ClerkT,* lines 1570–8, as well as *WBT,*
lines 1109–70, Boethius (III.pr.6), Dante, and *RR* (p 325/392).

458 Robinson, R.N. *Works.* 1957. See **12.**

The sentiments Chaucer expresses in *Gent* 'are sometimes treated by critics as if they were bold utterances, far in advance of the social philosophy of the age. But on the contrary the doctrine that gentility depends on character, not inheritance – *virtus, non sanguis* – was commonly received opinion. It might be described as the Christian democracy regularly taught by the church, though not regularly exemplified in Christian society' (p 522). See note on 'old richesse' (p 862).

459 Root, R.K. *Poetry of Chaucer.* 1900/1922. See **140.**

On *Gent*: 'Trite enough in a democratic age like the present, these thoughts were more novel in the day of Chaucer, particularly when they came from one who dwelt near the court, that great centre of all the "solemn plausibilities" of life' (p 74).

459a Schless, Howard. 'Chaucer and Dante.' In *Critical Approaches to Medieval Literature: Selected Papers from the English Institute, 1958–9.* Ed. Dorothy Bethurum. New York: Columbia University Press, 1960. Pp 134–54.

Gent borrows from Dante's third canzone in the *Convivio* several of its ideas, especially the phrase 'antica richezza.' But there is a 'fundamental question of the extent of association of Christ and *gentilesse* in the ballade' (p 150). Schless argues against glossing 'the firste stok' as Christ; rather the phrase refers to 'the first race of nobles, which is the "fader of gentilesse" in the same way that Chaucer is the father of English poetry' (p 152). What the poem loses in religiosity from this reading it gains in 'unity and comprehension that are otherwise lacking ... Dante's influence is one among many and depends chiefly on the "antica richezza" theme – the one original element from Dante that Chaucer added to his otherwise conventional view of *gentilesse*' (p 153).

460 Vogt, George McGill. 'Gleanings for the History of a Sentiment: *Generositas Virtus, Non Sanguis.*' *JEGP*, 24 (1925), 102–24.

On the sentiment that 'unto vertu longeth dignitee, / And noght the revers, saufly dar I deme,' Vogt concludes that the idea was not 'at all novel or striking in the fourteenth century, or, perhaps, in any century.' The truth seems to be that the sentiment is one which lends itself 'to poetic treatment in all ages and has little to do with the actualities either of the poet's criticism of life or of his practice' (p 102). Vogt cites passages expressing the sentiment in Seneca, Juvenal, Boethius, Wace, Andreas Capellanus, Guilielmus Peraldus, Gaydon, Jean de Meun, Frère Lorens, Baudoiun et Jean de Condé, various French proverbs, Robert of Brunne, Dante, Boccaccio, Richard Rolle, Langland, Wyclif, Dan Michel, Chaucer (eleven passages), Gower, and many other English writers on up into the nineteenth century. He finds six passages reflecting the opposite sentiment, namely that 'a gentleman will ever show himself a gentleman, and a villain a villain' (p 123).

Lak of Stedfastnesse

See also **39, 41, 46, 89, 103, 106, 444.**

460a *The Bannatyne Manuscript, compiled by George Bannatyne, 1568.* 4 vols.
Printed for the Hunterian Club, 1896; rpt New York: Johnson Reprint
Corporation, 1966.
Includes 'Sumtyme this Warld so Steidfast was' (f 67a), II, 181–2, as item
n 70, and 'The Song of Troyelus: Gif no luve is, O God, quhat feill I so'
(f 230a), III, 668–9, as item no 224, as well as eight other apocryphal
poems attributed to Chaucer.

461 Braddy, Haldeen. 'The Date of Chaucer's *Lak of Steadfastnesse.' JEGP*, 36
(1937), 481–90.
Braddy thinks Deschamps a more likely model than Boethius for the
type of balade Chaucer wrote. After reviewing various arguments on the
date of composition, he concludes that the political criticism in the poem
– the advice to Richard to cease doing his neighbour wrong and to give
up covetyse – seems more applicable to the 1390s than the 1380s; perhaps
the poem should be placed between 1396 (well after Clifford had brought
Chaucer Deschamps's balades) and 1399. 'It seems altogether probable
that while in a middle period Chaucer supported Richard, in his last
years he no less certainly was a partisan of the Lancasters, those generous friends of early days' (p 490).

462 — *Chaucer and the French Poet Graunson.* 1947. See **84.**
Braddy compares *Sted* to *Balade de Sens,* a political poem once attributed
to Deschamps, now claimed for Graunson. The *Balade* discusses
covetousness, pride, lack of truth and pity and 'tells how princes may
hold their people in true union' (p 67).

463 Brusendorff, A. *The Chaucer Tradition.* 1925. See **28.**
Sted was 'probably intended as a Machiavellian compliment to Richard
on his bold bid for supremacy [ca 1388] rather than as a somewhat commonplace reflection on his failure to do justice, a reflection which
Chaucer would hardly have dared to address to the king' (p 274).

464 Cohen, Helen Louise. *The Ballade.* New York: Columbia University Press,
1915.
Sted has 'an animus different from that found in his other *ballades* ... a
means of expressing the social confusion and the unrest of his day'
(p 242). Chaucer 'only occasionally reflects the social discontents of his
day; his outlook on life is plainly not that of a professional reformer, but
certainly in this *ballade* he pauses to analyse the source of evil in his age.
If the *general* idea ... be taken from Boethius ... one can only say that the
old philosopher's reflections merely furnished Chaucer with a point of
departure' (pp 242–3).

465 Cross, J.E. 'The Old Swedish *Trohetsvisan* and Chaucer's *Lak of Stedfastnesse* – A Study in Mediaeval Genre.' *Saga-Book*, 16 (1965), 283–314. Cross approaches *Sted* through its kinship with the *Trohetsvisan* (Song of Fidelity) and their shared relationships to the Latin *planctus* genre, to demonstrate that the study of Medieval Literature should go hand in hand with a study of genres. Cross describes various features of this kind of poetry in Germanic, French and Latin writers, features like the 'good old days' motif. 'Against such a background who can say that this simple contrast between past and present in *Lak of Stedfastnesse* is specifically Boethian' (p 296). Nor is there anything specific in the poem to suggest a debt to Deschamps. Cross includes in appendices a text and translation of the Troheten and a line by line comparison of *Sted* with various other literary works to reveal how commonplace the ideas are (pp 303–14). He does not attempt to illustrate the last stanza 'since there are no parallels of this feature within the genre except in poems written in ballade form,' which might suggest a French influence for the content. Cross warns against reading into the envoy a specific attack on Richard II or trying to date the poem in terms of it: 'There is no conclusive evidence within the poem of the identity of the recipient' (p 299). The accuracy of Shirley's statements on Chaucer's sending the ballade to Richard is 'difficult to assess' (p 301). It seems likely that 'John Shirley who was not only a (careless) scribe but a flourishing commercial publisher who had his eye to his customers when writing some of these gossipy headings, since he ran a kind of circulating library for a set of noble clients on strictly business lines. Of course he may have had special information since he was connected with court and literary circles but there is no certainty about this' (p 302).

466 Donahue, J.J. *Chaucer's Lesser Poems*. 1974. See **21**.
Though *Sted* is usually classified with the Boethian group, its connection with Boethius is 'too slight to justify the assignment.' The poem has a feeling for the 'real abuses of the poet's times, but [is] cool enough and broad enough to be shared by men of other times. Chaucer ... abandons his usual stance of devoted or amused bystander ... He is personal, but by avoiding narrow resentment and taking a moral stand against dishonor, he makes alliance with the aspirations of mankind' (p 244).

467 Donaldson, E.T. *Chaucer's Poetry*. 1958/1975. See **14**.
Sted is an 'exercise in the genre of advice to kings ... Chaucer should probably not be given too much credit for assuming this role of moral counselor to the monarch. Kings in the Middle Ages received a very large amount of good advice from court poets, probably as part of the poets' duties' (p 962/1126).

468 French, R.D. *Chaucer Handbook.* 1927. See **99**.
French reviews approaches to dating the poem in terms of the envoy;
notes that the poem uses only three rimes throughout.

469 Robbins, R.H. *Companion to Chaucer Studies.* 1968/1979. See **136**.
Sted, with Boethius II.m.8 as starting point, 'diverges from the Boethian
stress on love and presents the *un*-natural order of society ... The poem
approximates the evils-of-the-age tradition; one could almost rewrite
Chaucer from single lines of other jeremiads.' The envoy is also conventional, 'so conventional, in fact, that Lydgate incorporated this envoy in
his "Prayer for England," where "it satisfactorily dovetails into the whole
poem" (Robbins, *Hist. Poems*, p 389)' (p 326/393).

470 Schlauch, Margaret. 'Chaucer's Doctrine of Kings and Tyrants.' *Spec*, 20
(1945), 133–56.
Schlauch reviews the lively discussions of kings and tyranny in the
twelfth to fourteenth centuries – such topics as common profit, a ruler's
obligations, the recourses of the people, admissible forms of resistance,
and the validity of hereditary succession. Chaucer's admonition to the
King in the envoy to *Sted* is reminiscent of praises bestowed upon Edward I by an anonymous chronicle – mercy, peace, observance of law,
and just severity. The literature against tyranny was vast by Chaucer's
day – eg the political treatises of Marsilius of Padua, Dante, William of
Ockham, and Wyclif. It is not possible to say how much of the debate
Chaucer knew. He may have had extensive contact with the ideas on his
trips to Italy, however (pp 146–8). He introduces tyranny as a topic in
*LGW, KnT, MLT, ParsT, Mars, Pity, T&C, FA, ClerkT, MonkT, PhysT, PF,
Purse, Boece,* and, of course, *Sted*. The articles of Richard's deposition
show the larger issues clearly, issues which were 'already hoary from
centuries of debate' (p 155).

471 Skeat, W.W. *Oxford Chaucer.* 1894/1899. See **1**.
Skeat relates the general idea of *Sted* to Boethius, II.m.8, which he
presents in Chaucer's translation. He notes also that the Bannatyne ms
inserts a spurious fourth stanza which runs thus:

Falsheid, that sowld bene abhominable,
Now is regeing, but reformatioun,
Quha now gifis lergly are maist dissavable,
For vycis are the grund of sustentatioun;
All wit is turnit to cavillatioun,
Lawtie expellit, and al gentilnes,
That all is loist for laik of steidfastnes.

'This is very poor stuff,' Skeat concludes (I, p 556).

L'Envoy de Chaucer a Bukton

See also **102, 489, 490.**

472 Braddy, Haldeen. 'Sir Peter and the "Envoy to Bukton."' *PQ*, 14 (1935), 368–70.

Information in the Kirkstall Chronicle (1355–1400) supports Kuhl's suggestion (475) that Chaucer's Bukton was Sir Peter. When Richard II was confined at Knaresborough he was committed to the hands of Peter Bukton. There is no way of knowing whether Bukton had a part in the execution at Pontefract, but the fact that Bukton accepted custody of Richard gives convincing testimony that he was a partisan of Bolingbroke. The new king granted Bukton for life the office of steward of the lordship of Holderness. In 1400, as further appreciation, he was made constable of Knaresborough Castle. 'Chaucer's affiliations with Henry of Bolingbroke have long been recognized ... The evidence presented here would seem to suggest that Chaucer may have sponsored the cause of Henry a little earlier than we have supposed' (p 370).

473 Diamond, Arlyn. 'Chaucer's Women and Women's Chaucer.' In *The Authority of Experience: Essays in Feminist Criticism*. Ed. Arlyn Diamond and Lee R. Edwards. Amherst: University of Massachusetts Press, 1977, pp 60–83.

'An examination of Chaucer inspired by feminist concerns is not an historical perversity ... but a very natural way of approaching him, given the lively, even obsessive interest the later Middle Ages took in the problem of female nature' (pp 60–1). One Chaucerian stance toward women reflected in *Bukton* is 'clear enough in its jocular masculine cynicism' (p 64). On the other hand in works like *T&C* and *LGW* 'his equivocal nature, his tendency to create increasing complexity where other authors might seek resolutions, his preference for the dramatic as opposed to the lyric, all make him one of the most elusive friends women have ever had' (p 65). Chaucer was fascinated with Alisoun. 'He is both attracted and repelled by the idea of a vigor and independence stretching beyond the narrow range of categories open to him, and in her figure, and in his lifelong mining of the subject of women and love we sense his own discomfort with the categories ... He means to be women's friend, insofar as he can be, and it is this painfully honest effort, this unwillingness to be satisfied with the formulas of his age, which we as feminists can honor in him' (p 83).

473a Héraucourt, Will. 'What is Trouthe or Soothfastnesse?' *Englische Kultur in Sprachwissenschaftlicher Deutung*. Leipzig: Quelle and Meyer, 1936, pp 75–84.

Chaucer frequently redoubles nouns in his translations. But he also often reduplicates nouns when he is defining a moral value (p 76). In *Bukton*, line 2, he doubles *soothfastnesse* with *trouthe*. *Soothe* connotes an absolute moral value; *trouthe* has its roots in psychology and is more relative. It is a virtue realizable in the empirical world, as it approaches *soothe* through *soothefastnesse*. In the first stanza of *Bukton*, the gloss on Pilate's question to Christ, 'Quid est veritas?', implies that faith should manifest itself in works, not in some transcendental philosophy (p 84).

474 Kittredge, George L. 'Chaucer's *Envoy to Bukton.' MLN*, 24 (1909), 14–5.

It is hazardous to draw inferences about Chaucer's married life 'from so jocose a poem as the address *To Bukton*' (p 14). Kittredge compares the poem to various balades by Deschamps which praise the freedom of the celibate, mock the fool who would marry a second time, and dissuade a friend from wedlock. 'Chaucer's *Envoy to Bukton* may or may not be in good taste, but we are certainly not justified ... in allowing it any autobiographical significance ... Probably such utterances were no more seriously meant than the jests which are passed upon an intending bridegroom by his intimates at pre-nuptial "stag dinners" now-a-days' (p 15).

475 Kuhl, Ernest P. 'Chaucer's "My Maistre Bukton".' *PMLA*, 38 (1923), 115–32.

Kuhl reviews speculations on who Bukton was – Robert of Suffolk or Peter of Yorkshire? Peter was friend to Lewis Clifford, Philip Vache, and John Clanvowe, and part of the group closely connected with John of Gaunt. 'If Robert of Suffolk is "my maistre Bukton" then he is the only person in the poet's close literary circle, who, though more or less prominent in state affairs, was not a knight nor a follower of Gaunt or Derby' (pp 128–9). The reference to 'Frise' (line 23) implies some knowledge about the military and fits Peter, who while a youth served with Gaunt, could testify at the Scrope-Grosvenour controversy, and was one of a handful to accompany Derby on two Prussian expeditions. 'Life in the edge of perilous battle was not ... for Robert Bukton,' however (p 129).

476 Lowes, John Livingston. 'The Date of the *Envoy to Bukton.' MLN*, 27 (1912), 45–8.

'I do not wish categorically to assert that the date of *Bukton* is *not* the close of 1396 [ie, the date of the expedition of William of Hainault, alluded to in stanza 4]; but I do desire to point out that considerable caution should still be exercised in drawing exact chronological conclusions from the reference to being "take in Fryse"' (p 45). The reference to Fryse may itself be a commonplace; the Frieslanders enjoyed a certain proverbial notoriety in Chaucer's day. Still, it is likely that the Hainault expedition is a factor, though whether it is the preparation or the expedition itself which is alluded to is not clear. Chaucer's line would have little or no point after the expedition, so the poem was probably written sometime after 1393 but certainly before 1397 where Bukton's wife is mentioned in a grant.

477 Tatlock, John S.P. 'Notes on Chaucer: Earlier or Minor Poems.' *MLN*, 29 (1914), 97–101.

Concerning the folly of second marriage Chaucer could be borrowing from John of Salisbury's mocking of marriage, especially second marriage, in *Polycraticus* 8.11, a work Chaucer knew and used elsewhere. Salisbury quotes some of Chaucer's favourite passages on the subject from Theophrastus and St Jerome.

L'Envoy de Chaucer a Scogan

See also **88, 102.**

478 David, Alfred. 'Chaucer's Good Counsel to Scogan.' *ChauR*, 3 (1969), 265–74.

This 'most delightful and intriguing of Chaucer's shorter poems' is difficult to deal with because of its occasional nature, for which we do not know the occasion, and because it is often labelled as a begging poem, thus confusing its actual form (p 265). Both *Scogan* and *Bukton* belong to 'a tradition that may be called by the title given to Chaucer's *Truth* in several manuscripts: "Balade de Bon Conseyl".' The humour of these epistles 'depends partly on mocking the conventional seriousness of the moral ballade' (p 266). Perhaps *Scogan* is a witty response to some court poem which Scogan wrote. [Cf Alois Brandl, *Mittelenglische Literatur* in Hermann Paul, *Grundriss der germanischen Philologie* (Strassburg, 1893), II,i,684, who suggests that Scogan's blasphemy consisted in writing *The Court of Love*, which contains scurrilous lines that might have offended the god; also Kittredge (**485**, p 112), who notes that *CL* was written a century later than Scogan's *Moral Ballade*, but allows that Chaucer's poem could have been written in response to some other poem recited at court (David, p 268).] David analyses *Scogan* stanza by stanza, commenting on the tone as he proceeds to support his theory of wit and comedy in the poem. 'The humor as well as the point of Chaucer's advice turns upon the resemblances between Scogan and himself. Scogan is now as Chaucer was, and will become as Chaucer is now. Their fortunes as well as their figures may be alike, and Chaucer is afraid lest the God of Love make a scapegoat of anyone who resembles Scogan' (p 270). Chaucer's fear that Scogan's sin may deprive not only lovers but love poets of their reward is similar to jests in *LGW*. Though all three *Scogan* mss gloss 'stremes hed' as 'Windsorr' and its 'ende' as 'Greenwich,' 'on the primary level the stream must ... be taken not literally but metaphorically' to signify grace, honor, worthiness – that is, prosperity (p 272). The reference to Tully and friendship probably is meant to recall Cicero and Atticus, the 'paternal advice to a distinguished young man from a philosophically-minded older friend' (p 273). The poem has its serious side too: 'The fiction that Scogan's rash oath has brought about a deluge is comic and ironic, but the theme of mutability with which Chaucer plays is edged with seriousness' (p 273).

479 Donahue, J.J. *Chaucer's Lesser Poems.* 1974. See **21.**

Because of its wit, humour, and adroit shift from scolding to the self-pity of growing old, losing skill, and submitting to corrosive time, '*Scogan* does not suffer from being an occasional poem.' Donahue juxtaposes David's assessment of the poem (**478**) as one of Chaucer's most delightful shorter poems with Tatlock's calling it the most pathetic of them all (**495**), to see merit in both positions (p 261).

480 Farnham, Willard E. 'John (Henry) Scogan.' *MLR*, 16 (1921), 120–8.

Farnham argues that the Henry Scogan of Chaucer's time, a 'poet of respectable reputation,' and John Scogan the 'university-educated jokester and court fool,' who supposedly flourished a hundred years later, are one and the same person (p 120). Farnham discusses the bibliographical evidence available on *The Geystes of Skoggon,* published 1565–6 (no copy known), then republished in 1613 (one copy known), and again in 12° blackletter in 1626, and again ca 1655 and 1680. With each edition the editors extend his apocryphal life, giving him an Oxford MA, banishment to France, etc. The accusation by a Jesuit that his thinking was 'Protestant' is obviously apocryphal. His patron is said to be Sir William Neuil and Nevill; that must be Sir William Neville, who was witness for Chaucer in the suit brought by Cecily Chaumpaigne against the poet. He could be the patron of a Scoggin who 'engineers a characteristic bit of horseplay at a medieval Easter play in France' (p 125). A ms of 1480 includes an epitaph recalling John Scogan, a man of mirth who may have been a poet (p 126). The duality of Scogan simply cannot be argued from the duality of names. '*Lenvoy de Chaucer a Scogan* certainly admits the possibility that Scogan played "sporting parts," though probably, as Holinshed charitably remarks, "not in such uncivil manner as hath beene of him reported." Chaucer's *Envoy* is replete with affectionate banter ... The very spontaneity of Chaucer's banter seems to imply a subject who would repay the effort with an appreciative laugh' (pp 127–8). Henry Scogan must be the man we are searching for. After his death 'John' was bestowed upon him in confusion.

481 — 'Scogan's *Quem Quaerites*.' *MLN*, 37 (1922), 289–92.

The 1613 edition of *Scoggin's Jestes* contains a *Quem Quaerites* play amusingly spiced up by a priest and his one-eyed lemman. The compiler pretends he has translated the account out of the French. Undoubtedly

Scoggin's jests circulated before their first reported publication in 1565 [cf **480**]. 'Scoggin the jester was probably the same Scogan who lived in Chaucer's time and appears in Chaucer's *Envoy*' (p 291). In Scogan's play the secularization seems to have gone so far that some of the parts at least were played by townspeople.

481a Brooks, Neil C. 'Scogan's *Quem Quaeritis* and *Till Eulenspiegel*.' *MLN*, 38 (1923), 57.

A reply to Farnham **481**. The jest is taken from *Till Eulenspiegel*, translated ca 1560. The only alteration is the introduction of a pronounced anticatholic sentiment. The earliest preserved edition of *Till Eulenspiegel* is the Strassburg edition of 1515 in German. Certainly the tale is not of English origin; nor is there evidence of a French tie. Brooks cites studies which relate the episode to *Quem Quaerites*.

482 French, Walter H. 'The Meaning of Chaucer's *Envoy to Scogan*.' *PMLA*, 48 (1933), 289–92.

French objects to reading the poem as a begging poem; the plea occurs only in the last stanza. Rather, it is a refusal to write a conciliatory poem in Scogan's name. Chaucer may have been asked to write a poem smoothing over the matter hinted at in the poem. Disliking to interfere, the poet refuses. To do so without offence he assumes a jocular and plaintive tone, speaking himself like the injured party. 'His counterthrust is a sort of *a fortiori*' (p 290). The poem is thus a 'medieval *Rape of the Lock*. Like Pope, Chaucer was called upon to write something to bring together two persons at outs with one another; but unlike Pope, he declined the commission. As he hints in the poem, he may have attempted such tasks in the past; but in old age, he felt another such effort beyond his strength' (p 292). If this reading is correct, *Scogan* is 'unique in its type'; there is nothing like it in the extensive 'amatory literature of the period' (p 292). The whimsical independence is to be expected: 'The young clerk in the service of the house of Lancaster might have written love allegories to order; the retired courtier wrote what he pleased, and not even a good friend could command his services on any terms but Chaucer's own' (p 292).

482a Galway, Margaret. 'Geoffrey Chaucer, J.P. and M.P.' *MP*, 36 (1941), 1–36.

In discussing life records pertaining to Chaucer's service as J.P., Clerk of the Works, and Knight of the Shire, Galway comments on Henry Scogan, 'the friend to whom Chaucer addressed his Envoy' (p 8). She assigns the poem itself to 1391 or 1393 (p 16).

483 Goffin, R.C. 'Lenvoy de Chaucer a Scogan.' *MLR*, 20 (1925), 318–21.

Goffin does not think Chaucer had in mind any Latin work in the 'Tullius kindenesse' passage. Rather he draws from *RR* 5286. Goffin draws other parallels between the *Envoy* and the *Romaunt*, especially passages on the incompatibility of sex and old age. '"Fructifye" is Chaucer's *verbum sapienti*' (p 321).

484 Kean, Patricia. *Chaucer and the Making of English Poetry.* 1972. See **114.**
Scogan is a choice example of *divertissement* for the urbanites of the court,
'a magnificent set-piece of the mock-sublime' (I, 33) with its familiar
voice and mixture of plain, colloquial, blunt, conventional, witty, and
lively language (I, 33–7).

485 Kittredge, George Lyman. 'Henry Scogan.' *Harvard Studies and Notes,* 1
(1892) 109–17.
In response to Alois Brandl's suggestion that Scogan may be the author
of the pseudo-Chaucerian *Court of Love* (*Englische Literatur* II,i,684; see
478), Kittredge shows by linguistic evidence that *CL* belongs to the end
of the fifteenth century or later, when Scogan had been dead nearly a
hundred years. The poem of Scogan's that does survive is the *Moral Ballade to the Lords of the King's House,* which must have been written before
1407, when Scogan died. Chaucer's *Lenvoy* is too jocose a document to be
used as biographical evidence at all. Scogan's imagined reply, 'Lo! olde
Grisel list to ryme and pleye,' is 'just such a rejoinder as a young man
might well make to a friend twenty years his senior who had jocosely included him with himself in the class of antiquated gallants' (p 117). See
478.

486 — 'Chauceriana.' *MP,* 7 (1910), 465–83.
'The curious figure of a "Muse" conceived as "rusting" – in the *Envoy to
Scogan* – is a reminiscence of Alanus de Insulis, though Alanus is not
responsible for Chaucer's (half-jocose?) metaphor' (p 483).

487 Lenaghan, R.T. 'Chaucer's *Envoy to Scogan:* The Uses of Literary Conventions.' *ChauR,* 10 (1975), 46–61.
Lenaghan uses the envoy to explore the circumstances of civil servants
in the 1390s. *Scogan* is compared to the courtly begging poems by
Deschamps to reveal the practical facts of solicitation. Scogan is conventional in its rhetorical features and its subject, but at the same time the
envoy is a personal poem of one in Richard II's household, a call to a
friend in need. 'The statement of the poem is not, "Renew my pension,"
or "Don't defy love"; rather, it is something close to "We are friends; we
react the same way to the matter of love." Chaucer's tone projects a genial dignity. Without subordinating himself, he seeks a favour of his
friend by rehearsing the style of their equality' (p 57). The rhetorical
commonplaces about friendship reflect a civil servant seeking relief from
some of the stresses of his position.

488 Moore, Samuel. 'The Date of Chaucer's Marriage Group.' *MLN,* 26 (1911),
172–4.
Scogan was probably written in autumn 1393. The reference to Chaucer's
muse rusting in the sheath may refer to 'sober fact' (p 174). Chaucer
seems to have written in productive flourishes; *Scogan,* along with the
stimulus by Deschamps, got Chaucer going again, the result being the

marriage group of the *CT* (1393–6). *Bukton* must have been written at the end of that interval, since it mentions the Wife of Bath. But Chaucer did not write regularly. 'When his imagination was kindled by the dramatic possibilities of some new device, Chaucer worked at the *Canterbury Tales* with great energy; when he had exhausted these possibilities he laid the work aside until he could come at another device. It seems reasonable, therefore, to take Chaucer's utterance in the *Envoy to Scogan* as marking one of these periods in which he was not actively at work on the *Canterbury Tales*, but lying fallow' (p 174).

488a — 'The New Chaucer Items.' *MLR*, 22 (1927), 435–8.

Comments on documents which support the allusion in *Scogan* to Chaucer's residence in Greenwich in the early 1390's.

489 Norton-Smith, John. 'Chaucer's Epistolary Style.' In *Essays on Style and Language: Linguistic and Critical Approaches to Literary Style*. Ed. Roger Fowler. London: Routledge and Kegan Paul, 1966, pp 157–65.

Norton-Smith's 'exercise in sympathy' (p 157) reconstructs Chaucer's attitude toward the verse epistle on the basis of *Scogan*, *Bukton*, the two letters incorporated into *T&C* V, and those that appear in *LGW*. One strong influence is the *Heroides*, especially in *LGW*. In *T&C*, 'Chaucer's polite, graceful and conventional style,' a style which compares to that of verse epistles by Deschamps, 'sets the tone for the vast number of amatory verse epistles which was to be written in England in the fifteenth century' (p 159). The *Envoys* reflect Horatian influences. In *Scogan* Chaucer derives his image of pen-sword-rusting-in-sheath from Horace, *Satires* II, lines 39–44, a hitherto unsuspected source. This passage does not appear in the Horatian commentaries and does not seem to have been imitated by Medieval Latin poets, which 'is perhaps valuable in proving that Chaucer knew Horace' (p 162, n 14). In both *Scogan* and *Bukton* Chaucer captures 'the easy, conversational style of the Horatian epistle' in his imagery, syntax, and tone (p 163). The structure is not Horatian, however, at least not from his epistles, though there may be structural influence from Horace's *Odes* (p 164). 'Chaucer's achievement in the letter genre is stylistically distinct from that of his medieval forerunners and of his fifteenth- and sixteenth-century imitators. Only one English verse epistle of Charles of Orléans aims at a conversational style. It is only moderately effective for it fails to achieve easy intimacy' (p 164). 'In the *Envoi a Scogan* the command of urbane conversational syntax and style, of sly and playful use of mythology, of structural indirection, together with the Horatian borrowing, marks Chaucer out as the first English poet to master the essentials of the Augustan verse epistle' (p 165).

490 — *Geoffrey Chaucer.* 1974. See **361**.

Ch 7, 'The Envoi a Scogan and The Envoi a Bukton,' pp 213–25, relates these two 'genuine, independent, poetic epistles' (p 216), with their 'high degree of artistic craftsmanship' and 'kind of sophistication of tone,' to classical sources. In them we find 'a literary elegance and cultivation which we are more usually asked to associate with the Renaissance, or even with the Augustan temper of social verse of the eighteenth century' (p 213). 'Chaucer's ambiguous blend of playfulness and seriousness is typically Horatian' (p 218) in tone, though not in structure (cf **489**). Norton-Smith outlines the combination of rhetorical factors (enjambment, absence of tags and fillers) which contribute to the urbane, conversational effect. He then contrasts the tone of *Bukton* with Juvenalian indignation to reassert Chaucer's ties with the calm, quiet, gently jesting Horatian style (p 221). 'In Chaucer we meet a mind we cannot patronize ... a mind with immense technical resources in the arts of rhetoric and poetry, but with even greater resources in the art of reading literature at an excellent linguistic standard in at least four languages ... Chaucerian criticism on the whole seems happiest when relating Chaucer to the limitations of his contemporary writers, to tame conventions, to a range of ideas, complicated only in their being accommodated to the various academic arguments, otherwise narrow and largely unconsciously dismissive of the intellectual activity of the poet, his best-informed friends or the poetic fascinations of a great classical and late antique literature. Deschamps' contemporary praise and assessment of the living Chaucer always was nearer the truth' (p 225).

491 Phipps, Thomas M. 'Chaucer's Tullius.' *MLN*, 58 (1943), 108–9.

The Tullius reference in *Scogan*, line 28, is usually thought to refer to Cicero's *De Amicitia* or *Epistle VI ad Caecinam*, or perhaps the *Romaunt*, lines 5285 ff, on friendship. But none of these sources are very satisfactory. Perhaps the reference is to Tullius Hostilius who loved the poor and gave lands to those who had none. His generosity was well known to Chaucer and his friends. In *Bukton* Chaucer mentions the Wife of Bath, who in her tale speaks of 'Tullius Hostilius / That out of poverty roos to heigh noblesse.' Henry Scogan, who is probably the Scogan addressed in the *Envoi*, alludes to Tullius Hostilius in his *Moral Balade* when, after repeatedly referring to Chaucer as his master, he says, 'Take hede of Tullus Hostilius / That came from poverty to high degree' (p 109).

492 Polzella, Marion L. '"The Craft So Long to Lerne": Poet and Lover in Chaucer's "Envoy to Scogan" and *Parliament of Fowls*.' *ChauR*, 10 (1976), 279–86.

Polzella relates the detached narrator in the *Envoy* to other poems, especially *PF*, to show that although Chaucer's romantically backward narrator is a vehicle to evoke the world of love, he is also used to comment on the making of poetry. Both poems share the poet-lover's problems of time and craft. 'The "Envoy" itself is evidence that the poet, even while uncertain of his labor's "mede," remains devoted to his "craft"' (p 286).

493 Robinson, F.N. *Works.* 1957. See **12.**

Robinson suggests that the last stanza, with its personal message, 'has somewhat the effect of the envoy of a regular ballade' (p 523).

Cf, Maynard (**67**, p 59), who thinks of the poem as a double ballade with envoi.

494 Skeat, W.W. *Oxford Chaucer,* 1894/1899. See **1.**

Skeat discusses Henry Scogan along with Scogan's *Moral Balade* under his entry on *Gent* (I, pp 82–4). 'He is doubtless the very person to whom Chaucer's "Lenvoy a Scogan" was addressed, and Chaucer (line 21) there gives him an excellent character for wisdom of speech' (I, p 83). He is not to be confused with Thomas Scogan or the Scogin of that 'idle book called "Scoggins Iests"' (p 83). 'When Shakespeare, in 2 Hen.IV.iii.2.33, says that Sir John Falstaff broke Scogan's head, he was no doubt thinking of the supposed author of the jest-book, and may have been led, by observation of the name in a black-letter edition of Chaucer, to suppose that he lived in the time of Henry IV. This was quite enough for his purpose, though it is probable that the jester lived in the time of Edward IV ... On the other hand, we find Ben Jonson taking his ideas about Scogan solely from Henry Scogan's poem and Chaucer's Envoy, without any reference to the jester. See his Masque of the Fortunate Isles, in which Scogan is first described and afterwards introduced' (I, 83–4). On the deluge of the first two stanzas of Scogan, Skeat quotes an account of great rains in the autumn of 1393, recorded in Stowe's *Annales* of 1605, in which the walls of houses were borne down and 'men and women hardly escaped drowning' (I, pp 556–7).

495 Tatlock, J.S.P. *Mind and Art of Chaucer.* 1950. See **147.**

Bukton seems to be 'out of Chaucer's own experience,' as the poet advises against a second marriage. *Scogan,* though less serious, voices, nonetheless, 'the occasional pessimism of a man beginning to feel his years and the decay of his powers, and feeling forgotten by the great world. Of all Chaucer's poems it is the most pathetic' (p 85).

Merciles Beaute

Robinson **12** and Fisher **23** include *MB* among poems of doubtful authorship. But see **508.**

See also **55, 73, 89.**

496 Birney, Earle. 'Beginnings of Chaucer's Irony.' 1939. See **83.**
   MB is 'the expression of a gallant in a holiday mood, not the grimaces of
   a professional clown' (p 642).
497 Davies, R.T., ẹd. *Medieval English Lyrics.* 1963. See **16.**
   Davies presents *MB* as three related roundels on unreturned love. 'It
   would be unwise to regard either the humour or the colloquial vigour of
   the final roundel as peculiarly Chaucerian' (p 330).
498 Dodd, W.G. *Courtly Love.* 1913. See **96.**
   Though none but conventional ideas appear in *MB*, the poem exemplifies Chaucer's ability to revitalize conventional material with his own individuality. Only Chaucer could have written the last stanza (pp 101–2).
499 Donaldson, E.T. *Chaucer's Poetry.* 1958/1975. See **14.**
   MB 'has a characteristic Chaucerian ring' (p 960/1124).
500 Françon, Marcel. 'Note on Chaucer's Roundels and His French Models.'
   Annali Instituto Orientale, Napoli, Sezione Germanica, 9 (1966), 195–7.
   Musically, the *rondeau* is made up of two parts, the arrangement
   corresponding to the scheme STS–SSTST; in literary terms it is 'characterized by three stanzas and two rimes. The first stanza is used as a *refrain*,
   the first part of which is repeated at the end of the second stanza, while
   the complete *refrain* is repeated at the end of the third stanza. Originally,
   the first stanza was made up of only *two* lines, ... This – the simplest
   form of the *rondeau* – was called *triolet*' (p 196). There are other kinds of
   rondeau, according to number of lines in the first stanza – *rondeau tercet*,
   rondeau quatrain, rondeau cinquain, etc. Chaucer's 'Now welcom' at the end
   of *PF* corresponds to the *rondeau tercet*; *MB* is a series of *three rondeaux
   tercets.* 'The *rondeaux tercets* are comparatively rather rare, whereas the
   rondeaux quatrains and *rondeaux cinquains* are more often used, together
   with the *triolets*' (p 197).
501 French, R.D. *Chaucer Handbook.* 1927. See **99.**
   The tone of the poem suggests a date approximating that of the playful
   Bukton (p 105).
502 Hammond, E.P. *Bibliographical Manual.* 1908. See **37.**
   MB was first printed by Percy in his *Reliques,* 1767 (II, 11), as 'an Original
   Ballad by Chaucer.' Percy says in his introductory note, 'This little sonnet, which hath escaped all the editors of Chaucer's works, is now printed for the first time from an ancient ms in the Pepysian library, that

contains many other poems of its venerable author.' Hammond outlines
the fate of the poem in the hands of subsequent editors. Koch, *Chronology*, p 40, dated it about the same time as *PF*, or after *T&C* (pp 436–7).

503 Legouis, E. *Geoffrey Chaucer*. 1913. See **117**.

MB is 'mere amorous convention without a quiver of the voice' (p 62).
'Chaucer seems to scoff at the very style he has just employed' (p 63).

504 Lowes, John Livingston. 'The Chaucerian "Merciles Beaute" and Three
Poems of Deschamps.' *MLR*, 5 (1910), 33–9.

Deschamps's virelay (n 541, *Oeuvres*, SATF, III, 382) contains many
phrases of a conventional sort which relate to *MB* and are in the same
order and arrangement in which they appear in the Chaucerian poem.
Moreover, the two balades which precede the virelay in Deschamps belong to a Marguerite group, so 'there is some ground for thinking that
Chaucer may have known one of them.' The pair may have been among
the *euvres d'escolier* which Deschamps sent Chaucer. It is not known
whether the three poems have always been ordered as they now are in
the folio (p 35). Lowes finds some details of the roundel in the balades.
If the inferences are sound, 'Chaucer's authorship of "Merciles Beaute"
may be regarded as established beyond reasonable doubt' (p 37). There is
no evidence that any of Chaucer's English contemporaries who 'made of
sentiment' were interested in or knew Deschamps at all. 'That fact, taken
in conjunction with what has always been felt to be the genuinely Chaucerian ring of the lines, is, I think, practically conclusive' (p 37). Lowes
finds wit similar to Chaucer's in *Scogan* in the *Réponse* which follows
Deschamps's group. It may be then that the poems numbered 9, 540, 541,
536(?), 567, 568, 570, 569(?) were among the *euvres d'escolier* sent to
Chaucer, along with the famous balade. Probably the *Lay de Franchise*,
which Chaucer used in the Prol. to *LGW*, was included too, and the four
flour and leaf poems as well, though they may have reached Philippa of
Lancaster at an earlier date. The missive from Deschamps would require
some response from Chaucer. Perhaps there was an *Envoy de Chaucer a
Deschamps*.

505 Renoir, Alain. 'The Inept Lover and the Reluctant Mistress: Remarks on
Sexual Inefficiency in Medieval Literature.' In *Chaucerian Problems and
Perspectives: Essays Presented to Paul E. Beichner, C.S.C.* Ed. Edward Vasta
and Zacharias P. Thundy. Notre Dame: University of Notre Dame Press,
1979, pp 180–206.

Renoir discusses sexual frustration in the courtly literature of France,
England, and Iceland. His examples from Chaucer include *MilT* and
T&C, with asides on *LGW*, *PF*, and *MB*, where the lover proves himself
the exception by making 'a clean sweep of the fooleries of love with its
never-fulfilled expectations' (pp 180–1).

506 Renwick, W.L. 'Chaucer's Triple Roundel, "Merciles Beaute".' *MLR*, 16 (1921), 322–3.

The réponse of the Duc de Berry to the authors of the *Cent Ballades* (1389) has as its first line: 'Puiz qu'a Amours suis si gras eschapé'; to which Chaucer's refrain in the third roundel is precisely parallel: 'Sin I fro Love escaped am so fat.' Chaucer's line is 'little more than a comic embroidery on the *donnée* of this line, whose quaintness may well have caught the humour of the poet who so willingly made a jest of his own plump figure' (p 323).

507 Robbins, R.H. *Companion to Chaucer Studies*. 1968/1979. See **136**.

MB is a fine example of triple rondel. 'The catchy first line was quoted verbatim in a pseudo-Lydgate poem (Skeat, VII, 281).' After two conventional rondels on the wounded and dying lover, the third is a reversal, the lover giving thanks for not falling in love. 'Chaucer's obverted love lyrics ... were just as conventional (and as influenced by the French) as the direct complaints; and the fifteenth century saw the spread of this sub-genre' (p 325/392). For other observations see **134**, poems 207–12.

508 Robinson, F.N. *Works*. 1957. See **12**.

'In view of the Chaucerian contents of ms Pepys 2006, and of the thoroughly Chaucerian style and meter of the poem, *Merciless Beaute* may be accepted as authentic.' Robinson endorses the possibility of *prisoner* for *prison* in line 28, as suggested by Skeat **512**, but does not follow the suggestion in his text (p 866).

509 Robinson, Ian. *Chaucer's Prosody*. 1971. See **71**.

Commenting on half-line rhythms in balanced pentameters in Chaucer's Moral Balades, Robinson observes: 'If any stylistic evidence is needed for the attribution to Chaucer of *Merciles Beaute* it can surely be found in the rhythms ... This has just the kind of effective stress on the important places. 'If there is a perceptible metrical development in Chaucer it is almost certainly away from pentameter as usually understood towards an increased dependence on half-line movement' (p 174).

510 Root, R.K. *Poetry of Chaucer*. 1900/1922. See **140**.

MB 'is a charmingly graceful, but entirely conventional, love poem, after the French school, and perhaps imitated from a French original' (p 72).

511 Salomon, Louis B. *Devil Take Her*. 1931. See **286**.

The history of the farewell to love type begins with Chaucer. Old English verse contains little that can be called amorous at all. But in *MB* 'the third stanza celebrates the author's escape from the passion that ruled him in the first two ... It is a plain case of withdrawal due to disgust, and as such the forerunner of scores of later poems on the same theme' (p 67). The poem reverses the usual order by describing passion first, then rejecting it. 'Later writers, when they changed their attitude in the midst of a poem, generally began with bluster, but returned cowed in the end' (p 68). Salomon contrasts *MB* with the Lover's rejection of love at the end of Gower's *CA*. In *MB* 'the attitude is that of a released prisoner, celebrating his escape from a jailer for whom he cares not a bean, but under whose power, we feel, he will probably fall again at the first opportunity' (p 68). In *CA* the lover makes a clean break, for love profits naught. 'Chaucer's attitude sounds youthful and swaggering; Gower's suggests rather an old man who has thought the matter out. Between the two of them, they strike the keynote for at least half the anti-amorous poems in English' (p 69).

512 Skeat, W.W. *Oxford Chaucer*. 1894/1899. See **1**.
Skeat finds *MB*'s authenticity beyond question. The movement of ideas is that of Chaucer; the mastery of meter and rhymes are his; the phrases are his. Moreover, there is external testimony in Lydgate's *Ballade in Commendacion of our Ladie*, which quotes the opening line of *MB*. *MB* is the only poem Skeat admits into the set of Minor Poems with incomplete external evidence. 'If it is not Chaucer's it is by some one who contrived to surpass him in his own style. And this is sufficient excuse for its appearance here' (p 81). The allusion to *RR* points to Chaucer, and so does his statement that he wrote roundels. Except for *PF*, lines 680–92, and the three roundels in *MB*, no other Chaucerian roundels are known. Skeat gives titles to each of the three: I. Captivity; II. Rejection; III. Escape.

513 — 'The Chaucerian "Merciles Beaute".' *MLR*, 5 (1910), 194.
Skeat would emend, for metrical reasons, line 26, 'I neuere thenk to ben in his prison lene,' to read 'I neuere thenke ben his prisoun lene,' where *prisoun* means *prisoner*. See **508**.

Proverbs

Printed among the doubtful poems in Robinson **12**.

514 Brusendorff, A. *The Chaucer Tradition*. 1925. See **28**.
The authenticity of *Prov* has been doubted because of the rime *compas* / *embrace* (lines 5, 7). But that is the same rime as *Thopas* / *gras* and *place* / *solas*, which Chaucer uses in *CT* variously. Brusendorff cites a similar quatrain from Deschamps, which lends support to Chaucer's authorship (pp 284–5). See **520**.

515 Donahue, J.J. *Chaucer's Lesser Poems*. 1974. See **21**.
They 'suffice their modest purpose' (p 258).

516 Griffin, R.M. *Chaucer's Lyrics.* 1970. See **18.**

Griffin considers *Prov* to be early poems, Chaucer's first venture into 'contemplative moral verse' (p 27).

517 Hammond, E.P. *Bibliographical Manual.* 1908. See **37.**

Hammond places *Prov* among 'works printed as by Chaucer,' despite the fact that Fairfax 16 and Harley 7578 mark them as being by Chaucer. Shirley does not attribute the poems explicitly to Chaucer (Adds. 16165); he simply heads the two stanzas as 'Prouerbe.' Bradshaw (*Temp Pref.,* pp 107–8) and Koch (*Chronology of Chaucer's Writings,* p 78) doubted Chaucerian authorship on grounds of lack of Shirley's testimony. Skeat (**73,** p 145) says they are genuine, but Hammond follows Bradshaw's reasoning (p 449).

518 Kittredge, G.L. 'Chauceriana.' *MP,* 7 (1910), 465–83.

Kittredge cites French and Latin parallels for the phrase, 'No man caste his pilch away.' The proverb is also well known in German (pp 478–9).

519 Robinson, F.N. *Works.* 1957. See **12.**

Places *Proverbs* in the doubtful category. Robinson notes that two additional seven-line stanzas are added to the eight Chaucerian lines in Harl. 7578; these 'are certainly spurious' (p 867).

520 Skeat, W.W. *Oxford Chaucer.* 1894/1899. See **1.**

Skeat includes *Prov* with the genuine poems. He notes that the rime in line 7 *(embrace)* must be read as *embras,* pointing to a similar instance in *Sir Thopas* where Chaucer puts *gras* for *grac-e.* He also makes the 'most interesting point' of Chaucer's use of the proverb in line 7 in the *Mel,* where we read: "For the proverbe seith, he that to muche embraceth, distreyneth litel" (I, 564–5).

To Rosemounde

See also **40, 101a, 102, 143, 318.**

521 Birney, Earle. 'The Beginnings of Chaucer's Irony.' 1939. See **83.**

On the 'grotesqueries in style' of *Ros,* Birney observes: 'Far from parodying the form or burlesquing the viewpoint of the courtly balade, as some have thought, Chaucer enlivens both by the economical use of the more vivacious metaphors already dared by his masters. Chaucer had not yet prepared the court, or himself, for the out-and-out burlesqueries of *Sir Thopas;* but it is plain that he was already willing to relieve his ennui, and perhaps theirs, with an occasional whimsicality' (p 642).

522 Braddy, Haldeen. *Chaucer and the French Poet Graunson*. 1947. See **84**.
Braddy thinks that several of Chaucer's poems are addressed to actual
persons. 'One may conclude by asking: Who was Rosemounde?' (p 90).

523 Brewer, D.S. 'The Ideal of Feminine Beauty in Medieval Literature.' *MLR*,
50 (1955), 257–69.
'In the frigid little poem "To Rosemounde," Rosemounde shines like cry-
stal (1.3), her cheeks are like ruby (l. 4), and she has a seemly voice (l.
11). Chaucer, as always, is a typical man of his age' (p 269). See **85**.

524 Brusendorff, A. *The Chaucer Tradition*. 1925. See **28**.
Brusendorff would expel *MB* and *Ros* from the Chaucerian canon as examples of 'the more primitive forms of humour employed by lesser men'
(p 440).

525 Cohen, Helen Louise. *The Ballade*. 1915. See **464**.
Ros 'is *vers de société* in the gayest vein with mock-heroic touches' (p 239).

526 Coulton, G.G. *Chaucer and his England*. London: Methuen; Putnam, 1908;
8th ed, Dutton, 1950. Rpt New York: Russell and Russell, 1957. Illustrated with eight plates and other drawings in the text.
Coulton thinks *MB* and *Ros* must be utterances of Chaucer's infirmity
and disillusioned old age, because of their heavy irony (p 68).

527 Davies, R.T., ed. *Medieval English Lyrics*. 1963. See **16**.
Davies comments on the 'finely magniloquent' first stanza with its pleni-
tude of rhetorical figures which 'come naturally and with assured ease'
(p 328). But in the last stanza the tone is uncertain. There are other passages in Chaucer where the tone is uncertain too. 'It is not impossible
that these [passages] are poetically imperfect and that Chaucer was ex-
ceptionally insensitive to their bathos' (p 329).

528 Donahue, J.J. *Chaucer's Lesser Poems*. 1974. See **21**.
Ros is 'an adroit and enjoyable poem,' so witty with its incongruous imagery that 'it is possible to rid the poem of all dignity' (p 132). Donahue
objects to scholars who would take the poem 'sourly.'

529 Donaldson, E.T. *Chaucer's Poetry*. 1958/1975. See **14**.
'The extravagance of courtly images and attitudes is exaggerated and
transferred from the realm of the ideal to the realm of the real: the a-
bused courtly lover might well produce a flood of tears but he would
hardly measure them by the vatful, and he might be overwhelmed with
love, but not like a fish served buried in sauce. The images applied to
Rosamond make her perhaps a bit too crystalline and brittle, and while
the convention of the hopeless lover's everlasting fidelity is maintained,
the poet's presumably woeful state seems nevertheless to leave him rather comfortable, not to say downright jolly' (pp 960–1/1124–5).

530 Howard, Claud. 'The Dramatic Monologue: Its Origin and Development.' *SP*, 4 (1910), 33–88.

Howard suggests that *Ros* takes a first step in the transition from lyric to dramatic monologue by addressing emotional expressions to an individual who is 'visualized and spoken to directly' to conclude that 'this rudimentary form is the only element of the dramatic monologue, for its spirit is essentially that of the lyric' (p 45). Howard mentions also *MB*, but does not consider the more dramatic *Scogan* or *Bukton*.

531 Kitchin, George. *A Survey of Burlesque and Parody in England*. 1931. See **116**.

In *Ros* and *MB* 'the vulgar diction and imagery betray the burlesque intention' (p 14). 'To lower the tone of the poem by flat vulgarities was an obvious means to burlesque' (p 15).

532 Lewis, C.S. *The Allegory of Love*. 1936. See **118**.

The first stanza of *Ros* 'approaches most nearly to the aureate style of its successors.' The pike in 'galauntyne' is objectionable, however, because of the ambiguous tone. Is it comic? 'I feel no confidence. The conception of the "mocking" Chaucer must not be so used as to render it impossible for us to say Chaucer ever wrote ill – which is what follows if everything that cannot please as poetry is immediately set down as humour ... The pike is a case in point. As serious poetry it is bathos: as jest it is flat. What effect Chaucer intended is just one of those things which ... we shall never know, but which Gower or Scogan or John of Gaunt would have known at once and without question' (p 171).

533 Lowes, John Livingston. 'Illustrations of Chaucer Drawn Chiefly from Deschamps.' *RomR*, 2 (1911), 113–28.

Lowes would link *Ros*, line 20, to Froissart, *Oeuvres*, ed. Scheler, II.367: 'That I am trewe Tristam the secounde' / 'Nom ai Amans, et en surnom Tristrans.'

533a McCormick, W.S. 'Another Chaucer Stanza?' In *An English Miscellany Presented to Dr. Furnivall in Honour of his Seventy-Fifth Birthday*. Oxford: Clarendon Press, 1901. Pp 296–300.

The Rawlinson Poet. 163 copy of *T&C* includes the unique text of *Ros* on a flyleaf. The ms also includes an extra stanza of *T&C*, which indicates 'that this manuscript has descended from, or was influenced by, some original of which no other known ms bears the same trace' (p 298). The ms seems to be the work of four scribes, probably of the same scriptorium. McCormick follows Skeat's suggestion (**541**) that 'Tregentyll' or 'Tregentil' at the end of *T&C* and again at the foot of *Ros* is the signature of scribe D.

534 MacCracken, Henry Noble. '"Tregentil Chaucer" and "A. Godwhen."'
Athenaeum, Feb. 29, 1908, p 258.
E.K. Chambers, *Early English Lyrics* (1907), thought 'A. Godwhen,' which
appears in Cambridge ms Ff 1.6, to be a signature. But whenever it appears there is a space between 'God' and 'when.' MacCracken says it
must be a scribal motto – 'A God, when,' ie, the equivalent of 'O Lord,
how long. The motto occurs only with lovers' laments in this ms, and is
plainly a sort of scribal comment.' The signature 'Tregentil-Chaucer' on
p 22 of the ms must refer to Chaucer. A parallel to the expression occurs
in ms BL Sloane 1212, where reference is made on the end leaf to one 'I-
namyd tresgentyl Eger de Femenye.' 'Tresgentyl' is comparable to
'Hochwohlgeboren' in modern German society – 'an appellative recog-
nizant of some social position, little more.'

535 Reiss, Edmund. 'Dusting off the Cobwebs.' 1966. See **130**.
Ros has the same stanza structure, basic rhythm and much the same sort
of vocabulary as *ABC*. But 'while seeming to be polite and courtly' it is 'a
secular, playful and humorous poem' (p 63). The tone is controlled by
the *b*-rhymes which become too ludicrous to have been accidental. 'The
sound is far too heavy – too mooing even – for the praise of the lady and
the assertions of love that follow. It tends to suggest that what appears
as sincerity is really bantering and that the tone of the poem is playful
rather than sad or passionate' (p 63). The metaphors are exaggerated, the
emotion comically extreme: 'The comparison of the *walwed* fish with the
likewise-*walwed* lover could hardly be conducive to making the lady feel
any sadness or *pitee*. It is the height of the ludicrous, especially since the
galauntyne, the wine sauce the phallic pike is in, was, according to the
OED, connected in popular etymology with the term *gallant* – that is,
what the lover presents himself as being' (p 64).

536 Rickert, Edith. 'A Leaf from a Fourteenth-Century Letter Book.' *MP*, 25
(1927), 249–55.
Rickert suggests that *Ros* was written for the child-wife of Richard II,
who was in the keeping of Chaucer's sister-in-law, the newly made Duchess of Lancaster.

537 Robbins, R.H. *Companion to Chaucer Studies*. 1968/1979. See **136**.
Ros is 'a romp, full of fun-poking at the computermatch praise of a mistress – who might even be a little girl ... The chattiness is deceptive; the
poetry is artificial: the form rigid, the style rhetorical – in the first four
lines examples of *exclamatio, translatio, imago*, and *expolitio*' (p 324/391).

538 — 'Chaucer's "To Rosemounde".' *Studies in the Literary Imagination*, 4
(1971), 73–81.
'The language of the entire ballade is conventional, and the lady is addressed with the expected formulas of any *salut d'amour*. Robinson [**12**,
p 521] alone of all the critics stressed this interpretation: "a typical

complimentary poem in the spirit of courtly love"' (p 74). Robbins does
not use Robinson's text, however, but rather that of Kökeritz **40**. He
draws half a dozen parallels between *Ros* and other poems to demonstrate its conventionality and warns that 'a critic must be wary of
misreading his own modern interpretation into lines that cannot support
it.' Even the tyne of tears and pike in sauce have literary antecedents.
The only difference is that in Chaucer 'the fish-lover is cooked.' 'These
possibly dissident phrases have to be reconciled with the strict courtly
tone of the rest of the poem and justified in the overall context' (p 76).
From what is *not* in the description of Rosemounde Robbins thinks 'she
must be a sub-teenager' (p 78) and picks up on suggestions by Rickert
536 and others to suggest that the occasion and function of the poem is
'an aging Chaucer's graceful little compliment to the new queen [Prin-
cess Isabella of Valois, Richard II's seven-year-old bride] of the king who
had befriended him so much, and for whose first young bride, another
young girl (of fifteen), he may perhaps have composed, sixteen years earlier, the "Parlement of Foules" and the "House of Fame." The humor in
"To Rosemounde" consists in the dramatic irony of the application of the
terminology of courtly love to a queen who was but a child and to a
child who was a queen' (p 78). Robbins notes contemporary accounts of
the princess' beauty. Her embroidered robe 'may have suggested to
Chaucer the name Rose (of the world) – and the need for finding eight
rhyming words!' (p 79). From Richard's point of view the marriage was
completely economic. Robbins imagines a grand occasion with Chaucer's
friends and the king present at which the ballade might be presented 'to
delight the child consort' (p 81).

539 Root, R.K. *The Poetry of Chaucer*. 1900/1922. See **140**.

Ros was written at the same time as the longer poems and 'breathes the
same spirit of mingled seriousness and irony' (p 73).

540 Skeat, W.W. 'An Unknown Poem by Chaucer.' *Athenaeum*, April 4, 1891,
p 410.

Announces discovery of the poem in Bodleian ms Rawlinson Poet. 163.
See **541**.

541 — Oxford Chaucer. 1894/1899. See **1**.

'This poem was discovered by me in the Bodleian Library on the 2nd of
April, 1891. It is written on a fly-leaf at the end of ms Rawlinson Poet.
163, which also contains a copy of Chaucer's Troilus. At the end of the
"Troilus" is the colophon: "Here endith the book of Troylus and of
Cresseyde." This colophon is preceded by "Tregentyll," and followed by
"Chaucer." On the next leaf (n 114) is the Balade, without any title, at
the foot of which is "Tregentil" – "Chaucer," the two names being written at a considerable distance apart. I believe "Tregentil" to represent
the name of the scribe. In any case, "Chaucer" represents the name of

the author. It is a happy specimen of his humour' (I, 81). In his notes Skeat gives a recipe for galantine sauce (I, 549–50). He also notes that Cotgrave says a tyne is an open tub holding four or five pailfuls and borne by a 'stang' between two men. 'We picture to ourselves the brawny porters, staggering beneath the "*stang*," on which is slung the "tine" containing "four or five pailfuls" of the poet's tears' (I, 549).

541a Spearing, A.C. and J.E. *Poetry of the Age of Chaucer.* Port Melbourne, Australia: Edward Arnold, 1975. Pp 199–200.

Ros is a courtly parody similar in tone to the turtle-dove's assessment of love in *PF*. The absurdity of the lover's posture is brought 'by elements of excess in the poem's imagery ... It is usually lips, not cheeks, that are compared to rubies, and if her cheeks are round as well as shiny red she must be more like a country girl than a courtly lady' (p 200). The tubful of tears, the 'squeakiness' of the 'out-twining' of the Lady's voice, the ludicrous image of the pike in sauce, and the gross exaggeration of the lover's comparison of himself with Tristram characterize the uncourtliness of the self-depreciating lover whose postures of romantic love verge on farce, 'but with carefully calculated clumsiness' (p 200). The text of *Ros* is printed with glosses pp 218–19.

542 Vasta, Edward. '*To Rosemounde:* Chaucer's "Gentil" Dramatic Monologue.' In *Chaucerian Problems and Perspectives: Essays Presented to Paul E. Beichner.* Ed. Edward Vasta and Zacharias P. Thundy. Notre Dame: Notre Dame University Press, 1979, pp 97–113.

Vasta thinks the 'tregentil' refers to Chaucer and reflects the scribe's perception of Chaucer's achievement, 'more complex than we find it, more delicate and graceful, and thus poetically more noble ... more pleasing, more "gentil"' (p 98). Vasta analyzes the poem from three points of view: I. *The speaker* marks the first perspective. He would praise the lady, complain of lover's pains, profess great love, move her to admiration, sympathy, affection, love, and final solace. His rhetorical strategy is to attract her by 'a display of mental dexterity' (p 99). His tone is one of 'verve and confidence with a distinct sense of self-satisfaction, even a certain pride' (p 101). II. *Rosemounde, receiving the address,* enjoys the second perspective. She is beautiful, courteous, intimate, and dances. The logic of the address projected upon her as audience is to move her toward the enjoyment of her favours, 'replete with intimations of sexual union' (p 102). But from her point of view, if she is the standard lady of such poems, she will be put off, perhaps insulted, possibly shocked and in the end 'laugh at the fool and dismiss him from her mind because his language, his logic, and his tone reveal such limitations of character and talent as to make his cause hopeless. His "unliklynesse" in love ... is everywhere apparent' (p 102). The tub and fish metaphors reveal his incompetence by his language, which is colloquial and bathetic. 'Lady

Rosemounde would find him as unlikely a suitor as can be found anywhere among the first-person speakers of Chaucer's works' (p 106). III. *The Author's* perspective reveals a multilayered satire, a satire of the style of love poetry, a satire of character (ie, the persona himself), and a mocking of the ideology of love. For the reader the poem is 'a dramatic monologue in the full definition of the genre' (p 107). Chaucer's 'introduction of his self-mocking sanity, embodied in the authorial *persona* so familiar and distinctive in his works, was a creative decision of radical originality. It transformed the ballade into a work of a new genre which proved felicitously adaptable in his *CT* prologues for the Reeve, the Wife of Bath, and the Pardoner, and whose potential as an independent literary form would be fully explored centuries later' (p 108). Vasta would date the poem early, ca 1369–70, along with *BD* and the *Romaunt*.

Truth: Balade de Bon Conseyl

See also **34, 41, 42, 45, 67, 79, 88, 89, 141, 197.**

543 Braddy, Haldeen. *Chaucer and the French Poet Graunson.* 1947. See **84.** Braddy discusses Sir Philip de la Vache as one of the circle of friends Graunson and Chaucer had in common. Vache visited Savoy in 1362 (pp 36–7).

544 Brusendorff, A. *The Chaucer Tradition.* 1925. See **28.** Among the Minor Poems *Truth* has been handed down in the largest number of mss – twenty-two, plus two noteworthy old prints. Its genuineness is above suspicion, though the Envoy occurs only in a single ms (Addit. 10340), and it is there in questionable circumstances. Though it may be by Chaucer, it was probably added later by one of his friends (p 245). Shirley, whose copies lack the envoy, says the poem was written at the end of Chaucer's life when he was dying. A French *Balade moral et de bone counseylle* is found in Shirley's Trin.R.3.20. There must be some connection between the poems ('mys en press' and 'On a asses mais oon ait souffisaunce'), 'though it may be doubtful which imitates the other' (p 252).

545 David, Alfred. 'The Truth about "Vache".' *ChauR,* 11 (1977), 334–7. David challenges Lampe's exegetical interpretation (**555**) of Vache (cow=ox) as a patristic symbol of humility and sacrifice, noting various interpretative distinctions within the exegetical tradition; he then emphasizes that the Envoy is 'missing from twenty-nine of the thirty textual authorities we have for the poem': 'Any interpretation that attributes crucial significance to the line about Vache ought to explain why that line is absent from all but one of the surviving copies of Chaucer's most popular short poem. If Chaucer really meant to attach exegetical significance to Vache, that meaning was lost to the overwhelming majority of readers until Furnivall turned up the envoy in British Museum ms Additional 10340' (p 336).

546 Donaldson, E.T. *Chaucer's Poetry.* 1958/1975. See **14.**

'The story that Chaucer composed *Truth* on his deathbed is highly improbable, but it does point up the high regard the poet held for the quality of *trouthe* throughout his literary career' (p 963/1124).

547 Du Boulay, F.R.H. 'The Historical Chaucer.' In *Writers and their Backgrounds: Geoffrey Chaucer.* Ed. Derek Brewer. London: G. Bell & Sons, 1974; Athens, Ohio University Press, 1975, 33–57.

Du Boulay compares the tone of *Truth* and Clanvowe's *The Two Ways* (pp 46–7).

548 Flügel, Ewald. 'Chaucers Kleinere Gedichte.' *Anglia,* 23 (1901), 195–224.

After commenting on the large number of *Truth* mss Flügel glosses key words and phrases in the poem: *suffise* (v 2), similar to sentiments in Gower and Occleve; *tikilnesse* (v 3); *blent* (v 4); *reule wel thyself* (v 6), cf Dunbar and Deschamps; the refrain (v 7), cf a proverb from Lekynfeld on deliverance by truth, as well as passages in Wyclif, Langland, Gower and Deschamps; *tempest the noght* (v 8); *here is non home* (v 17), cf Boethius, Cicero, Plotinus, and also Dunbar; *forthe beste out of thy stall* (v 18), cf Boethius on man's bestiality; *loke up* (v 19), cf Boethius, Cicero, and attitudes in *Handlyng Synne* and Lydgate; *hold the heye weye* (v 20), cf Deschamps, Boethius, and several Biblical passages; *Vache* (v 22), cf Biblical admonitions, especially Amos 4:1; *cry hym mercy* (v 24), ein Gallicismus; *draw unto him* (v 26), cf Boethius and Matt. 11:28. Flügel suggests that the envoy may have been part of a separate redaction, possibly one intended exclusively for Sir Philip (pp 222–3); perhaps the envoy alone was written when Chaucer was dying.

549 Gillmeister, Heiner. 'The Whole Truth about *Vache.*' *Chaucer Newsletter,* 2 (Winter, 1980), 13–4.

Vache is a reference to Chaucer himself, not Sir Philip de la Vache. The exhortation 'Vache, leve!' is the poet's French name CHAVSIER ('shoemaker') written backwards and partly anglicized: Reis Vach. (cf O Fr. *reis, vache!* 'leave, cow!' where the singular imperative of OF *reissir* corresponds to that of Modern French *sortir, sors.*) 'Chaucer thus, by means of a conversion of his name, draws attention to the fact that he has undergone a conversion in real life, an interesting instance of the concept of *praesagium nominis*, the medieval belief in the prophetic force inherent in a person's name' (p 13). Gillmeister sees I Sam. 6 to be the ultimate source of the *vache* simile. See also Heiner Gillmeister, *Discrecioun, Chaucer und die Via Regia.* Studien zur englischen Literatur, band 8. Bonn: Bouvier Verlag Herbert Grundmann, 1972, pp 201–5, where he first discussed 'Vache' and the 'heye wey.'

550 Green, A.W. 'Structure of Three Minor Poems.' 1963. See **106.**
Green emphasizes the tripartite structure of the balade and suggests that
Vache may be 'swordpoint satire at himself,' rather than 'a friendly name
for Sir Philip la Vache,' and thus 'another excellent example of self-
ridicule by Chaucer, or ridicule of Everyman including Chaucer' (p 80).

551 Hammond, E.P. *Bibliographical Manual.* 1908. See **37.**
See especially discussion of titles to the poem and notes on early opinions on genuineness of the envoy. Tyrwhitt was the first to question
Shirley's heading that the poem was written on Chaucer's deathbed
(pp 401–3).

552 Jefferson, B.L. *Chaucer and the Consolation of Philosophy of Boethius.* 1917.
See **453.**
Jefferson discusses *trouthe* and *sothfastnesse* as a prominent motif
throughout Chaucer's writings (pp 104–7) and contrasts treatments of the
idea in *Truth* (a lofty abstract conception) and *Sted.* He quotes and gives a
synopsis of *Truth,* a poem which 'stands out as one of the most sincere
and noble of Chaucer's utterances. No stronger evidence of the lasting
influence of the *Consolation of Philosophy* upon Chaucer could be shown
than that it is the dominating influence of this poem. It shows that the
Consolation had entered into the very fibre of his thought ... *Truth* sums
up in a nut shell the teaching of the first three books of the *Consolation'*
(pp 108–9). The poem juxtaposes universal truth with man's relation to
the world. The 'flee from the press' motif is precisely the theme of
Plato's *Republic* (Bk 6) and of the entire *Consolation,* an idea Jefferson explores in detail, along with 'dwelle with sothfastness' and 'trouthe shal
delivere' (pp 109–19).

553 Jones, Claude. 'Chaucer's "Truth" Modernized, 1756.' *NQ,* 171 (1936), 455.
Jones reprints a translation of *Truth* by an anonymous author in the
Universal Visiter and Memorialist, 1756. The translation is in three 10-line
stanzas, rhymed ababcdcdee.

554 Koch, John. 'Chaucers Boethiusübersetzung: Ein Beitrag zur Bestimmung
der Chronologie seiner Werke.' *Anglia,* 46 (1922), 1–51.
Koch argues that Boethius III.m.11 is a source for *Truth.* He thinks the
envoy may have been part of a later separate redaction intended exclusively for Sir Philip Vache (pp 22, 47–8).

555 Lampe, David E. 'The Truth of A "Vache": The Homely Homily of
Chaucer's "Truth".' *PLL,* 9 (1973), 311–4.
'"Vache" = cow = man is not simply a comic undercutting of the moral
earnestness of the poem ... The related metaphors in the poem also
operate as an appropriate part of the homiletic pattern of the poem if
they are understood in terms of medieval iconography and bestiaries'
(p 312). Lampe relates Vache, beste, heye (hay), stal, and mede (meadow)
as diverse figures pertinent to bestiality. Noting the importance of beasts

in church decoration, Lampe suggests *vache* implies not simply cow, but ox, *vacca* being 'a transferable generic name' (p 313). Patristic glosses on the tropological significance of ox suggest humility but also 'the necessity of worldly renunciation,' an idea apt to the pilgrim metaphor in the poem. 'Thus rather than being a satiric signal for self-ridicule, the usage of "Vache" in this ballade is instead an example of what Edmund Reiss terms the "unusual and interesting combination of the homiletic and the homely"' (p 314. [cf **130**, p 65]).

556 Manly, John M. 'Note on the Envoy of *Truth*.' *MP*, 11 (1913), 226.
Manly supports Rickert's theory (**560**) that Vache refers to Sir Philip de la Vache. Her discovery disposes of two problems: 1) the authorship of the poem, which some have doubted; 2) the improbability of Shirley's assertion that the poem was made by Chaucer on his deathbed. 'That Shirley knew little about the poem is indicated by the absence of the Envoy from the two copies made by him. The improbability of a death-bed composition is perhaps increased by the presence of the pun on Vache's name' (p 226).

557 Owen, Charles A. 'Thy Drasty Ryming ...' *SP*, 63 (1966), 533–64.
Truth, 'perhaps Chaucer's most successful lyric,' shows 'a bold exuberance of word and image that miraculously enhances the solemnity of the poem' (p 534). Owen also points out Chaucer's remarkable handling of the *–al* rhyme.

558 Patch, Howard Rollin. 'Desiderata in Middle English Research.' *MP*, 22 (1924), 27–34.
Beginning with James Russell Lowell's wondering whether anyone can hope to say anything fresh or new about Chaucer, Patch expresses hope and outlines important new work (like Kittredge's noting of northern forms in the *Romaunt*) and areas for fresh study. 'Any study of Chaucerian manuscripts is likely to be rewarding. In dating *Trouthe* scholars have sometimes ignored the fact that the envoy with the dedication to Sir Philip La Vache appears only in one manuscript' (p 33).

559 Ragan, James F. 'The *Hevenlich Mede* in Chaucer's "Truth".' *MLN*, 68 (1953), 534–5.
'Hevenlich mede' is usually interpreted to mean 'heavenly reward,' but for both stylistic and philological reasons "mede" could mean 'meadow.' The gloss would not only be 'in keeping with Chaucer's jocular mood in the poem, but also with the poet's practice in riming' (p 534). 'What is more logical than Chaucer's exhortation to a "Vache" [cow] than that he pray for a heavenly meadow? For this is surely one case in which a mead is at the same time a meed' (pp 534–5). Cf riming of *drede* and *mede* as well as *rede, dede, lede,* all of which are open [ae] phonemes rather than the close [e] of meed (reward).

560 Rickert, Edith. 'Thou Vache.' *MP*, 11 (1913), 209–25.

Vache (line 22) puns on the name of Sir Philip la Vache, who married Elizabeth, the daughter of Chaucer's friend Sir Lewis Clifford (p 209). Rickert reconstructs abundant details of his family and his life going back to 1265 and Sir Richard la Vache who later in life was made Knight of the Garter (1355) and then Constable of the Tower for life. The first reference to Philip is in 1358 when his father petitioned a benefice from the Pope on behalf of his twelve-year-old son, a petition which was granted. Sir Philip was a courtier and soldier, keeper of the royal jewels, keeper of the royal manor and part of Woodstock. He became Knight of the Garter himself in 1399 and was given the stall of none other than John of Chamberlain of the household of the child Queen Isabel. Clanvowe was one of the supervisors of his will, the details of which Rickert lists. Rickert gives a reading of the poem in terms of the biographical information; she suggests a date of composition between 1386–90, which would tie the poem to a period of stress in Vache's life. In commenting on Vache's notable hospitality, Rickert wonders if he might not have been a model for Chaucer's Franklin (p 225).

561 Robertson, D.W., Jr. 'Historical Criticism.' *English Institute Essays*. Columbia University Press, 1950, pp 3–31.

In this essay on the interpretation of medieval literature, including Middle English lyrics, Robertson comments briefly on the pilgrim metaphor in *Truth* (p 18). The essay is reprinted in D.W. Robertson, Jr., *Essays in Medieval Culture* (Princeton: Princeton University Press, 1980), pp 3–20, accompanied by a headnote which revises several salient points: eg, 'I no longer think that charity and cupidity are "opposites," since love is basically a motion of the will toward something and varies in nature with the character of its object. Man's "quest," moreover, is not "eternal." The word *levels* applied to tropological, allegorical, and anagogical interpretations is convenient but misleading. The meaning ascribed to the primrose in "The Maid of the Moor" is perhaps dubious' (p 3).

562 Robinson, F.N. *Works*. 1957. See **12**.

'Dr. Jefferson [**453**] goes rather too far in calling it an epitome of the Consolation ... Biblical influence, direct or indirect, is also to be noted in both language and thought.' Ragan's suggestion (**559**) is 'worth considering,' though the argument from rime is 'not conclusive, since Chaucer did not consistently avoid riming close and open –*e*'s and –*o*'s' (p 861).

563 Root, R.K. *The Poetry of Chaucer*. 1900/1922. See **140**.

'The balade of *Truth* is the best answer one may give to the charge that Chaucer was incapable of "high seriousness." Though suggested in part by Boethius, the poem is essentially original, and expresses, I think, the substance of Chaucer's criticism of life ... The poet is gifted with a delicate and sensitive soul, which, kept untainted, can give forth life and beauty to his own age and to the ages in store. To spend it all in mad protest against a wicked world – what shall it profit?' (p 73).

564 Shanley, James Lyndon. 'The *Troilus* and Christian Love.' *ELH*, 6 (1939), 271–81.

'The ultimate reason for Troilus' woe was not that he trusted in a woman but that of his own free will he placed his hope for perfect happiness in that which by its nature was temporary, imperfect, and inevitably insufficient' (p 272). After consideration of false happiness in Thomas à Kempis, Dante, and St Augustine, Shanley clinches his argument with Chaucer's 'Balade de Bon Conseyl' and the folly of 'wrastling for this world' (p 281).

565 Skeat, W.W. *Oxford Chaucer.* 1894/1899. See **1**.

Suggests that the third stanza of the balade was based on Boethius I.pr.5. Shirley's note on the deathbed, so frequently repeated, 'is probably no better than a bad guess' (I, p 550). Though the envoy appears in only one ms 'there is no reason at all for considering it spurious' (I, p 553). Chaucer probably chose vache (cow) as a less offensive 'beast' than those mentioned by Boethius, viz wolf, hound, fox, lion, hart, ass, and sow (p 553).

565a Spearing, A.C. and J.E. *Poetry of the Age of Chaucer.* 1975. See **541a**. Pp 198–9.

Relates the refrain-line to John 8:32. 'It is not only that the man who follows the poem's injunctions will be liberated from bondage to "this world," but that his own integrity will draw down the help of Christ, who is Truth, and bring him to salvation' (p 199). The first two stanzas are marked by 'a kind of pessimistic conservatism;' the third is more optimistic and dynamic. The text of *Truth* is printed with glosses pp 216–17.

Womanly Noblesse: A Balade That Chaucer Made

See also **73**.

566 Brusendorff, A. *The Chaucer Tradition.* 1925. See **28**.

WN is Skeat's title which seems to Brusendorff 'too abstract to be quite relevant' (p 277). He refers to the poem as *Envoy to a Lady*. The poem occurs only in the late Addit. 34360, copied from Shirley. The text is 'very unsatisfactory.' Brusendorff prints the text as it occurs in the ms as an antedote to Skeat's corrections.

567 Dodd, W.G. *Courtly Love.* 1913. See **96**.

Both *WN* and *BC* 'have a ring of sincerity that surprises' and produces 'an impression of genuine feeling' (p 99). Dodd considers autobiographical readings of the poems but then discredits them: 'Poets of the period were always writing in the first person and complaining of the misfortunes of love' (p 100).

568 Donahue, J.J. *Chaucer's Lesser Poems*. 1974. See **21**.
WN 'contains little more than one pleasing touch' (p 118).

569 Griffin, R.M. *Chaucer's Lyrics*. 1970. See **18**.
Griffin places *WN* and *AWU* among the middle lyrics, when Chaucer is at his most graceful. Most of his lyrics of this period are straightforward moral poetry with a strong Boethian influence. But in these two he seems temporarily unconcerned with the deeper problems of existence (pp 86–96).

570 Hammond, E.P. *Bibliographical Manual*. 1908. See **37**.
Skeat, in his letter to *Athenaeum*, 1 (1894, part I), 742, announced the ballad as his discovery; Pollard *ibid*, p 773, however, replied that its existence was known to the Museum before purchase of the ms Hammond reviews attitudes of scholars on the poem's authenticity (p 463).

571 Moore, Arthur K. *The Secular Lyric in Middle English*. 1951. See **124.**
Moore finds *WN* 'deficient in figures which should measure the depth of the poet's distress' (p 131).

572 Robinson, F.N. *Works*. 1957. See **12.**
'Although called a ballade in the manuscript and accompanied by the unusual envoy, *Womanly Noblesse* has a difficult rime scheme not elsewhere adopted by Chaucer in poems of the type. In spite of the scribe's ascription to Chaucer, his authorship has been questioned. The poem is less characteristic of him than the *Rosemounde*, but there seems to be no good reason for rejecting it from the canon' (p 521).

573 Root, R.K. *The Poetry of Chaucer*. 1900/1922. See **140.**
In *WN* the *a*-rhyme is repeated twenty-two times. 'It should be noticed, however, that Chaucer has prudently chosen very easy rimes' (p 79).

574 Skeat, W.W. *The Student's Chaucer*. 1894. See **2.**
Skeat includes *WN* as the last of the Minor Poems in this volume, with the note: 'This genuine poem was first printed in June, 1894' (p 129). That printing was a leaflet issue of the poem by Skeat himself. He claims to have discovered the poem, as he did *Ros*, though Pollard contests the claim (**570**). Skeat suggests that it was composed before *Pity* and *AA*, in the mid-1370s (p xiv). The poem was included in Vol 4 as an addition to the Minor Poems of Vol 1.

575 Stillwell, Gardiner. 'Chaucer's Eagles and their Choice on February 14.' *JEGP*, 53 (1954), 546–61.
Stillwell examines *PF* in light of the Valentine tradition, considering first Chaucer's other Valentine Poems (*Mars*, *CD*, and *WN*), then four poems by Graunson, Gower's *Cinkante Balades* (n 34 and n 35), three Lydgate poems, and Charles of Orléans' 46th balade. *WN* is not specifically a Valentine poem, yet it is very like that of the first eagle in *PF*, though

more gentle. It is no wonder that the maiden formel blushes and has to have nature's reassurances that no would-be-lover will pounce on her and carry her off (unless she so desires it).

❧ Index

Numbers in boldface type indicate authorship or primary entry. 'r' indicates review entry. A boldface number in parenthesis indicates a subdivision of the preceding entry outside parenthesis. For example: Donaldson **14 (168) (210), 58r**, 77 indicates that Donaldson wrote item 14 and that items 168 and 210 are by Donaldson also but are part of item 14. Item **58r** is a review by Donaldson, while item 77 makes mention of him. On the other hand, Bannatyne ms 39, **460a**, 471 indicates that the Bannatyne ms is mentioned in entries 39 and 471 while **460a** is a primary entry, in this instance an edition of the manuscript.